Bloomsbury and Modernism

American University Studies

Series IV
English Language and Literature

Vol. 94

PETER LANG
New York • Bern • Frankfurt am Main • Paris

Ulysses L. D'Aquila

Bloomsbury and Modernism

PETER LANG
New York • Bern • Frankfurt am Main • Paris

Library of Congress Cataloging-in-Publication Data

D'Aquila, Ulysses L.
 Bloomsbury and modernism / Ulysses L. D'Aquila.
  p. cm. — (American University studies. Series IV,
English language and literature ; vol. 94)
  Bibliography: p.
  Includes index.
  1. English literature—20th century—History and
criticism. 2. Bloomsbury group. 3. Modernism
(Literature)—Great Britain. 4. Forster, E. M. (Edward
Morgan), 1879-1970—Criticism and interpretation.
5. Woolf, Virginia, 1882-1941—Criticism and
interpretation. I. Title. II. Series.
  PR478.B46D34   1989   820.9'1—dc20   89-31947
  ISBN 0-8204-1017-9   CIP
  ISSN 0741-0700

CIP-Titelaufnahme der Deutschen Bibliothek

D'Aquila, Ulysses L.:
Bloomsbury and modernism / Ulysses L. D'Aqui-
la. — New York; Bern; Frankfurt am Main; Paris:
Lang, 1989.
 (American University Studies: Ser. 4, English
 Language and Literature; Vol. 94)
 ISBN 0-8204-1017-9

NE: American University Studies / 04

© Peter Lang Publishing, Inc., New York 1989

Printed by Weihert-Druck GmbH, Darmstadt, West Germany

TABLE OF CONTENTS

I

INTRODUCTION:

BLOOMSBURY AND THE CLIMATE OF MODERNISM

We have embarked into the final decade of the twentieth century, our own *fin-de-siècle*. By now the revolutionary movements in art and literature which rocked the early 1900s seem as remote from us as, say, Pre-Raphaelitism or Art Nouveau, and the baffling proliferation of schools and manifestos – Cubism, Fauvism, Futurism, Vorticism, Imagism, Surrealism – spawned by this revolution evokes for most people visions of a world long since vanished. The Jazz Age Paris of Picasso and Josephine Baker; the atelier of Gertrude Stein, its walls lined with canvasses by Matisse, Cézanne and Gauguin; the transcontinental high-life of Hemingway and the Fitzgeralds; the Montparnasse of bereted Ezra Pound with its innumerable bistros; the London of T. S. Eliot, elegant in his neat suit, or of Virginia Woolf and her friends in their Bloomsbury flats, smoking and talking intently over pale gas fires – these are the scenes which most often come to mind when we think of the avant-garde art world of the early years of this century. Behind these tableaux lies a vague assumption that the innovative art and the radical ideas promoted by these artists and thinkers were in some respect all of one piece. Such a notion, appealing as it does to the desire for a comprehensive and ordered perspective on the past, is at once both true and deceptive.

It is one of the virtues as well as one of the pitfalls of historical thinking that it can smooth a gloss of clarity and uniformity over periods that were in fact rife with profound fissures, paradoxes and differences. This is especially the case with the Modernist era when the clash of old and new was more abrupt and dislocating than any transition of the past had been. The diversity of opinion among some of the leaders of the various movements when seen close-up almost defy any attempt to draw parallels and relationships between them. Unquestionably, in aesthetic theory as well as in politics, the spokesmen for this emergent world spanned a wide range from left (Leonard Woolf, Edmund Wilson) to far right (Marinetti, Wyndham Lewis), and such divergence was sharp enough to provoke the occasional fierce verbal combat.[1] And yet, our present distant and retrospective view does allow and indeed encourage the attempt to see a pattern and some common themes behind the manifold activities of the Modernists.

Speaking in particular of those Modernists centered in London, Malcolm Bradbury has said that "what, despite their extraordinary differences of temper and intention, unites them is a prevailing sense of dislocation from the past, and a commitment to the active remaking of art." They would all of them be spurred by a Nietzschean desire to establish a new order upon new values, and by a commitment to re-form contemporary ethics as well as the prevailing social and political sphere through their aesthetic efforts. Bradbury goes on to distinguish an "English brand of Modernism, founded in the sense of transformation, often of liberation, affecting those who believed

---

[1] Italian Futurism, which was nationalistic in character, Wyndham Lewis's Vorticism and Apollinaire's Orphism were all especially pugnacious in the dissemination of their ideas.

the era of Victorianism was ending, a new phase in society, art and thought beginning."[2]

This latter, English phase of Modernism is what will concern us primarily in the present study. Because of this, some of the manifestations of international Modernism – the technophilia of the Italian futurists, Dadaist Absurdism, the bleaker visions of German Expressionism, for instance – will be hardly mentioned, whereas the impact of contemporary French art and letters, of Freud, of Henri Bergson's philosophy, or of William James's psychology will bear more closely upon the writers discussed here. Of course, even among the English avant-garde there existed relationships that were from the outset more adversarial than conspiratorial. The well-known antagonism of Wyndham Lewis and T. E. Hulme to the Bloomsbury Group is a case in point. Their anti-romantic, exteriorized methods, not to mention their authoritarian politics were in most ways antithetical to Bloomsbury humanism and liberal pacifism.[3] Yet even here there were surprising resemblances, from the pervasive influence of Bergson to the impact upon all

---

[2] Malcolm Bradbury, "London 1890-1920," *Modernism 1890-1930*, ed. Malcolm Bradbury and James McFarlane (Harmondsworth, Middlesex, England: Penguin, 1976) 178-79.

[3] Before they quarreled, Wyndham Lewis's works had figured in Roger Fry's Second Post-Impressionist exhibition as well as in the Omega Workshops. The aesthetician and philosopher T. E. Hulme was, like Bloomsbury, a disciple of G. E. Moore. A leading figure in the Imagist movement that included Pound and Lewis, Hulme sought, along with T. S. Eliot, to revive objective classical values as a corrective to the formlessness and subjectivity of late romanticism. He was an ardent militarist, and he died in combat in 1917.

of them of scientific relativism, that in retrospect overshadow some of the apparently irreconcilable differences.

All of the Modernists, it should be remembered, were products of the late nineteenth century. The literary culture out of which they emerged to maturity was very much that of the *fin-de-siècle* and no matter how radically they may have reacted against some of its tenets, the roots of their original thinking must inevitably be located in this common inheritance. Writing at the tail-end of high Modernism, Edmund Wilson observed that ". . . both the strength and the weaknesses characteristic of much of the literature since the [First World] War derive naturally from the Symbolist poets . . . . The literary history of our time is to a great extent that of the development of Symbolism and of its fusion or conflict with Naturalism."[4] The need of the Modernists to throw off the bonds of the past, then, can never be entirely separated from the inevitable dynamic engagement with those very conditions out of which these artists saw themselves as struggling. The Bloomsbury writers, especially, maintained a peculiar allegiance to Victorianism even as they excoriated it; pioneers of the new, they were nonetheless, as Roger Fry so wisely remarked, "the last of the Victorians."

Though their history has been written and rewritten, much confusion yet remains as to the nature of Bloomsbury. In essence an alliance of close friends (not a joinable club or society, not a "school" with a well-defined aesthetic program, hardly a cult, religious or otherwise), Bloomsbury can be

---

[4] Edmund Wilson, *Axel's Castle: A Study in the Imaginative Literature of 1870-1930* (New York: Scribner's, 1931) 27.

said to constitute one of those rare instances in culture when mutual intellectual, artistic and emotional affinities so harmoniously coalesced as to form, organically, a distinct and remarkable aggregate.

The roots of the Bloomsbury Group were at Cambridge University and more specifically at Kings and Trinity Colleges where, of the men, all but Duncan Grant had been educated. Most of them belonged to a select club, the Cambridge Conversazione Society, whose elected members were known as the Apostles.[5] Gathering on Saturday evenings, the Apostles would read papers upon various subjects, usually philosophical or political, and discuss current topics. There was little talk of aesthetics, though literary and classical interests were a tradition within the society.[6] This habit of evening meetings and intimate discussion was carried over into the post-collegiate lives of these young men – naturally, they were all young men, for though Cambridge had

---

[5] Neither Clive Bell nor Thoby Stephen were elected to the Apostles, but they were at the core of another club, the Midnight Society, all of whose members were later part of Bloomsbury.

[6] This needs to be somewhat clarified. Roger Fry (who during his Cambridge years was a student of science) and G. E. Moore certainly occupied themselves with such subjects as the nature of beauty, but this was largely in an abstract way. There was very little concern, at this time, with paintings. The achievements of the French Impressionists and Van Gogh had as yet made no impact; in fact, they were probably unknown to them. At Oxford, where the mood was more aesthetic than that of intellectual Cambridge, Symbolism, Art Nouveau, Whistler and Beardsley were still the order of the day. Virginia Woolf has written, "There is no evidence, apart from McTaggart's early reference to Rossetti and from one visit in his company to the Royal Academy, that the young men who read so many books and discussed so many problems ever looked at pictures . . . ." Virginia Woolf, *Roger Fry* (New York: Harcourt, 1940) 51.

established in the nineteenth century two colleges for women, Girton and Newnham, there was still little casual social intermingling of the sexes.

That is, not until Thoby Stephen began to gather his Cambridge friends at the London home he shared with his two sisters, Vanessa and Virginia, and his brother, Adrian. These newly liberated orphans were the progeny of that eminent Victorian man of letters, Leslie Stephen. Stephen had died in 1904, nine years after his second wife, Julia, leaving the four offspring of this marriage, all in their early twenties, to fend for themselves. The timing was opportune for they had come to a decision to live life on their own terms, to turn their backs on the century recently left behind, and to go forth into the new one free of the social inhibitions which had bound and restricted their adolescence. Upon their father's death, they moved out of the family residence in Hyde Park Gate, Kensington to what was then a rather less respectable address in Bloomsbury, that area of London which borders on the British Museum. They determined to make their new home, 46 Gordon Square, a place where their friends could easily meet and talk at all hours, and where the Apostolic code of candor would be the rule.

The young women, both of them beautiful, highly intelligent and somewhat formidable in their aloof sensitivity, were initially shy and silent in the unaccustomed male company. In time, however, their presence began to be felt in the altered tone and matter of the conversation. The high-minded logic and austere intellectualism of Cambridge was to give way to an easier, more humorous form of discourse. Formalities of address were dispensed with, and finally even that most taboo of subjects for the Victorians, sex, became one of their chief topics for debate. It might be mentioned that neither of the sisters had achieved, at this point, any notable accomplishment, but they had long before decided between them that Vanessa was to be the painter, Virginia the writer. Determined on this course, Vanessa enrolled in the Royal Academy Schools to study art, and Virginia began a literary apprenticeship by submitting anonymous reviews to *The Guardian* and *The Times Literary Supplement*.

Open as it was to the various modern art movements then stirring the air, what was especially avant-garde about Bloomsbury would not at this early period (1904-1906) have been very evident. Only in its general ethos – that friendship and the contemplation of beauty were life's highest goods – can we see the germ of the aesthetic radicalism that came to be associated with the group. This ethos, which in so many ways came to define Bloomsbury, derived in great part from one slim volume, *Principia Ethica* (1903), by the Cambridge philosopher G. E. Moore.

The influence of the ideas contained in this book had an immeasurable impact on the young generation of Cambridge intellectuals, and no study of Bloomsbury or its various members can ignore it. Leonard Woolf has written that

> There have often been groups of people, writers and artists, who were not only friends, but were consciously united by a common doctrine and object, or purpose artistic or social. The Utilitarians, the Lake poets, the French Impressionists, the English Pre-Raphaelites were groups of this kind. Our group was quite different. Its basis was friendship, which in some cases developed into love and marriage. The color of

> our minds and thought had been given to us by the climate
> of Cambridge and Moore's philosophy.[7]

G. E. Moore's philosophy provided a foundation, a rationale upon which these eminently rational and decidedly skeptical young people were able to base a world-view and way of life profoundly different from that of their parents. Briefly, Moore had asserted that

> by far the most valuable things, which we know or can imagine, are certain states of consciousness, which may roughly be described as the pleasures of human intercourse and the enjoyment of beautiful objects.[8]

Eager as they were to jettison the old proprieties, the tiresome social duties and rituals, the repressive sexual standards of their upbringing, the friends were as yet tied to deeply ingrained late-Victorian intellectual and moral patterns. Moore's *Principia Ethica* seemed to give license to an invigorating freedom of thought and to a far less hampered sort of behavior. So while the members of early Bloomsbury had no formal agenda like that, for instance, of the Fabian Socialists, they came to share a common allegiance to ideals of rationality, a passion for truth-seeking, and a belief in the supreme importance of human relationships.

Out of this lightly-woven fabric, a pattern of more definite aesthetic notions was soon to emerge. Certainly, in the field of painting, with which Cambridge had so little concerned itself, Bloomsbury was to exert a deep and

---

[7] Leonard Woolf, *Beginning Again* (New York: Harcourt, 1963) 25.

[8] G. E. Moore, *Principia Ethica*, quoted in J. K. Johnstone, *The Bloomsbury Group* (New York: Farrar, 1978) 23.

lasting influence. It was in 1910, the year in which Virginia Woolf later said "human character changed," that Roger Fry launched the first Post-Impressionist exhibition.[9] This event marks a crucial stage in early Modernism, for it signals the first major importation of modern Continental ideas about art into insular Great Britain.

It is difficult for us to imagine today that the paintings of such now well-established artists as Cézanne, Seurat, Picasso, Gauguin and Van Gogh could have been the objects of so much derision and incomprehension eighty years ago, but such was the case. Roger Fry had been engaged by London's prestigious Grafton Gallery to inaugurate a show of modern French painting. He himself came up with the inadequate label, Post-Impressionist, to distinguish the early work of these Modernists from that of the Impressionists who had immediately preceded them. It was a catch-all term, for the exhibit included a wide variety of styles, from the Symbolism of Maurice Denis to the Fauvism of Vlaminck and Rouault. There were twenty-one Cézannes, thirty-seven Gauguins, and twenty-two Van Goghs. Matisse and Picasso were only sparsely represented, though they were to figure more prominently in the 1912 exhibit. Although many of these paintings had been executed twenty or thirty years before, only Manet (1832-1883) was at the time a recognized Master. He was included to demonstrate the line of ancestry of

---

[9] Roger Fry (1866-1934) had been at Cambridge where he was a member of the Apostles and a great friend of McTaggart and G. Lowes Dickinson. Older by nearly a generation than the rest of Bloomsbury, he did not become intimate with the group until shortly before the Post-Impressionist exhibition.

the younger painters, especially of Cézanne. The official title of this first exhibition became "Manet and the Post-Impressionists."

All records indicate that no fewer than four hundred people attended the gallery every day, among them England's most eminent art critics and dealers. The furor and the general disapproval left Roger Fry, who was entirely confident of the worthiness of this modern art, not only undaunted but more than ever convinced of the relationship between aesthetics and the social order. Expressions of outrage went well beyond that of a purely visual incomprehension. Wilfred Scawen Blunt, for example, wrote that the paintings were "works of idleness and impotent stupidity, a pornographic show." The critic, J. Comyns Carr opined that the exhibit "seems to me to indicate a wave of disease, even of absolute madness; for the whole product seems to breath not ineptitude merely but corruption."[10] Finally, Robert Ross, writing in the *Morning Post* (7 Nov. 1910), claimed that the Post-Impressionist show gave evidence of "the widespread plot to destroy the whole fabric of European painting." These rabid and paranoiac vilifications suggest the threat such deeply subversive art posed to the settled convictions of the Establishment.

Although Roger Fry had already gained a considerable reputation as a scholar and connoisseur (he was a curator of New York's Metropolitan Museum and an advisor on Old Masters to J. P. Morgan), he decided to abandon these activities to devote himself entirely to the promotion of Modernism. Together with his close ally, Clive Bell, Fry began to publish

---

[10] Quoted in Frances Spalding, *Roger Fry: Art and Life* (Berkeley: U of California P, 1980) 136 & 139.

books and articles explaining the heterodoxies of the new art, giving theoretical justifications for the distortions and abstractions which had so undone the viewers of the paintings. They wanted, in short, to educate the public toward an acceptance of non-representational art which they believed required "a special orientation of the consciousness, and, above all, a special focusing of the attention."[11]

If, as a result, England's official art establishment might reject him, for the young and innovative, Fry would become both spokesman and arbiter. Virginia Woolf wrote,

> So long as the young trusted him, he cared nothing for the enmity of officials. What mattered was that the young English artists were as enthusiastic about the work of Cézanne, Matisse, and Picasso as he was. The first Post-Impressionist Exhibition, as many of them have testified, was to them a revelation; it was to affect their work profoundly. And to explain and to expound the meaning of the new movement, to help the young English painters to leave the little backwater of provincial art and to take their place in the main stream, became from this time one of Roger Fry's main preoccupations.[12]

Of the young painters, Vanessa Bell and the very promising Duncan Grant soon left behind their naturalistic and somewhat Whistlerian styles to embrace wholeheartedly the brilliant colorism and bold abstraction of Post-Impressionism. By the time Roger Fry launched his second exhibition in

---

[11] Quoted in Johnstone 46.

[12] *Roger Fry* 159.

1912, they themselves had produced work of the kind and quality to be exhibited alongside that of Picasso, Matisse, Braque and Derain.

The infusion of Modernist art theory as well as the centrality which painting came to hold among the group is important to this literary study of Bloomsbury because these provided what Cambridge had not; whereas Cambridge and G. E. Moore had given an abstract and intellectual impetus to the creative activity of Bloomsbury, Fry and Bell helped to imbue it with a real and sensual mode of living and working. What had been merely of the mind was now the very heart and blood of Bloomsbury. Clive Bell's doctrine of significant form, with its emphasis upon texture and other formal values as the source of aesthetic pleasure, could not fail to appeal to the writers who in their own way were challenging the bulky naturalism of such writers as Galsworthy and Wells. Fry himself had literary interests, and his long-term project of translating Mallarmé arose out of a belief that the poet was an early Cubist involved in an effort to break down words into relations of "pure poetical necessity," and determined to divest his verse of all elements extraneous to the design. This subjective retreat from external reality and the notable departure from narrative elements which had for so long dominated English art exerted a tremendous impact on the writers associated with Bloomsbury.

And this shift in style, however theoretical in origin, was in fact extremely vitalizing to the Bloomsbury artists. On the whole, the creative activity and success of the group accelerated to the point that new outlets were sought for the dissemination of their work. In 1913, Roger Fry opened his Omega Workshops, a commercial enterprise designed to promote all the plastic arts – painting, pottery, weaving, textile design – and also to provide a showroom where these productions might be sold for profit. By 1917, Leonard and Virginia Woolf had started their own publishing concern, the Hogarth Press.

The close connection between the various figures of Bloomsbury went well beyond a merely artistic sympathy of aim; in 1906, following the tragic and premature death of her brother, Thoby, Vanessa Stephen married Clive Bell. When, after a few years and the birth of two sons, their marriage developed into an open, but non-conjugal friendship, Vanessa began a love affair with Roger Fry.[13] After 1916, Vanessa Bell became closely allied with Duncan Grant, with whom she lived and worked until her death in 1961. Together they were responsible for a veritable revolution in design and the decorative arts in England. They exhibited widely, took commissions to paint and decorate both private homes and public spaces and, as the years went on, they gained increasing renown. Duncan Grant, in particular, has been called England's own Matisse. In 1911 Leonard Woolf, Lytton Strachey's closest friend at Cambridge, returned from civil service in Ceylon and proposed to Virginia Stephen. Their marriage in effect sealed the bond of affection and sympathy that united the various friends. The Bloomsbury Group had truly come into being.

While it is probably fair to say that literature is, in some respects, a more conservative art than painting and one more intricately linked to what has gone before, it is not difficult to see how much the Post-Impressionist

---

[13] Fry was married to the artist Helen Coombe. She suffered from severe mental illness and was eventually committed to an asylum.

ferment affected a writer like Virginia Woolf. Stressing as it did form over content, and attempting, in Fry's words, to capture "that overpowering significance which ordinary men can only find in [everyday] things at rare moments of imaginative exaltation,"[14] Post-Impressionist art coincided in many respects with Woolf's own essential desire to convey epiphanous moments of being. Certainly there can be little doubt that the more experimental writing of this period shows as remarkable a departure from late Victorian and Edwardian models as Picasso's painting style does from that of John Singer Sargent.

But the change, nonetheless, was slower and more tentative. Forster's *The Longest Journey* (1907), Lawrence's *Sons and Lovers* (1913), Joyce's *Dubliners* (1914), and Virginia Woolf's *The Voyage Out* (1915) do not at first glance seem especially innovative set beside the work of Hardy, or Conrad, or Samuel Butler. It really takes a closer examination of their purposes, something as much of matter as of style, to discern the Modernist qualities of these early twentieth century novels.

The last-mentioned figure, the Victorian eccentric Samuel Butler, is an important precursor. He, along with such radicals of his generation as Edward Carpenter and Havelock Ellis, began a process of dismantlement which his literary successors – Lawrence, Forster, Joyce, and Virginia Woolf – were to continue. Butler's posthumously published masterpiece, *The Way of All Flesh* (1903), supplied a direction for the Modernist novel in its sharp criticisms of Victorian social and sexual mores and in its frank condemnation

---

[14] Quoted in Spalding, *Roger Fry* 74.

of that most sacrosanct institution of Victorian life, the family. Rarely had a novel treated so unsentimentally and with such psychological acuteness the painful development of a young man into independent maturity out of the stifling repressiveness of his nineteenth century childhood. Only Dickens among the Victorians had managed as incisive an indictment of the social system, but Dickens, with his hand always on the pulse of popular sentiment, had done so without bite or offense to his public. Butler's book, on the other hand, came as a shock and a revelation, and it came just as the waning century drew to its close.

Queen Victoria died in 1901 and by the time her son, that middle-aged playboy, Edward Prince of Wales, ascended to the throne, a new tone of liberality, of social freedom, of relaxed manners and morals (some would say immorality) was already in the air. This is not to suggest that the slate was suddenly wiped clean; the accretions of Victorianism and the might of British Imperialism were far too deeply entrenched and too formidable to be easily swept away, but the rumblings of dissent were distinct and becoming more so.

Butler's *The Way of All Flesh*, Havelock Ellis's *Studies in the Psychology of Sex*, and Edward Carpenter's *Love's Coming of Age* each in its way attacked Victorian sexual and moral attitudes, as well as the oppressiveness of patriarchal family life. All of these books contained implicit criticisms of those other legacies of the nineteenth century, Benthamite Utilitarianism and an excessively mechanistic determinism that had come about as Darwin's ideas took hold. These materialist philosophies had eventually permeated every aspect of Victorian life, reverberating into its educational system, its social values, its legal and economic workings, and not least into its literature.

Such continuously admired writers as George Eliot and Thomas Hardy, the one a disciple of Spencer, the other a staunch biological determinist, seemed burdened with the need to express in their novels some faith in positivist social philosophy and science, as if in recompense for the religious faith they could no longer endorse. The obsession with morality which is rife in Victorian literature points to a central crisis of that age, the crisis of Belief versus Unbelief.

If one was, like Newman, among the believers, the urge was to vent the conscience in public, to explain and excuse one's religion. If among the latter – Leslie Stephen and Matthew Arnold, for instance – the need was to constantly reaffirm one's adherence to and belief in morality. As Nietzsche wrote scathingly of the English,

> They are rid of the Christian God and now believe all the more firmly that they must cling to Christian morality. . . . In England one must rehabilitate oneself after every little emancipation from theology by showing in a veritably awe-inspiring manner what a moral fanatic one is. That is the penance they pay there.[15]

So while it is true that Darwin, Huxley, Spencer, and Mill were themselves instrumental in bringing about the slow death of many Victorian sacred cows, not least the theological, by the end of the nineteenth century they too had become the engines of a *Weltanschauung* the Modernists were to find extremely uncongenial.

---

[15] Nietzsche, *Twilight of the Idols* in *The Portable Nietzsche*, ed. Walter Kaufmann (New York: Viking, 1968) 515.

A pervasive desire to find some way out of the oppressive moral impasse and to finally settle the feud between science and faith began to be felt toward the end of the century. The 1890s, in particular, are characterized by a search for a more accommodating world-view. We get hints of it in Walter Pater's hesitant style, with its intimations of a more fluid, subjective and evanescent perceiving consciousness:

> At first sight experience seems to bury us under a flood of external objects, pressing upon us with a sharp and importunate reality, calling us out of ourselves in a thousand forms of action. But when reflexion begins to act upon those objects they are dissipated under its influence; the cohesive force seems suspended like a trick of magic; each object is loosed into a group of impressions – colour, odour, texture – in the mind of the observer.[16]

Similar ideas are reflected in William James's psychology and his Edinburgh lectures published as *The Varieties of Religious Experience* (1902) established a basis in human psychology for mystical feelings and experiences that had little to do with either orthodox religion or morality. In France, Henri Bergson was formulating a philosophy of intuition which on one hand rejected the materialism and positivism of nineteenth century science and on the other found in Einstein's theories a scientific corroboration of his own views. Little by little, such ideas gained a footing among avant-garde artists and intellectuals, giving to their efforts in prose, poetry and the plastic arts

---

[16] From the "Conclusion" to *The Renaissance: Studies in Art and Poetry* (3rd ed. 1888), in *Selected Writings of Walter Pater*, ed. Harold Bloom (New York: NAL, 1974) 59.

a new rigor and toughness that had been absent in the work of the Symbolists and Decadents.

Perhaps no figure outside of the art world proper could have had as much influence within it as that beleaguered Viennese psychologist, Sigmund Freud. A not inconsiderable prose stylist himself, Freud served to link the biological and materialist science of the nineteenth century to a peculiarly twentieth century predilection for interior exploration. His insights into the unconscious motives of behavior and his daring exposure of the formerly unspeakable sexual component of personality pushed open a new window on human nature. Freud's *magnum opus*, *The Interpretation of Dreams* (1900) and his seminal *Three Essays on the Theory of Sexuality* (1905) both purported to describe and explain in a scientific manner the bizarre and irrational manifestations of the mind;[17] yet viewed in another way, they seem a continuation and development of the Symbolist, and later, Modernist impulse to delve into mysterious areas of the psyche, including the tendency to multiply meanings through association, to give credence to dreams and hallucinatory experiences, and to allow play to erotic fantasy. In any event, the contribution Freud's insights made went far beyond the technical field in which he was working; just as Darwin's monumental and ground-breaking book, *The Origin of Species* (1859), had altered the Victorians' way of looking at the world, so too did Freud's work insinuate itself into all areas of

---

[17] Anticipating its revolutionary impact upon the coming age, Freud purposely dated his *Interpretation* (which actually appeared in 1899) to conform with the first year of the new century. *Three Essays* was published the same year as Einstein's *Special Theory of Relativity*.

twentieth century culture, and especially that of literature. It became, as W. H. Auden so rightly said, part of our "climate of opinion."

It is as a general climate of opinion that all the aforementioned ideas must be seen in their relation to the creative writers discussed in this study. Certainly, Virginia Woolf's psychology can have derived as easily from Dostoyevsky as from Freud, while E. M. Forster's philosophy is no more a transcription of G. E. Moore than it is of Plotinus or the *Bhagavad Gita*. Yet the atmosphere in which the writers lived was saturated with ideas that their acute and sensitive minds could hardly fail to absorb, and these ideas were concentrated to a degree we in our more diffuse and technological age might find hard to imagine.[18]

That there are inevitable continuities as well as sharp breaks with the past is axiomatic to any historical study; Modernism, in particular, lends itself to the bi-polar view, for its thinkers and artists were as occupied in laying to rest what lay behind as in creating new alternatives for the future. There was in Modernism a certain hyper-subjective self-consciousness, absent among the Victorians. With the old certainties torn away, the Modernists felt convinced they had arrived at some unique juncture of destiny. What lay ahead might be frightening and horrific or sublime and transcendent, but it most certainly would be like nothing seen before.

Despite the bows to classicism and the anti-romantic stance of a Wyndham Lewis or a T. S. Eliot, it seems clear that insofar as Modernism is

---

[18] Even so, a parallel might be found in the immense influence that the ideas of Marshall McLuhan, Herbert Marcuse and Norman O. Brown exerted on a later generation, even upon those who did not actually read their books.

concerned with interior consciousness, with subject-object relations, and with the heightening and intensification of experience, it shares something crucial with Romanticism. Irving Howe claims that subjectivity is

> . . . the typical condition of the modernist outlook. In its early stages, when it does not trouble to disguise its filial dependence on the romantic poets, modernism declares itself as an inflation of the self, a transcendental and orgiastic aggrandizement of matter and event on behalf of personal vitality. In the middle stages, the self begins to recoil from externality and devotes itself, almost as if it were the world's body, to a minute examination of its own inner dynamics . . . . In the late stages, there occurs an emptying-out of the self, a revulsion from the wearisomeness of individuality and psychological gain.[19]

Certainly this is true for the three writers treated in this study. Their work exemplifies, in one way or another, all of the stages here outlined by Howe.

Forster, establishing a "filial dependence on the romantic poets," invoked Shelley in calling his second novel *The Longest Journey*, while his last borrows both the title and metaphysics of Whitman's "Passage to India." All of his works evince a desire to break down social boundaries that inhibit the self's expansion. Strachey's biographies reject the objective and event-centered methods of Victorian historiography in order to pursue a more subjective probing into the "inner dynamics" of his famous characters. And Virginia Woolf, who ranks among the great innovators of Modernist fiction, pioneered techniques whereby the interior flow of consciousness, and the evanescent subterranean nature of personality might gain priority over "the

---

[19] Irving Howe, "The Idea of the Modern," *The Idea of the Modern in Literature and the Arts*, ed. Irving Howe (New York: Horizon, 1967) 14-15.

old stable ego of the past." Her novel *The Waves* tunnels to the limit of solipsism, and finds there "an emptying-out of the self" that is, epistemologically, profoundly disquieting, and yet seemingly mystical in implication. Far from being a place from which the novel could no longer develop, *The Waves* can be seen as the parent of such later prose experiments as those of Beckett and the *roman nouveau*.

This predominant subjectivity was, for the Bloomsbury writers, in no wise a cancellation of the liberal and humane rationalism that was so much a cherished part of their Cambridge inheritance. Whatever of prophecy or mysticism there may be in the work of E. M. Forster and Virginia Woolf, these are always tempered and balanced by the analytic vigor and clear-eyed skepticism that were the hallmarks of the Moore legacy. Certainly, in the case of Lytton Strachey, who modelled himself on the French neo-classical writers and the English eighteenth century, the romantic/subjective element remains only problematically resolved in his work. If the world can indeed be divided between Aristotelians and Platonists, classicists and romantics, Benthamites and Coleridgeans, Lytton Strachey would be among the most troublesome of writers to place.

The books to be discussed in the following chapters are ordered more-or-less chronologically. Of Forster's six novels all but *A Passage to India* (1924) were written before the first World War. Lytton Strachey's *Eminent Victorians* (1918) made its appearance with the first books of the post-war period, and established a new standard for future biography. His *Queen Victoria* (1923) consolidated the territory opened up in the previous book and completed his anatomization of the Victorian Age. Though she had written many essays and reviews, Virginia Woolf's writing career began in earnest with the publication of *The Voyage Out* in 1915. Her remarkable productivity can be conveniently divided into three somewhat distinct periods, the first ending with the publication in 1922 of *Jacob's Room*. The second begins with the appearance of her book of essays *The Common Reader* in 1925 and culminates seven years later in 1932 with another volume of criticism, also called *The Common Reader*. The final extends from the publication of *Flush* (1933), an imaginative biography of Elizabeth Barrett Browning's dog, to *Between the Acts* which came out shortly after her death in 1941. During the second of these periods she wrote what are generally considered her best novels, *Mrs. Dalloway* (1925), *To the Lighthouse* (1927), and *The Waves* (1931), as well as a humorous mock-biography, *Orlando* (1928), and a deeply-felt feminist polemic, *A Room of One's Own* (1929). These, along with two important essays, "Modern Fiction," and "Mr. Bennett and Mrs. Brown," will form the core of the present discussion.

By reviewing their varied works, each in its turn, it is hoped that some sense of a common temper and inheritance among these three Bloomsbury writers might come into focus without for a minute diminishing their unique individuality. That the writings of Forster, Strachey and Woolf have at last achieved a status within "the great tradition" from which F. R. Leavis was so anxious to exclude them is attested by the continued interest they provoke and the relative popularity they still enjoy. As we make our way uneasily toward a new millennium, we may yet find in these writers not only pleasure, but some key to our future.

II

CAMBRIDGE, FORSTER AND "THE NEW LIFE"

When E. M. Forster came up to Kings College, Cambridge in 1897 he arrived at a university in the throes of an intellectual renaissance. Like so many exceptional men of his generation, Forster had hated his public school, feeling out of place in its rough and tumble, often brutal atmosphere.[1] Cambridge, on the other hand, was to prove, once Forster got his bearings, in every way congenial to his spirit. Here he was to meet a group of men whose companionship and influence upon him would be of lifelong duration, and here Forster was to discover a style of thought and being that in a sense recreated him, and made his subsequent writing possible.

Kings College itself had been until not too many years before a sort of private country club for Etonians, a place where privileged young gentlemen might come and enjoy a period of pleasant idleness without the slightest intellectual effort. So lax were its rules that a Kings "scholar" could obtain a degree without taking examinations, and if he remained unmarried, could pass automatically into a life-fellowship. University reforms initiated in the 1850s slowly changed this state of affairs. Though the academic standard remained low for some years, by the time Forster arrived, Cambridge was beginning to distinguish itself intellectually both in research and in the quality of its teaching.

---

[1] One of these, Tonbridge, Forster pilloried as Sawston School in *The Longest Journey.*

The Cavendish Laboratory was already gaining the international reputation it would maintain, attracting to it such minds as that of Ernest Rutherford whose pioneering studies in atomic theory helped bring about the new science of nuclear physics. And in philosophy Cambridge had entered one of the most fertile periods in its long history. Several names in particular stand out: Alfred North Whitehead (1861-1947), John McTaggart Ellis McTaggart (1866-1925), Bertrand Russell (1872-1970), and G. E. Moore (1873-1958), all associated with Trinity College.

Each of these men was to make a decided mark on philosophy, and it can be said without exaggeration that Bertrand Russell was to become one of the most influential and widely read intellectual figures of the twentieth century. Whitehead, too, has remained a thinker of considerable importance and his works are still easily available in inexpensive editions. As for McTaggart and Moore, though they are now far less generally familiar than either Russell or Whitehead, they were, at the turn of the century, definitely forces to be reckoned with; it is to their ideas that we can trace a large portion of what was to become the Bloomsbury ethos.

McTaggart stood for Transcendental or Absolute Idealism, a current of thought which, though running counter to the native empiricist tradition, had gained a noticeable momentum in British philosophy during the first half of the nineteenth century. This foreign Idealism, flowing out of Germany and the pens of Fichte, Hegel and Schelling, taught in brief that the phenomenal world, including matter, space and time, had no independent existence, but were rather the transitory shadows of immutable transcendental essences. It held that the movement of history was a dynamic process of the Absolute or World Spirit which proceeded dialectically toward ever greater synthesis.

This was not a philosophy that would greatly appeal to a nation intent on industrial expansion and dedicated to mercantile values. Its tenets smelled vaguely of sedition and of the rumblings of revolution. In fact, the early British proponents of Transcendental Idealism were neither politicians nor philosophers, but the poets of a new Romantic Age; Blake, Coleridge, Wordsworth and, later, Shelley became the voices of this passionate philosophy of the imagination which, setting itself against the secular rationalism of the Enlightenment, offered a "natural supernaturalism" and a revolutionary alternative both to Christian orthodoxy and to eighteenth century materialism.

But this Romantic reaction was not to last and by the 1840s it had fairly much spent its force, at least outside the universities. The chaos of the French Revolution and the Napoleonic Wars that followed put the government as well as the land-owning oligarchy of Great Britain in a mood of reaction. Anxious to preserve the stability of the monarchy and to consolidate the material gains industrialism and colonial expansion had brought, the English turned to a type of social and political philosophy more in harmony with these aims. Certainly by McTaggart's day Transcendental Idealism had sustained innumerable buffetings from the more naturalistic ideas associated with Victorianism, such ideas as Darwin's Evolutionism, Herbert Spencer's positivist social theories, and Mill's Utilitarianism. These scientific philosophies, more in the mainstream of British thought, to a great extent drove the alien German doctrines underground.

But while the fervent and revolutionary Romanticism of an earlier time faded away, a chastened Idealism did nonetheless persist throughout the Victorian era, especially in imaginative literature and poetry. Such mid-century movements as the Pre-Raphaelite Brotherhood are evidence of this continuity, and evidence too of the tenuous nature of Romantic heterodoxy against the prevailing tide of scientific materialism.

McTaggart himself, like Shelley before him, had begun his philosophical career a materialist and an atheist, but by the early 1890s he had become converted to the Idealist posture from which he never wavered. Though this was to a degree a maverick position, it is also true that during the *fin-de-siècle* some of the suppressed currents of Idealism began to bubble forth astonishingly. The Celtic Twilight, Madame Blavatsky's Theosophy, French *Symbolisme* were all a part of the exotic variety of movements spawned by the Romantic resurgence. At Oxford, a receptive place for new doctrines, the influential F. H. Bradley was preaching his own particular brand of Idealism to a generation already steeped in the Aesthetic Movement. All in all, it was an extraordinary confluence; streams of thought that had for so long run parallel but not touched – natural science, mysticism, theology, analytic philosophy – suddenly rushed in and commingled. In the heady atmosphere of pluralism, everything began to be questioned; time-honored codes of behavior, social institutions, religious practices, and sexual mores were all held up to scrutiny. The Victorian Age was, in a clamor of old and new, drawing to a close.

Even at Cambridge, with its strong rationalist bias, and where such aesthetic and religious movements as had often stirred Oxford seldom made much incursion, there was evidence of a growing dissatisfaction with the answers of both science and theology. Here F. W. H. Myers' respectable Society for Psychical Research attracted some of the university's most formidable minds, while radicals like George Bernard Shaw and Edward Carpenter advanced dress-reform, feminism, vegetarianism, and a cult of back-to-nature. It was in this milieu of change and experiment that McTaggart's Idealism, including his beliefs in reincarnation, immortality, and a sort of heaven without God where souls would be united in a communion of love, won for a time the serious regard of his Trinity colleagues.

This is not to suggest that rationalism was abjured; the fact is that McTaggart's exposition of his philosophy was solidly within the Cambridge analytical tradition. If anything, McTaggart was responsible for initiating a style of philosophical writing that aimed always at lucidity and precision, rejecting to a certain extent the obfuscation of his German sources. It may have been this, as much as the substance of his teaching, that attracted Moore, Whitehead and Russell to him. Many years later G. E. Moore was to write in his autobiography, "that many of the comparatively clear doctrines which he [McTaggart] attributed to Hegel were very unlike anything which Hegel could possibly have meant – certainly Hegel never meant anything so precise."[2] And Moore went on to say that long after he had ceased to find value in the work of Hegel, he continued to study and lecture upon McTaggart.

In the end all three men would repudiate McTaggart's Transcendental Idealism as well as the Hegelian dialectics which formed its backbone, but it

---

[2] Quoted in Paul Levy, *Moore* (New York: Holt, 1979) 108.

is evident that many of the features of his system were to remain embedded in their subsequent thinking. Certainly in the case of Moore, who is truly the philosophical prophet of Bloomsbury, the cogent reasoning, the clarity of expression, and the famous phrase associated with him, "What exactly do you mean by that?" are all legacies from McTaggart.

Some writers on Forster have tended to underplay the influence of Cambridge philosophy and G. E. Moore, in particular, upon him. Their points of view are well-taken if one is excessively literal about the notion of influence. Forster was by no means an abstract thinker, and the humorous irony with which he presents the Cambridge scenes in the first paragraphs of *The Longest Journey* – presumably an accurate recreation of an Apostolic get-together – would suggest his real distaste for the sort of unapplied cerebration he here portrays. But G. E. Moore's impact issued, by all accounts, from something other than just the intellectual authority of his speech and writing, great as that was. He seemed to exemplify for his fellow Apostles the real human value of philosophy. As with the ancient Greeks, Moore's reasoning had not only made him wise, it had made him good.

Leonard Woolf, who had known many eminent people, claimed at the end of his long life that G. E. Moore was "the only great man whom I have ever met or known in the world of ordinary, real life. There was in him . . . a combination of mind and character and behavior, of thought and feeling which made him qualitatively different from anyone else . . . ."[3] Others, too, saw in Moore a kind of saintliness in his passion for truth and

---

[3] Leonard Woolf, *Sowing* (New York: Harcourt, 1960) 131.

in his kindly demeanor. It would seem, finally, that it was the force of Moore's personality, his simplicity and moral integrity, as much as the power of his mind, that proved most potent to those who were drawn into his circle. Among these, we must include Forster who, if not precisely an intellectual disciple of Moore, was in profound ways affected by the moral ambiance of this man's teaching and character.

Moore's major work, *Principia Ethica*, published in 1903, is a short book with the stated purpose of discovering "the fundamental principles of ethical reasoning; and the establishment of these principles." In a series of carefully reasoned arguments Moore presents his case for an ethical pluralism in which a person should be at liberty to decide for himself the best mode of conduct. Moore states that "instead of following rules, . . . the individual should rather guide his choice by the direct consideration of the intrinsic value or vileness of the effects which his action may produce." This assertion, buttressed as it was by an impeccable logic, had an extraordinarily tonic effect both upon all subsequent work in formal Ethics, and even more so upon the minds of its most enthusiastic readers. Lytton Strachey was stunned. He wrote to Moore, ". . . I am carried away. I think your book has . . . wrecked all writers on Ethics from Aristotle and Christ to Herbert Spencer and Mr Bradley . . . ."[4] Maynard Keynes and Leonard Woolf would be equally swept into the fervor that surrounded the book's publication; thinking back on the effect it had upon them, Keynes said it was in the nature of a new faith or religion, while Woolf conversely claimed it was the book's eminent

---

[4] Quoted in Michael Holroyd, *Lytton Strachey: The Unknown Years 1880-1910* (New York: Holt, 1967) 180.

common sense that made its greatest appeal. These somewhat conflicting views are to our present purpose, for they suggest an important source for the creative dynamic that propelled the work of all the Bloomsbury Group. In one way or another, Moore's ethical reasoning entered into Keynesian economic theory, into Roger Fry's aesthetics, into Leonard Woolf's political writings, and into the biographical history that Lytton Strachey produced. Furthermore, the dialectical play of reason and mysticism, the belief in human relationships, the yearning toward higher states of mind, and the hope that is held out for transcendence – those factors which become so apparent in the final two chapters of *Principia Ethica* – are in every way at the core of the fiction Virginia Woolf and E. M. Forster were to write.

If indeed Forster never actually read *Principia Ethica*, it is certain that he knew of its essential contents through his avowedly Mooreist friends, Hugh Meredith and A. R. Ainsworth.[5] And though the rigorously analytic chapters are not likely to have appealed to him, the startlingly revolutionary message of the pages in which Moore launches into a discussion of states of consciousness and the nature of good, would have spoken more directly to Forster at this formative stage of his thinking. In effect, this message was a call to freedom, to a liberation of behavior from bourgeois repressions, and to the unbinding of the senses from their centuries of moral strangulation.

---

[5] Interesting discussions of this question can be found in S. P. Rosenbaum, "*The Longest Journey*: E. M. Forster's Refutation of Idealism," *E. M. Forster: A Human Exploration*, ed. G. K. Das and John Beer (London: Macmillan, 1979) 32-54; and in P. N. Furbank, "The Philosophy of E. M. Forster," *E. M. Forster: Centenary Revaluations*, ed. Judith Scherer Herz and Robert K. Martin (Toronto: U of Toronto P, 1982) 37-51.

To those still in thrall to rigid late-Victorian social codes, Moore's conclusion was more than a breath of fresh air; it was the beginning of a New Birth, and it emerged with all the promise of the coming century.

In the first chapter of Forster's *Where Angels Fear to Tread* (1905), after the hilarious scene of Lilia Herriton's departure by train, Philip, her brother-in-law, utters the phrase, "Here beginneth the New Life." He is being funny, and the more so as he has no idea how prophetic those words are to be. Released from the stifling grip of her in-laws and the atmosphere of their middle-class suburb, the high-spirited but very foolish Lilia will indeed encounter a new life in the warmer, more sensual climate of Italy.

On the surface of it, this first novel is a bright comedy of manners. The plot, if on occasion improbable, moves swiftly from crisis to crisis, and the characters are all of them well-drawn, though with easy strokes. For the most part, Forster gives us "round" rather than "flat" people, and even his caricatures – old Mrs. Herriton, for instance – are apt to reveal unexpected dimensions. Throughout, the reader is kept at sufficient distance from the protagonists to allow comedy to happen. Instinctively, Forster must have felt the danger of too great an empathy by which the tragic sense and his deeper intent would have overwhelmed the novel. For it is apparent almost immediately that some other force is at work here; its catch-words are "the New Life," "transfiguration," "conversion."

These terms are repeated at crucial points as a way of announcing the story's philosophical purpose, and yet, in the Apostolic manner, the profundities inherent in the idea of conversion or transfiguration are handled very lightly. What Forster knew, in his precocious wisdom, is that, yes, conversion, a New Birth might be possible (if unlikely), but it would come not in a blinding flash, with trumpets sounding, but rather in the ordinary course of life's events. It is important in Forster's essentially realist (though not materialist) view of the world that the various spiritual transformations toward which we are bent come about in utterly common as well as in uncommon ways. In other words, the birth of a baby (or the desire for such) is part of the yearning for immortality; a voyage to a foreign country may be analogous to a spiritual journey into unknown parts of oneself; love, friendship, marriage are outer symbols of the *coniunctio oppositorum*; and then death, which happens with so little fanfare in Forster's novels, is the final transfiguration, which comes when we have outgrown or can no longer sustain our present form and circumstances. This is not to say that a more dramatic and more truly spiritual conversion might not happen as well, though it is much rarer.

In that extraordinary scene at the end of *Where Angels Fear to Tread* when Philip Herriton comes to tell Gino that his kidnapped baby has been killed, and then, after a violent scuffle, watches as Caroline Abbott comforts the distraught man, "he was assured that there was greatness in the world. There came to him an earnest desire to be good through the example of this good woman. He would try henceforward to be worthy of the things she had revealed. Quietly, without hysterical prayers or banging of drums, he underwent conversion. He was saved."[6] Philip, the detached aesthete, achieves spiritual salvation by learning to embrace real life, the life of the

---

[6] E. M. Forster, *Where Angels Fear to Tread* (New York: Vintage, 1958) 173.

senses and the true life of the emotions. For Lilia who has married impulsively, mistaking physical attraction for love, transformation can only come after her descent into a hell of harsh realizations. This is the fate of other Forster heroines who suffer the same flaw, that of an undeveloped heart. In the case of Lilia, who is too foolish to become wise, her final moral triumph is to bring forth a new life into the world before she herself sinks into death. And this baby, brief though its existence is, becomes for its father Gino, for Caroline Abbott, and for Philip Herriton the agent of their individual redemptions.

It is evident, even without too carefully analyzing this slightest of Forster's novels, that in addition to displaying its author's formidable gifts as a writer of social comedy, *Where Angels Fear to Tread* also shows his desire to express a quite definite and mature ethical vision. That he had decided to wed this vision to comedy may itself be part of Forster's debt to his Cambridge and Apostolic alliances.

Among the Apostles, especially during the ascendancy of Lytton Strachey, levity as well as frankness were the general rule. Solemnity and pomposity were likely to be hooted down as hold-overs from the rejected Victorian past. Even the titles of those papers delivered before the Society tended to be clever and humorous rather than academic.[7] In one of these by G. E. Moore, "Is Conversion Possible?" the philosopher (who had by this time refuted McTaggart's Idealism) posed the question of whether or not the Philosopher's Stone might be found by which finally all doubt would be laid

---

[7] "Ought the father to grow a beard?" and "Does Absence Make the Heart Grow Fonder?" are the titles of two of Strachey's surviving papers.

to rest and a state of constant Truth achieved. The problem itself was meant absolutely in earnest, and the paper, like all of Moore's work, was very carefully reasoned. Yet when the issue was put up for vote, it was stated as "Can we turn Monday mornings into Saturday nights?" (Saturday nights being the Society's appointed meeting time). Here, both the matter and the tone are not at all unlike Forster's when he achieves, as he so often does, a balance between vision and humor.

Of course, Forster had precedents in earlier English novelists for the sort of fiction he wished to write. Jane Austen, George Meredith, Samuel Butler all combine social satire and humor with a decidedly moral tone. But with Forster it went further than the usual aims of satire, for he wished to express through his fiction a much richer, more complex philosophical outlook than any of these three predecessors had attempted. When queried late in life about his influences, Forster admitted the debt to Jane Austen whose penetrating domestic comedy had very much suited his temperament, but he went on to say that his bent was more ambitious, and that though he had used comedy, he had "tried to hitch it to other things."[8]

Among these "other things" is a feeling for landscape and nature that owes a great deal to Romanticism. While on occasion this can appear to be no more than the usual English love of the countryside and a lyrical appreciation of it, more often Forster sees place and its objects – houses, ruins, ancient sites, trees, rocks – as having their own superior life, amidst which the doings of human beings can either seem petty and false or else be

---

[8] P. N. Furbank and Francis Haskell, "The Art of Fiction: E. M. Forster," *Paris Review*, No. 1 (Spring 1973).

altered by the contact. In *The Longest Journey* (1907), for instance, there is the secluded sacred dell which for Rickie Elliot is "a kind of church – a church where indeed you could do anything you liked, but where anything you did would be transfigured."[9] Later, in the same book, we are transported to Cadbury Rings, a mysterious site harking back to the Druids or beyond. Here Rickie, Mrs. Failing, Stephen Wonham, and Agnes Pembroke retreat as an antidote to the Anglican service they've just attended. And here Rickie learns from Mrs. Failing that Stephen is his illegitimate half-brother, a fact so abhorrent to him that he faints as he stands in the center of the ancient Rings. Like the spirals in Dante's *Commedia*, those of Cadbury seem to symbolize stages along the road of purgation and self-awareness. Apparently the spiritual potency of such pre-historic sacred places can remain effective long after the original inhabitants have disappeared, for as he is brought to, Rickie, whose repressions have hidden so much from him, has a revelation: "The earth he had dreaded lay close to his eyes, and seemed beautiful. He saw the structure of the clods. A tiny beetle swung on the glass blade. . . . There broke from him a cry, not of horror but of acceptance."[10] Rickie's momentary descent into the Unconscious seems to have brought about a symbolic embracing of his long-denied sensual nature. Unfortunately, as so often in Forster, it is a salvation manqué, and Rickie Elliot must face many another trial and many another failed atonement before his sad end.

In addition to this innovative use of place, Forster comes closer in this novel than in any other to a representation of the specific philosophical issues

---

[9] E. M. Forster, *The Longest Journey* (New York: Vintage, 1922) 19.

[10] Forster, *The Longest Journey* 142-43.

which had been so hotly debated by the Cambridge Apostles in their late night discussions. Cambridge itself represents all that is high-minded and unworldly in contrast to the bourgeois philistinism of Sawston. To be sure, the Cambridge scenes in *The Longest Journey* often contain elements of satire, for Forster wants to poke fun at the sophomoric intellectualizations of these young men who have had so little real experience of the world. But if he seems to make light of the perennial question of whether or not the cow one observes in the field has an existence apart from one's perception of it, he uses this as a spring-board for concerns of even greater moment. *The Longest Journey* is indeed almost too packed, overloaded one might say, with symbolic incident.

The main protagonist, Rickie Elliot, is lame, a deformity we are told is hereditary, and which has caused him to decide he must remain unmarried and childless. We learn, in addition, that he intensely disliked his father who cared even less for him, while for his mother Rickie had an entirely docile reverence. This troubling set of emotions is made even more problematic by the fact that both parents have died by the time Rickie is fifteen. Like Oedipus, Rickie Elliot must endure a series of painful revelations, chiefly centering on the fact of his kinship to Stephen Wonham. He is able to maintain his posture of disgust so long as he believes the crude and earthy Stephen is the bastard son of his hated father, but when he at last learns the truth, that Stephen is his beloved mother's illegitimate child, he cannot support the fact and is undone. The contrasts in this novel between realism and idealism, asceticism and sensuality, intellect and emotion, and between various types of love makes it perhaps one of the most dialectical works of fiction ever written, and yet we are left unsatisfied and unsettled at the conclusion.

Where Angels Fear to Tread succeeds where *The Longest Journey* does not by maintaining its humor and keeping a fine balance between the demands of social satire and the author's deeper moral intent. The second novel, on the other hand, seems swamped and confused in its motives. All the right ingredients are there – a plot full of dramatic events, social issues, ethical crises – but the mix is imperfect. Interestingly, there is more of Forster himself here than in the previous book. It is evident that he drew closely on his own experience as well as on his own dilemmas; in fact, the trouble may be that the novel is too "personal" in that sense that the author hasn't sufficient distance on his material. Forster, it would seem, is one of those writers who writes best when his attention is focused somewhat outside himself. As with Jane Austen, acute observation is his strongest suit, while excessive introversion turns his work morbid and neurotic. There is, of course, much to admire in *The Longest Journey* and for the author himself it paved the way for the greater success that was to follow.

In *A Room with a View* (1908) Forster returned to the comedic strategy he had so successfully deployed in his first novel. It seems he had actually outlined the plot much earlier and had even done some of the writing, but what resulted was a definite advance on the two previous books. Here is all the brightness and spirit of the first and a good deal of the profundity of the second, yet more closely knitted into a unified pattern. The characters are, all-in-all, better realized, more firmly anchored in their fictive world, and (unlike the paler intelligences that had preceded them) vibrating with organic life. Italy, here again, is the great good place where all the proprieties, repressions, and frozen emotions brought down from the British Isles either come undone in a great muddle, or melt altogether. Of course, Florence is primarily a stage set for a very English comedy, and any Italians who appear are in the nature of props; even Englishmen, like Reverend Eager, who have made Italy their home are in no sense assimilated. Indeed, the expatriots have a good deal more distrust and distaste for the average Italian than the tourists who are always yearning for a taste of "the real Italy." For the former, it is the Medieval and Renaissance art, the postcard views across the Arno, and the secluded villas to which they retire that make Italy worthwhile. The brawling, begging, love-making natives are but a nuisance to be endured, or sent on their way.

Forster presents his characters in contrasting pairs: Charlotte Bartlett and Lucy Honeychurch, a fussy spinster and her attractive but naive and unformed young cousin; the Emersons, father and son, the elder a socialist and freethinker, the younger handsome but maladjusted; two Anglican clergymen, a Rev. Beebe representing the more benign aspect of his calling, and a Mr. Cuthbert Eager who signifies everything that is snobbish, false, worldly and unkind about his religion. There are also the two elderly unmarried sisters, the early Victorian Miss Alans, and standing alone, a lady novelist, Eleanor Lavish, who fancies herself unconventional and adventurous. They are all of them types Forster knew well, and he gets their patter perfectly, revealing through their seemingly inconsequential remarks the fiber of which these people are made.

Yet no character here is too intimately Forster himself. In this novel he maintains an admirable critical distance, so crucial to the comic tone, while allowing the characterizations and the plot to carry the freight of social commentary, and the ironic style to bear the burden of meaning which he had delivered over to an intrusive authorial voice in *The Longest Journey*.

The mood of *A Room with a View* is one of lightness and rapidity, especially in Part One which takes place in Italy (and which was apparently drafted several years earlier than Part Two). The complexities and ambiguities of *The Longest Journey* are not initially in evidence here, the plot being much more straightforward in its movement. Nonetheless, from its initial scenes the novel reveals the psychological and social forces which propel it forward. The setting is the Pension Bertolini, situated in Florence, a hostel neither shabby nor elegant which caters to the English tourist. Charlotte Bartlett and Lucy Honeychurch have arrived to discover that they've been given, not the promised rooms with views, but rather rooms which look out upon a courtyard. Hearing their complaint, Mr. Emerson, to whom they have not been introduced, offers to exchange rooms with them, for he and his son, he claims, care little for views. This unsolicited and generous offer is seen by Miss Bartlett as a gross violation of propriety, one that would put her and her young charge somehow under obligation to the strangers, and she curtly rebuffs it. Then, through a curtain, the genial Rev. Beebe appears who after a time assures the lady that she might with impunity make the exchange, for Mr. Emerson, though "rather a peculiar man. . . . has the merit – if it is one – of saying exactly what he means."[11]

Honesty and directness are, in this world of gentility, carefully modulated small-talk, and behavior dictated by sacrosanct social codes, highly suspect, and can only reveal the Emersons as people of inferior status. Lucy, upon whom the novel is chiefly focused, becomes the example of a crippling bifurcation of inward feeling from outer demeanor that these inviolable codes enforce. She is treated by her creator, though, in a more sympathetic manner than either Lily Herriton or Agnes Pembroke, for Lucy at least has a chance of salvation. She plays Beethoven with feeling, and occasionally she senses inchoate currents of emotion trying to break through. Unfortunately, when these threaten to surface, she quickly stifles them, until she can "re-enter the world of rapid talk, which was alone familiar to her" (*RV* 30).

While Lucy does have a certain sensitivity to visual art, she requires guide books to buttress it with dates, classifications, and the approval of recognized art historians. For instance, when Miss Lavish runs off with her Baedeker, Lucy in dismay realizes she will have to tour Santa Croce without it. "She walked around disdainfully, unwilling to be enthusiastic over monuments of uncertain authorship or date" (*RV* 25). In a very comical but significant scene which propels Lucy toward her next fateful encounter with the Emersons, she wanders over the sepulchral slabs that cover the floor of the cathedral's transept, wondering which "was the one that was really

---

[11] E. M. Forster, *A Room with a View* (Harmondsworth, Middlesex, England: Penguin, 1955) 13. All subsequent references, cited within the text, will be to this edition.

beautiful, the one that had been most praised by Mr Ruskin" (*RV* 25). It of course does not occur consciously to her that she is walking over graves, and that the dead past of an Age of Faith lies beneath her feet; she is too peevishly concerned to acquire the "proper" aesthetic sensation. But even this eludes her. There is for Lucy Honeychurch not a shred of spiritual feeling, either positive or negative, among the statues and paintings of the ancient church.

Growing weary of art, Lucy begins to observe both the red-nosed tourists and also the natives who come to make their ablutions. A little Italian boy, apparently in the church to pray, stumbles over the stone slab of a recumbent bishop. Mr. Emerson rushes over to help him, and as he dusts the boy off, enjoins him to leave the dark damp church and to "go out into the sunshine . . . and kiss your hand to the sun, for that is where you ought to be" (*RV* 26). It is the first time we hear of the old man's "natural religion" which plays such a large part in *A Room with a View*. Certainly, his belief has nothing to do with the Christian God, or with sin, or saints, or prayer books. Rather, it seems a compound of Classical paganism, the Transcendentalism of Emerson and Thoreau, and the Democratic Socialism of Edward Carpenter. It is, whatever else, a counterpoise to body-denying Christianity, both to that of the medievalism which surrounds him in Santa Croce and to the Calvinism of his British compatriots.

We see this especially in the encounter with the unpleasant Rev. Eager, who is at that moment lecturing to a group of tourists on the frescoes of Giotto. Eager tells them (perhaps in refutation of Ruskin and Pater) not to appreciate Giotto for his tactile, but rather for his spiritual values. Then he reminds them that Santa Croce was built "by faith in the full fervour of medievalism, before any taint of the Renaissance had appeared" (*RV* 28). Hearing this, Emerson exclaims, "Built by faith indeed! That simply means the workmen weren't paid properly. And as for the frescoes, I see no truth in them. Look at that fat man in blue! He must weigh as much as I do, and he is shooting into the sky like an air-balloon" (*RV* 28). Rev. Eager's reference to the Middle Ages is important, for "medieval" and its adjunct "chivalry" are part of the novel's shorthand for everything that is flesh-denying, ascetic, opposed to the body and to the senses.

Meanwhile, Lucy has come forward to the fallen child's aid as well. She, no more Papist than Mr. Emerson, suddenly finds herself in uneasy league with him against medieval superstition, but very perplexed. Her discomfort makes her say all the correct-sounding things, but her Edwardian manners and the studied proprieties of her speech are quickly punctured by the tactless and truth-telling Mr. Emerson. As Mr. Eager and his offended audience move away, Lucy begins to feel "that she ought not to be with these men; but they had cast a spell over her. They were so serious and so strange that she could not remember how to behave" (*RV* 28). While George gazes entranced at a fresco of the ascension of St. John, Mr. Emerson confides to Lucy his concern over his son's evident unhappiness, imploring her to see what she might do for him. He explains George's "world sorrow" and perplexity, declaring that while they both understand that "life is perhaps a knot, a tangle, a blemish in the eternal smoothness" (*RV* 32), he sees no reason why this should make his boy so unhappy. But all of this is too much for Lucy and she retreats to her old formulas about hobbies and the salutary effects of foreign travel. Her salvation, and George's, are yet to come.

Shortly thereafter, in the late afternoon of a wet Florentine day, Lucy saunters forth alone into the Piazza Signoria vaguely hoping for some sort of adventure. There, she stops to buy a packet of art photographs, notably one of Botticelli's "Birth of Venus" which to her mind is spoiled only by the nudity of its central figure. Forster's description of the Piazza, as Claude Summers has pointed out,[12] is suffused with sexual symbolism: the phallic palace tower, the womb-like loggia, and brooding over it all, the muscular naked figure of Neptune, beneath whom sport a group of satyrs. These monuments, produced during the height of the Renaissance, are the antithesis of the medieval ideal against which Lucy is in half-hearted rebellion. As she starts back to the Pension Bertolini, rather disappointed that nothing exceptional has occurred, a fight breaks out between two men over a small debt. In the fray, one is hit on the chest. Stumbling in Lucy's direction, it appears "as if the man had an important message for her. He opened his lips to deliver it, and a stream of red came out between them" (*RV* 47). Lucy immediately faints.

Just before she blacks out, Lucy sees George Emerson looking at her "across something." The next moment, he is holding her in his arms. There is an instant conflation of George with the dying man and his aborted message. Like Rickie Elliot, Lucy returns from this semi-death with a new vision: "The whole world seemed pale and void of its original meaning. . . . The thought occurred to her . . . that she, as well as the dying man, had

---

[12] Claude J. Summers, *E. M. Forster* (New York: Ungar, 1983) 84.

crossed some spiritual boundary" (*RV* 48-49). The event seems also to have triggered in George, who is still peering at Lucy, "but not across anything," a life-affirming revelation. Confessing to her that he has thrown the blood-bespattered photographs into the Arno, he says, "something tremendous has happened; . . . . I shall probably want to live" (*RV* 50-51). For George, cognizant to the point of suicide that life is not only a great enigma ("the everlasting Why"), but perhaps an insoluble one, the inner conversion precipitated by the dramatic occurrences in the piazza is incalculably important. Lucy, on the other hand, once she has collected herself, immediately pulls back from the realm of meaning, the "spiritual boundary," toward which she had made so close an approach. Begging George (who she fears "lacked chivalry") not to tell the others about the strange adventure, she breezily asserts, "how quickly these accidents do happen, and then one returns to the old life!" (*RV* 51). Yet the image of death and resurrection remains to haunt her. George, the more percipient of the two, is willing to attribute his rebirth at least in part to Lucy. But Lucy, who cannot yet admit to consciousness the possibility of a passion for the peculiar young man, must marshall all her defenses toward denying both deeper meaning and sensual love, which in Forster's present scheme go hand in hand.

The next episode brings to a sort of culmination the previous movements. Rev. Eager, who knows all the "best" people of the English colony, arranges an outing but plans to exclude the undesirables, especially the despised Emersons and the too eccentric Miss Lavish. The respectable and snobbish curate (one of Forster's best satiric achievements) is the antithesis of everything his author cherishes as right and good. His manner oozes a subtle malice and insincerity. In Santa Croce we overhear him lecture on the virtues of St. Francis – ". . . full of innate sympathy . . . quickness to perceive good in others . . . vision of the brotherhood of man . . ." (*RV* 30) – just after snubbing the kindly if perhaps too blunt Mr. Emerson. Later, when he meets Lucy and Charlotte in the Piazza Signoria, he fishes greedily for details of the previous day's tragedy, while rudely shooing away vendors and bemoaning the fact that such a frightful thing should happen in the city of Dante and Savonarola.

Through all of this, we realize that Lucy, however benighted, has moved a few steps closer to the truth. At once she perceives both the pretentiousness of Miss Lavish's self-advertised claims to art and originality and the hypocrisy of Mr. Eager's piety and culture. These latter two characters, though not on good terms with one another, are definitely linked by a shared complacency and egotism.

Foiled the following day by the rival arrangements of Reverend Beebe, Mr. Eager is obliged to ride in a carriage with both Miss Lavish and Mr. Emerson. They are driven by a handsome Italian, the embodiment of Phaethon, who stops to collect his "sister," a lovely Persephone. Noticing after a while that their driver has his arm around the young woman, Eager insists, against the protests of the others, that Persephone must be let off. Mr. Emerson, of course, warmly champions the cause of love: "Do we find happiness so often that we should turn it off the box when it happens to sit there? To be driven by lovers – a king might envy us, and if we part them it's more like sacrilege than anything I know" (*RV* 69). The rest are in a turmoil; should they be on the side of Nature or on the side of Propriety? Mr. Eager is victorious and the party proceeds.

Reaching their destination, the tourists are scattered in various directions. Restless, Lucy wanders off in search of Mr. Beebe and Mr. Eager. She is guided by Phaethon to a gorgeous terrace covered with a profusion of violets. Here she encounters, not the two clergymen, but George Emerson who upon seeing her rushes up and gives her a passionate kiss. This brief love scene is immediately interrupted by the intrusive figure of Charlotte Bartlett, standing "brown against the view" (*RV* 75).

Concerned for Lucy's reputation and even more so for her own as chaperon, Charlotte flees with Lucy to Rome, and thence back to England. What happens in Rome we are not specifically told, but we do find that Lucy has got on terms of formal intimacy with Mr. Cecil Vyse, a cultured dandy and aesthete. Just as the first chapter of Part One begins in the shaded and very English rooms of the Pension Bertolini, the beginning of Part Two is set in the heavily curtained drawing-room of the Honeychurch home, Windy Corner. Each location is an enclosure guarding the proprieties, shielding its inhabitants from the unpredictability of unwelcome intruders, as well as from Nature itself. Outside, on the private terrace of Windy Corner with its two neat flower beds, Cecil Vyse is attempting to win Lucy's hand in marriage. Within, Mrs. Honeychurch and Lucy's young brother, Freddy, await the outcome.

Cecil has antecedents in Forster's two previous novels. Like Philip Herriton and Rickie Elliot, he is a man caught up in ideas of art and beauty, and yet unable to really live:

> He was medieval. Like a Gothic statue. Tall and refined, with shoulders that seemed braced square by an effort of the will, and a head that was tilted a little higher than the usual level of vision, he resembled those fastidious saints who guard the portals of a French cathedral. Well-educated, well endowed, and not deficient physically, he remained in the grip of a certain devil whom the modern world knows as self-consciousness, and whom the medieval, with dimmer vision, worshipped as asceticism. A Gothic statue implies celibacy, just as a Greek statue implies fruition . . . . (*RV* 93)

This character type is very important to Forster, and he likely included himself, reluctantly, among those with this particularly modern disease of self-consciousness. The "naturals" – Gino, Stephen Wonham, George Emerson – may have their own deficiencies, but there is usually an implied superiority of their lives, governed by physical passion and emotion, over those lives ruled by sterile intellect and artificially cultivated sensibility. Here again, the medieval is seen as an obstructing wall between a pre-Christian pagan ideal, and some new order struggling to emerge out of the Victorian past.

That Lucy should accept Cecil's proposal shows how much she is still in the grip of "the medieval"; fearful of passion, anxious to submit to Cecil's aesthetic superiority, in no sense "in love," Lucy would rather be "like a woman of Leonardo da Vinci's, whom we love not so much for herself as for the things that she will not tell us" (*RV* 95) – Cecil's view of her – than to attempt the more arduous task of becoming herself.

It is one of the wonderful ironies of the novel that its celibates are made to play an inadvertent part in uniting and bringing to life the stifled passions of those characters destined for redemption. Onto this particular scene of chaste betrothment appears the Reverend Beebe. He has taken up his post as rector of Summer Street, the little village where Windy Corner is situated. Before he discovers the engagement, he repeats to Cecil the sentiment he had expressed to Lucy some time before at the Pension Bertolini, to the effect that if she ever took to living in the manner in which she played the piano, "the water-tight compartments in her will break down, and music and life will mingle. Then we shall have her heroically good, heroically bad . . ." (*RV* 99). But Mr. Beebe, the voice of Pauline virginity, does not suspect just how prescient his words will be.

An amusing series of events follows: Sir Harry, the principle squire of Summer Street has acquired a pair of unattractive new villas, considered eyesores by the townsfolk, and is in the position of letting them. Lucy suggests the Miss Alans, and begins to make arrangements with the elderly spinsters. Cecil, who is contemptuous of Sir Harry and the whole population of Summer Street, decides to play what he thinks will be a clever trick upon them. Having met at the National Gallery a man and his son, a pair he presumed to be, if not vulgar, at least sufficiently lacking in gentility, he too arranges the tenancy of the Summer Street villa. In the way of things, these men happen to be Mr. Emerson and his son, George.

With their appearance, Truth and passion reassert themselves among the staid civilities of Lucy's present life. For one, her brother Freddy, a likeable young man, quickly takes to George. He and Rev. Beebe together pay a call at the villa as the Emersons are moving in. Piled in the sitting-rooms are tokens of the Emerson creed: a volume of Byron, Housman's *A Shropshire Lad*, Butler's *The Way of All Flesh*, Schopenhauer, Nietzsche, while in the passage is a wardrobe crudely inscribed with the Thoreauvian motto, "Mistrust all enterprises that require new clothes." Freddy immediately suggests that they go for a swim, and he leads Mr. Beebe and George to his cherished pond, a place he and Lucy call The Sacred Lake. Whether or not he has sloughed off his previous melancholy, George knows, just as surely as he knew he'd crossed some spiritual threshold in Italy, that Fate has brought him to this place. While he and Freddy splash about, urging Mr. Beebe to join them, "a change came over them" (*RV* 139), all restraint is let loose, and they race wildly around the pond, tossing one another's clothes into the water, until they are surprised by the unexpected appearance of Mrs. Honeychurch, Lucy and Cecil, who happen to be taking a walk in the woods. Funny as the scene is, it bears comparison to those previous moments of epiphany – Philip Herriton's in Monteriano, Rickie Elliot's at Cadbury Rings, and George's in the Piazza Signoria – for this naked return to Nature "had been a call to the blood and to the relaxed will, a passing benediction whose influence did not pass, a holiness, a spell, a momentary chalice for youth" (*RV* 141).

But while George passes into a state of grace, the unfortunate Lucy grows more and more muddled. Faced with the prospect of marriage to Cecil whose supercilious manner has begun to put off those closest to her, Lucy has now to confront George Emerson and the unsettled business between them. Though she is disturbed by memories, Lucy "never gazed inwards. If at times strange images rose from the depths, she put them down to nerves" (*RV* 151). At this point, the final ironic agent of her fate arrives.

Charlotte Bartlett, her plumbing at Tunbridge Wells in disarray, has been invited by the sympathetic Mrs. Honeychurch to stay at Windy Corner. As usual, calamity seems to follow in her wake. While Lucy, George, Freddy and his friend gather on the tennis lawn, Cecil begins to mockingly read an atrocious novel he has picked up from the library. Entitled *Under a Loggia*, it describes a group of English tourists in Florence, in particular a young woman named Leonora who on a bank carpeted with violets is suddenly kissed by a romantic young man. Immediately aware both of the pseudonymous novel's provenance, as well as the source of this scene, Lucy moves to confront cousin Charlotte with the accusation of having revealed to Miss Lavish their mutual secret. But as she walks toward the house just ahead of George and Cecil, the latter falls back to retrieve the forgotten book while George Emerson advances on Lucy and steals another kiss.

Trying to remain indignant, Lucy scolds Charlotte and then attempts to upbraid George for his misconduct, but even as she is ordering him from her house, she feels him beckoning "over the rubbish, the sloppy thoughts, the furtive yearnings that were beginning to cumber her soul" (*RV* 175). He replies by eloquently spelling out for her just the sort of man he believes Cecil Vyse to be, the sort who can "know no one intimately, least of all a woman," and who takes pleasure in "playing tricks on people, on the most sacred form of life that he can find" (*RV* 177). After George leaves, Lucy returns to the terrace in the grip of powerful emotions. Freddy, unaware of what has just occurred, calls for Cecil and her to take George's place at tennis. Hearing Cecil refuse in his usual haughty tone, "the scales fell from

Lucy's eyes. How had she stood Cecil for a moment? He was absolutely intolerable, and the same evening she broke her engagement off" (*RV* 180).

The denouement is swift, and brought about in part by the machinations of the two virgins, Charlotte Bartlett and Reverend Beebe. Lucy, forever confused, acts to escape her problems by planning to go to Greece with the Miss Alans, enlisting Charlotte's help in persuading her mother. Surrounded by these guardians of chastity, she feels she might avoid the prying of her family and their servants, the questionings of curious neighbors, the further importunings of George Emerson, and her own tumultuous emotions. In the midst of all Lucy's prevarication, Mrs. Honeychurch, a paragon of good sense, accuses her daughter of behaving exactly like cousin Charlotte. Brought up short by this remark, Lucy little by little begins to see the terrible result of her obtuseness and confusion: "Waste! That word seemed to sum up the whole of life. Wasted plans, wasted money, wasted love . . . . Was it possible that she had muddled things away? Quite possible" (*RV* 208).

Lucy and her mother drive to pick up Charlotte who has been visiting Mr. Beebe's mother. They notice that the Emerson's villa has been put up for let, and find out from the driver that the old man is ill with rheumatism and has decided to move to London with his son. As Charlotte emerges from the rectory and goes on with Mrs. Honeychurch to the church, Lucy, who does not wish to join them, is led by a maid into Mr. Beebe's study to wait. There she is surprised to find a very disconsolate and weary Mr. Emerson to whom she must repeat the same lies she has been telling the others. As always, he sees through her subterfuge and begs her to clear up the muddle before it's too late. In tears, Lucy refuses at first to understand.

It is significant that Lucy has declined to go up to the church with her mother and Charlotte, and yet she finds herself here confronted by Reverend Beebe's volumes of theology which "surrounded the visitors on every side; they were piled on the tables, they pressed against the very ceiling" (*RV* 213). It seems dreadful to her that poor Mr. Emerson, an impious freethinker, should have to take refuge here. She is unable to see that "Mr Emerson was profoundly religious, and different from Mr Beebe chiefly by his acknowledgement of passion" (*RV* 213). The juxtaposition of the two spiritual perspectives is crucial, for the former, the medieval, is one of the "water-tight compartments" blocking Lucy's self-awareness, while Mr. Emerson's religion, which admits passion and bodily love, is to be the source of her salvation.

Trying to bring her round to clarity and truth, Mr. Emerson implores Lucy to realize that she has loved George all along, and that only her fear of physical love has prevented her from seeing it. At first, Lucy "could not understand him: the words were indeed remote. Yet as he spoke the darkness was withdrawn, veil after veil, and she saw to the bottom of her soul" (*RV* 216). As so often in Forster, psychic transformation comes a bit too suddenly for what has gone before, but this is due, perhaps, to his belief that generally conversion was an instantaneous and unexpected (if undramatic) process, an abrupt reordering of the soul. Mr. Emerson's revelations have "robbed the body of its taint, [and] . . . shown her the holiness of direct desire. . . . It was as if he had made her see the whole of everything at once" (*RV* 218).

Her eyes at last opened, Lucy is ready to embark on "the New Life," a life of the awakened senses. She marries George Emerson and returns to honeymoon in Florence. The Comic Muse who had for a moment seemed to desert the novel, in the final chapter reappears; the couple find themselves reestablished at the Pension Bertolini, laughing over the curious course of events that has brought them back to the same pension and the same room with a view. They reflect how narrowly they had gained this happiness, and George remarks on the irony that Charlotte's unwitting (or perhaps not so unwitting) collaboration had, in effect, brought them into one another's arms.

Earlier, invoking George Meredith, Cecil Vyse had commented that "the cause of Comedy and the cause of Truth are really the same" (*RV* 124). In the moral universe of *A Room with a View*, no maxim could be more apt.

III
"ONLY CONNECT . . .": *HOWARDS END* AND *MAURICE*

Though only two years separate the publication dates of *A Room with a View* (1908) and *Howards End* (1910), they were years in which a certain watershed was crossed. As Virginia Woolf so decidedly put it, "On or about December, 1910, human character changed." In the history of Modernism, other dates might as easily be picked to indicate important demarcation points: certainly 1900 is one (though Queen Victoria did not die until a year later), 1918 (the end of the first World War) is another and, further on, 1929 (the year of so many crises) might be chosen to denote a culmination of this era. But in 1910 King Edward VII died, and with him an older order seemed to pass away. That brief idyll known as the Edwardian period was in many ways only Victorianism with its stays loosened. The social structure was as yet organized much as it had always been, with a landed aristocratic ruling class occupying the large county estates, an ever widening (and increasingly rich) industrial middle-class, and then the vast legions of the working-class and the very poor from whose ranks came the nobles' footmen, cooks and serving maids as well as a labor force for the coal mines and factories of the wealthy capitalists.

The age-old gap between rich and poor had perhaps not greatly widened, but the darker side of industrial capitalism, which had brought about the decline of the old agrarian feudal order, was becoming ever more apparent. The size and squalor of London's slums had increased enormously during the nineteenth century, rendering poverty more visible and its degrading results far more difficult to ignore. The burgeoning power of

Socialism and of the Labor Party, along with the militant movement for women's suffrage were all part of the political response called forth by these various economic forces and by the resultant change in consciousness that Virginia Woolf had remarked.

This change is evident in *Howards End*, a novel which both directly and subtly confronts some of the major social issues of this transitional period. In no other of Forster's books, for instance, does money play so large a part, and the question of inherited versus newly-acquired wealth is one of the important dynamics of this particular work. Where *A Room with a View* depends in many ways upon Edwardian conventions and expectations – chaperonage, sexual reticence, the assumed delicacy of young ladies – to propel its comedy, *Howards End* is much more modern. It could, in fact, be brought in imagination even closer to our own times. The houses might need to be shrunk a bit and some of the servants dismissed, but otherwise it doesn't greatly betoken a too distant past. Helen and Margaret Schlegel are far more liberated heroines than any of Forster's previous women, and we take it for granted that they should go about London alone, administer their own love affairs, attend meetings, operas and plays, or travel to Germany unescorted.

Even the landscape seems to have changed. The Suburbia of the former novels has been notably modernized: "It was new, it had island platforms and a subway, and the superficial comfort exacted by business men."[1] One must go yet farther afield to find unspoiled nature, and the

---

[1] E. M. Forster, *Howards End* (Harmondsworth, Middlesex, England: Penguin, 1967) 16. All subsequent references, cited within the text, will be to this edition.

insidious encroachment of "development" is always just over the next hill. Where not too many years before horse-drawn carriages had conveyed a fairly stable population from one town to the next, now motor cars (in this novel especially associated with Charles Wilcox) roar through the landscape stirring up dust and leaving the roads clogged and smelling of petrol. Those ugly semi-detached villas that had so upset the citizens of Summer Street here do not raise an eyebrow, while the well-established residential neighborhoods of London are razed with little protest to make way for massive blocks of flats.

The classes, too, are mingling and mixing as never before, their boundaries becoming ever less distinct. We get a beginning of this in *A Room with a View*: Mr. Honeychurch, we are told, was a prosperous local solicitor who, having built an impressive home, was soon taken by newer residents moving in from London as the remnant of an indigenous aristocracy, an error Mrs. Honeychurch has done nothing to dispel. And Lucy's inability to recognize her feelings for George Emerson results as much from class snobbery as from sexual repression; Cecil Vyse, if unlovable, is a much better match than a poor railway clerk with no connections. The merger of classes is carried in *Howards End* a step further. Like Jane Austen, Forster seldom ventures either too far up or too far down the social scale,[2] but within its broad middle range he is willing to tackle the important question, as Lionel Trilling put it, of "who shall inherit England?"

---

[2] He even admitted, in the *Paris Review* interview with P. N. Furbank, that his description of the Bast's home-life was rather a stretch for him.

In this social sense, especially, the sisters Schlegel are infinitely more advanced than any female characters we have yet met. Forster claimed that they were based on the sisters of his friend, Goldsworthy Lowes Dickinson, and it seems clear that they also have affinities with Vanessa Bell and Virginia Stephen. If not in personality, at least in their activities, Margaret and Helen remind us of the two young Stephen women who, set free by the death of their parents and privileged with independent incomes, pursued liberal political causes and art and personal relationships with such enthusiasm. Even the presence of the Schlegel's unmarried and rather passive brother, Tibby, suggests the sort of arrangement one might have encountered at Fitzroy or Gordon Square, Bloomsbury around 1910.

It is important in the scheme of *Howards End* that the Schlegels are not, any more than are the Wilcoxes, landed gentry. They are, instead, members of the intellectual upper middle-class with sufficient money and leisure to allow them to act out their social and aesthetic ideals with little concern for the harsher realities of money-getting. For this, Margaret feels grateful and inclined to remind her less practical younger sister of the economic foundation upon which their liberalism is built. The Wilcoxes, in contrast, are well-to-do industrialists – they have a rubber company based in Africa – and are very much involved in every aspect of finance and speculation. Deficient in poetry, they are nonetheless the epitome of those values and qualities which, now more than ever, have come to stamp the business world: competitiveness, egoistic self-assertion, and the urge to profit and dominate. Unattached to the land, the Wilcoxes tend to view its traditional values with disdain. Their attitude to property, to people and to ideas is at best, utilitarian, at worst, exploitative.

Mr. Wilcox, to be fair, has retained something of the benevolent paternalism and decent manners of an earlier day. He arranges everything with remarkable efficiency and has a gentlemanly concern for the welfare of others. His older son, Charles, on the other hand, is completely reprehensible. Spoiled, rude and very selfish, he is seldom seen except when bullying a servant or abusing a porter or dismissing his very silly wife. So unredeemed and unredeemable is he that by the end of the novel we find him behind bars, the only one of Forster's characters to be quite so severely punished. The other two Wilcox siblings, Paul and Evie, are more shadowy figures – Paul we hardly see at all – and they are tempered with some good qualities, as if to say that surely a woman of Mrs. Wilcox's temperament and breeding would not have produced solely obnoxious offspring.

For Mrs. Wilcox, though we never get to know her very well, is a thoroughly good woman. Unlike all the others, she *is* rooted to the land, and can be identified with everything Forster loves about England. When we first meet her she is

> trailing noiselessly over the lawn, and there was actually a wisp of hay in her hands. She seemed to belong not to the young people and their motor, but to the house, and to the tree that overshadowed it. One knew that she worshipped the past, and that the instinctive wisdom the past can alone bestow had descended upon her . . . . (*HE* 22)

Like Mr. Emerson in *A Room with a View* and Mrs. Moore in *A Passage to India*, Mrs. Wilcox is one of those mystic and prophetic figures Forster incarnates in order to give voice to the transcendent realm beyond this world where all true and eternal values are lodged. She never really utters anything extraordinary, and on occasion deflates the airy idealism of others with a dose of common sense, but her presence invariably suggests a kind of balance and proportion (with a bias toward the unworldly) that Forster holds out as exemplary. Even her closeness to death, as that of the other two "prophets," seems to symbolize the unseen and invisible of which she is the mouthpiece.

The house to which Ruth Wilcox belongs is Howards End, but it is some time before we learn that it is her own ancestral home. The significance of the house can not be overstressed; it is as much an actor in this novel as any of the characters. Forster had spent the formative years of his childhood at the house in Hertfordshire upon which Howards End is based, and his loving description of it in Helen's letter is very like the actual place, Rooks Nest, where he had been so happy. Just as this novel is about money, so too is it about houses, and no fewer than five of them figure prominently in these pages.

Of these, Howards End and Oniton Grange are country houses with a great deal of English history behind them, and if houses (and their grounds) can be regarded as symbols of the Feminine Principle, they might be said to represent those aspects of this archetype that a modern, predominantly masculine and hyper-rational consciousness has been wont to reject. At Howards End, for instance, there is a beautiful wych-elm shading the old house, and embedded in it are some pigs' teeth placed there long ago by country people who believed that by chewing the bark one could cure toothache and other maladies. Among her family, only Mrs. Wilcox now knows of this, or cares, though Margaret, hearing about it, declares humorously: "I love folklore and all festering superstitions" (*HE* 68). Later, at Oniton in Shropshire over which broods an ancient ruined castle, Margaret is enchanted by the landscape, and feels herself a part of its turbulent past. While for Henry Wilcox the estate is merely an investment, and one he now rather regrets for its inconvenience, Margaret deeply identifies with some spirit that hovers over the place, for "it, too, had suffered in the border warfare between the Anglo-Saxon and the Kelt, between things as they are and as they ought to be" (*HE* 215). If, in *Howards End*, English common-sense is pitted against Germanic idealism, so too is Anglo-Saxon practicality and efficiency seen in contrast to Celtic poetry and mysticism.

But the Forsterian *Weltanschauung* is far too wide-reaching to allow for one without the other. Wilcox enterprise might turn Howards End into a warehouse and build a garage where its paddock once was, but by the same token it is Henry's money and entrepreneurship that have preserved the place when it might otherwise have been lost. The message that echoes over and over in this novel is the need to somehow integrate the two perspectives, for "the business man who assumes that this life is everything, and the mystic who asserts that it is nothing, fail, on this side and on that, to hit the truth." And it is not merely the compromise of "halfway" that is wanted, but rather to achieve a state of balance by "continuous excursions into either realm" (*HE* 182).

Howards End begins with a letter, and the letter precipitates a muddle. Out of this muddle, resulting from the confusions of an undeveloped heart (in this case that of Helen Schlegel), come the eventual transfigurations of the novel's principle characters. It is Forster's signature device and he uses it again and again, for he sees a great part of human interaction as guided by no more than the fortuitous stumblings of one being against another. So tenuously does he draw the line between muddle and mystery, and so precariously does he balance his skeptical humanism against his belief in an ideal and transcendental world, that it has been possible to read his fiction, as many have, as a sort of paean to nihilism. But the seeming ambivalence of Forster's world-view is crucial. It links him to the other British Modernists and lends a sharp edge to the prophetic voice so clearly discernible over the rattling noise of the new.

The only one of the Bloomsbury writers to have managed a friendship with the difficult D. H. Lawrence, Forster was well aware of the pitfalls of prophecy. A recognizable similarity in outlook had initially drawn the two writers together. In their individual fashions, each endorsed a chthonic and Dionysian religion of sensation, sexuality and transformative emotion. And both of them believed that only some Nietzschean transvaluation of values could possibly circumvent the stultifying repressiveness of Christian orthodoxy or of the caste-bound intellectualism which stifled the emergence of a new and truly liberated humanity. But Lawrence was considerably more extreme in his views. In one letter he actually accused Forster of "glorifying" the business people in *Howards End* and of skirting the profundities which the book seemed to hint at. Lawrence felt that Forster would not come out, as he himself had done, absolutely on the side of a revolutionary spiritual vision in which "man" would be enjoined to "yield himself up to his metamorphosis, his crucifixion, & so come to his new issuing, his wings, his resurrection . . . ."[3] And, indeed, this was so. Forster had nothing like Lawrence's loathing for mankind and all its works, and the idea of artificially forming a new society by rejecting entirely the surrounding one is a notion Forster entertains only in *Maurice*, which he did not publish. But this is not to say that the prophetic and the revolutionary are not embedded in Forster's work. They quite obviously are, though Forster has to a certain degree confined them to that cherished sphere of personal relations, out of which he felt any change in the world at large must flow.

This, in a way is what happens at the close of *Howards End* and it is a vision worthy of Lawrence, for the message here is both spiritually and socially radical. Margaret (the *new* Mrs. Wilcox) embraces a reformed Henry, whose serious psychosomatic breakdown has effected at last a reconciliation of his worldly values with his wife's transcendentalist convictions. Then, as in a poster vision of the Chinese Revolution, Helen holding her out-of-wedlock baby, and Tom, the reaper's boy, emerge ecstatically from a field of newly-mown hay. Henry Wilcox has decreed that the farm will pass to Margaret, then to Helen's son. It is he who will inherit England, or at least this part of it. But the social alteration this implies, profoundly significant though it is, rests upon a precarious and tentative

---

[3] Quoted in P. N. Furbank, *E. M. Forster: A Life*, vol. 2 (New York: Harcourt, 1978) 7.

stewardship of the land, while the menace of another kind of world, perhaps an Orwellian one, looms on the horizon.

It is Helen, the most purely idealistic of the characters, whom we hear from first when she writes joyfully to tell Margaret about the Wilcoxes and Howards End. These letters reveal a great deal about Helen, whose romantic enthusiasm has wrapped the Wilcox family in a halo of perfection (though all but Mrs. Wilcox suffer from hay fever), and made of their house and its grounds a paradise. When the youngest son, Paul, arrives, Helen immediately falls in love with him. We learn, too, that Helen and Margaret had met the Wilcoxes at a German hotel where they were all vacationing, and that Mr. Wilcox, a conservative, has shot down all of Helen's modern notions about women's equality, though apparently without offending her.

Concerned that Helen's love affair is serious, Margaret dispatches her aunt, Mrs. Munt, to go and see what needs to be done. After Mrs. Munt has left on this errand, Margaret receives a telegram from Helen saying that the affair is over. Thus begins the muddle that causes Helen to fall out with the Wilcox family and drives the deep wedge between the Schlegel and the Wilcox sensibilities that it will become Margaret's duty to reunite. Back in London, Helen realizes what had happened, that she had really been in love with the family, or her idea of them and had taken perverse delight in having her liberal beliefs challenged and overthrown by Mr. Wilcox. Like most romantic idealists, she has a propensity to disillusionment, and seems to encourage it, if only to spring back toughened and more sure of herself. The fact is,

> . . . she had liked being told that her notions of life were sheltered or academic; that Equality was nonsense, Votes for Women nonsense, Socialism nonsense, Art and Literature, except when conducive to strengthening the character, nonsense. . . . When Mr. Wilcox said that one sound man of business did more good to the world than a dozen of your social reformers, she had swallowed the curious assertion without a gasp . . . . (*HE* 24)

We are made aware that Helen's ideas, "the Schlegel fetiches," are inherited ones. Her father, now deceased, was a German intellectual and Idealist who had left his native country when its militancy and Imperialism began to trouble him. He was "the countryman of Hegel and Kant" (*HE* 28), and his surname, as much as Mr. Emerson's, is to remind us of the literary and philosophical tradition he represented and has passed on to his children. Though "it was his hope that the clouds of materialism obscuring the Fatherland would part in time, and the mild intellectual light re-emerge" (*HE* 29), he had feared that Germany was heading a very dangerous direction.

The Schlegels are, like Lucy Honeychurch, also great devotees of German Romantic music, especially Beethoven, and it is at a concert in Queen's Hall that they first encounter Leonard Bast, a young insurance clerk anxious to improve himself through culture. Helen, deeply moved by the Fifth Symphony, and rejecting the upcoming Brahms and Elgar, has left early, accidentally taking with her Leonard Bast's umbrella. Margaret, apologizing for Helen's carelessness, asks him to walk with her to their house where he might retrieve it. This is among the most comic scenes of the book and the one that best illustrates the genteel bohemianism of the Schlegel milieu.

They discuss, along with the season's opera, the new art – Monet, Debussy ("something about a Faun in French"); they smoke cigarettes; they laugh about the late Queen Victoria; they make irreverent jokes about the Royal Family ("How inconceivable it would be if the Royal Family cared about Art"). The mere fact that Margaret has brought home a strange young man about whom she knows nothing serves to indicate how very far these women have advanced from the world of Lucy Honeychurch.

And yet there is something disturbing, something almost condescending in their attitude toward Leonard Bast. When he leaves, their vaunted democracy seems suddenly a veneer, and it presses in upon them that

> . . . all is not for the best in the best of all possible worlds, and that beneath these superstructures of wealth and art there wanders an ill-fed boy, who has recovered his umbrella indeed, but who has left no address behind him, and no name. (*HE* 44)

This "goblin footfall," heard first in the strains of Beethoven at Queen's Hall, presages the unusual events which are to follow, events which prophetically foretell some of the changes about to befall England itself.

Mrs. Munt, a busybody, has discovered that the Wilcox family has moved into one of the expensive new flats in the building opposite the Schlegel's Wickham Place. Worried that the old affair between Helen and Paul might be stirred up again, Margaret has an uncharacteristically curt exchange with Ruth Wilcox. In the process, the two find they quite like one another and develop a short-lived friendship, a friendship abruptly cut asunder by the unexpected death of Mrs. Wilcox. The cause of her death is as mysterious as it is sudden; psychologically, if not physically, it appears related to her being uprooted from Howards End, the source of her inner strength and the real passion of her life. On the last occasion of their being together, the two women go Christmas shopping, and Mrs. Wilcox on impulse asks Margaret to dash down to Howards End with her. Margaret declines, not at first realizing the importance of the invitation, and that in refusing it she has hurt Mrs. Wilcox. As they return home in silence, Margaret suddenly has a horrible Blakean or Dickensian vision of London:

> The city seemed Satanic, the narrower streets oppressing like the galleries of a mine. No harm was done by the fog to trade, for it lay high, and the lighted windows of the shops were thronged with customers. It was rather a darkening of the spirit which fell back upon itself, to find a more grievous darkness within. (*HE* 80)

Even in their momentary estrangement, some profound rapprochement seems to occur between the women, and Margaret understands that the city, with its "craving for excitement" and its "hordes of purchasers" is an infernal prison which will soon prove fatal to her friend. At the funeral and after, a scene most revealing of the emotional frigidity and greediness of the surviving Wilcoxes, we learn that Ruth has left Howards End to Margaret. The male Wilcoxes, of course, suppress this bequest and Margaret hears nothing of it until she has already taken Ruth's place as the house's mistress and heir.

In the meantime, the Schlegels are obliged to move as Wickham Place is to make way for redevelopment. All of London, in fact, is in flux, and if Dickens had painted its Victorian aspect in *Bleak House*, Forster will do the same for its Georgian in *Howards End*.

> One visualizes it as a tract of quivering grey, intelligent
> without purpose, and excitable without love; as a spirit that
> has altered before it can be chronicled . . . . It lies beyond
> everything: Nature, with all her cruelty, comes nearer to us
> than do these crowds of men. (*HE* 102)

This picture of modern urban life is important not only in Forster but in all modernist literature which, as Malcolm Bradbury points out, was very much "an art of cities."[4] Virginia Woolf offers a similar vision at the end of *Orlando* when that novel's hero/heroine emerges into the twentieth century. The most remarkable thing about the modern city is its transitory and mobile character, its rootlessness. Certainly it is an atmosphere of excitement, change, hurry, even creativity, but then, "London only stimulates, it cannot sustain" (*HE* 141).

Forster's stated antidote is one he acknowledges as out-of-date, for "to speak against London is no longer fashionable. The earth as an artistic cult has had its day, and the literature of the near future will probably ignore the country and seek inspiration from the town" (*HE* 102). The ironic tone of this suggests what Forster knew – that a genuine connection to the land and its agrarian values was nearly a thing of the past. Any revival would be in the nature of "an artistic cult" such as those which had cropped up during the Romantic resurgences of the latter nineteenth century. Indeed, when Leonard Bast comes to impress the Schlegels with his rustic hiking adventure, he must invoke books and writers to describe it. So it is with only a modest

---

[4] See Malcolm Bradbury, "The Cities of Modernism" and other essays in his collection *Modernism*, ed. Malcolm Bradbury and James McFarlane (Harmondsworth, Middlesex, England: Penguin, 1976).

hope that Forster pits the tranquility and attunement with nature attainable in the country against the prevailing "nomadic civilization which is altering human nature so profoundly" (*HE* 243).[5]

A series of sordid but comical contretemps brings Leonard Bast, this time with his sluttish wife Jacky, back into the lives of Margaret and Helen. Leonard and Jacky form an unlikely bridge over which Helen and Margaret must pass in order to redeem Henry Wilcox, with whom Margaret is soon romantically involved, from his materialist heresy. Leonard, rather defeated by poverty and a miserable marriage, becomes Helen's special project. Paradoxically, he needs her as his link to a desired social and cultural life, while she sees in him the potential natural man, "grandson to the shepherd or ploughboy whom civilization had sucked into the town; as one of the thousands who have lost the life of the body and failed to reach the life of the spirit" (*HE* 109).

Henry Wilcox, whose wealth has doubled since his wife's death, has since let Howards End and taken Ducie Street in London and bought Oniton Grange, an estate in remote Shropshire. Outwardly successful and exhibiting the usual composure of the extrovert, Mr. Wilcox is inwardly more adrift than he can admit to himself. He has, it is true, his utilitarian values – concentration, for instance – which allow him to maintain a semblance of order, but beyond the ill-digested religious teachings of his childhood, his

---

[5] It is worth comparing in this instance Jane Austen's *Mansfield Park*, written during a not dissimilar period of transition, where Fanny Price's yearning for rural stillness is threatened by the Crawfords' modern craving for excitement and "improvements."

70

inner-life is in chaos. "And it was here that Margaret hoped to help him" (*HE* 174).

> She would only point out the salvation that was latent in his own soul, and in the soul of every man. Only connect! That was the whole of her sermon. Only connect the prose and the passion, and both will be exalted, and human love will be seen at its height. Live in fragments no longer. Only connect, and the beast and the monk, robbed of the isolation that is life to either, will die. (*HE* 174-75)

But Henry is too obtuse to absorb her sermon. Unable to kindle such a light within himself, Henry must make the connection from without,[6] so he and Margaret become engaged, much to the disapproval of Helen and Mr. Wilcox's children.

Having offered the information that the Porphyrion Fire Insurance Company (Leonard Bast's firm) is to go under, and this information, passed on to the luckless Leonard, resulting in his quitting and going on to another but disastrous post, Mr. Wilcox inadvertently sets the stage for the climax of *Howards End*. It is a climax that rivals that of *Where Angels Fear to Tread* in violence, coincidence and extremity. Furious at the ruin Henry's information has caused her protégé, Helen appears at Evie Wilcox's wedding with the unfortunate man and his disorderly wife. This scene, while drawing a connection between the widely disparate characters, also serves to reveal Forster's various views on the institution of marriage.

---

[6] Earlier we are told that Ruth Wilcox came from Quaker stock and that while she submitted to joining the Church of England on her marriage, she continued to wish for "a more inward light" (*HE* 85).

Only in *A Room with a View* are we offered a picture of marriage that could be called romantic, and this goes no further than the honeymoon chamber. In all the other novels marriage, with few exceptions, is seen as the enemy of friendship, passion and the deeper forms of love.[7] Here, that of Evie and Percy Cahill, like that of Charles and Dolly, is pure convention, the sort of union that Ibsen had damned a decade before. That of Margaret and Henry will be a marriage of two older people, almost an alliance of convenience, and one not really connected with procreation. But the unhappy marriage of Leonard and Jacky is the most degrading of all, and when it is revealed that Jacky had once been Henry Wilcox's mistress, "this was only one new stain on the face of a love that had never been pure" (*HE* 220).

The exposure, exhibiting as it does the shoddiness of Henry Wilcox's soul as well as the weakness of Leonard's, makes a brief rupture in Margaret's engagement. But after some apologies and expressions of remorse, Henry is forgiven and the two are married. Margaret settles into married life, spending her time studying theosophy, and only occasionally missing the excitement of new art movements. But if Wedekind and Augustus John slip by her, she is nonetheless content, for "she had outgrown stimulants and was passing from words to things" (*HE* 244). Henry, a bit chastened though unregenerate, continues with his business of amassing money, but he is living off of spiritual currency borrowed from his wife, and his inward bankruptcy is about to tell. Helen, very upset by the whole affair,

---

[7] *The Longest Journey*, in fact, takes its title from Shelley's poem, "Epipsychidion," a polemic against monogamy.

72

travels to Germany, leaving her former protégés to sink further into poverty. Despite her apparent concern,

> Helen forgot people. They were husks that had enclosed her emotion. She could pity, or sacrifice herself, or have instincts, but had she ever loved in the noblest way, where man and woman, having lost themselves in sex, desire to lose sex itself in comradeship? (*HE* 290)

The ultimate nobility of her love might be questionable, but that she had lost herself in sex with Leonard Bast, if only for half an hour, soon becomes evident. In Germany she discovers that she is pregnant, and being emancipated, decides to have her child and to remain outside of England. Only the serious illness of her aunt calls her back. It is no exaggeration to say that this was a very daring theme for a novelist in 1910, and his sympathetic treatment of it, with no hint of moral censure, must have shocked more than a few of Forster's readers.[8]

In fact, when Helen returns and admits her condition, she is taken by everyone as mad and a scheme is plotted to have her brought into custody. Howards End, by now just a warehouse for the Schlegels' furniture, becomes the setting for this trap. Only at the last moment does Margaret grow horrified at the implications of her own collaboration. By refusing to take part, and instead insisting that her sister be given refuge at Howards End, Margaret causes a serious breach between herself and Henry. He, who had sinned and been forgiven, was now, in the fortress of his respectability,

---

[8] His mother, Lily, was indeed very offended and much worried about how her son's other female relatives would react to the scandalous subject.

unwilling to forgive Helen or to recognize his part in what had happened. In fury, Margaret cries

> You shall see the connexion if it kills you, Henry! You have had a mistress – I forgave you. My sister had a lover – you drive her from the house. Do you see the connexion? . . . A man who ruins a woman for his pleasure, and casts her off to ruin other men. And gives financial advice, and then says he is not responsible. These, man are you. You can't recognize them because you cannot connect. (*HE* 287)

One must see here another of the many ways in which *Howards End* enjoins us to connect. It is not only the prose and the poetry of life, the material and the spiritual, common sense and the imagination, the male and the female which must be brought into harmony, but also, and perhaps more importantly, it is the crucial connection between action and its consequences which must be made fully conscious. That the wealth and social standing of a Henry Wilcox are related to the poverty and lowliness of a Leonard Bast; that the imperialism of England involves the enslavement of Africa or India; that the hegemony of an acquisitive and overly materialistic way of life must destroy all hope of a society built on equity and communal spiritual values – these dichotomies, Forster subtly insists, are at the heart of our modern malaise, and no collective redemption will be possible until a link between them is made.

This universal struggle, the struggle over who will inherit the earth, is symbolized in *Howards End* particularly by the disastrous encounter between Leonard Bast and Charles Wilcox. Leonard, in deep remorse, decides to seek out Margaret. After some trouble, he tracks her down to Howards End, never guessing he is to find Helen there, and much less Charles Wilcox.

On his way, he passes cultivated fields and the laboring farmers who "are England's hope" (*HE* 301). Three types of humanity are outlined here: the tillers of the soil who, if not perfect, live at least within the natural rhythms; the uprooted and dispossessed like Leonard Bast who have lost the earth and have little share in the city's bounty; and, finally, the type represented by Charles Wilcox, the Imperial who "hopes to inherit the earth. . . . But the Imperialist is not what he thinks or seems. He is a destroyer. . . . and though his ambitions may be fulfilled, the earth that he inherits will be grey" (*HE* 301). Charles, seeing Leonard, attacks him and in the scuffle a bookcase topples over, a German sword falls, Leonard's heart fails. It's all a confused muddle, but in the end, Leonard lies dead on the ground.

The inquest finds Charles Wilcox guilty of manslaughter and sentences him to prison. This final blow breaks Henry Wilcox completely and as Margaret makes plans to flee to Munich with her sister, he prevails upon her once more to take him back. Her sermon, earlier preached in vain, at last penetrates through the shattered walls of his ego. In the ensuing months he, Margaret, Helen and Helen's new-born infant settle into Howards End and the deserted place returns to life. Love and connectedness have saved Henry Wilcox. Helen's son, a natural child of the earth, will inherit what's left.

Maurice

After the publication of *Howards End*, another 14 years were to pass before Forster produced another novel for the public. Considering that he had delivered within the course of five years four remarkable books, this long hiatus seemed puzzling. Very few, even among his closest friends, guessed the cause, and Forster himself, working away at an abortive novel, could not easily figure the source of his malaise. Even the renown that began to come his way after the success of *Howards End* was met by Forster with a certain alarm, and then silence. Though he did manage to get out a book of short stories, *The Celestial Omnibus*, the following year, his mood of apathy and creative frustration was to continue for quite some time. In a diary entry of 16 June 1911, he tried to probe the roots of his inability to write:

> Weariness of the only subject that I both can and may treat
> – the love of men for women & vice versa. Passion &
> money are the two main springs of action (not of existence)
> and I can only write of the first & that imperfectly. Growing
> interest in religion does not help me.[9]

Certainly the urge to write fiction had not abandoned him, but the distance between what he really wished to say – something of those passions that burdened his own heart – and what it was permissible to say must have seemed to him insuperable.

The scandal that had destroyed Oscar Wilde only a decade earlier was still fresh in collective memory, and the public taboo against homosexuality, in England much more so than on the Continent, was enforced by stringent laws. Though Forster moved in a world that included many homosexuals, the need for general secrecy and concealment was not merely a personal inhibition, but one demanded by circumstance. His own sexual development

---

[9] Quoted in P. N. Furbank, *E. M. Forster: A Life*, vol. 1, 199.

had been late in coming and his satisfying affairs few in number, but Forster did believe in, and lived by, a code of passion.

Despite overwhelming constraints, there were champions of the love that had for so long dared not speak its name, and the late nineteenth century produced a number of liberated voices. John Addington Symonds, an eminent critic and man of letters, and Havelock Ellis, the psychologist and pioneering sexologist were two of the most prominent challengers of the prevailing Victorian view that homosexuality (or "inversion") was a morbid condition, symptomatic of a severe moral degeneracy. Symonds argued from the historical position that "homogenic" love had a long and noble past, and had indeed been considered by the Hellenes as the superior human affection.[10] Ellis, in his ground-breaking study *Sexual Inversion*, attempted to demonstrate scientifically that homosexual practice was both common and universal, hence it deserved to be regarded sympathetically as an alternate form of normal human sexual expression.[11] But it was another figure, that of Edward Carpenter, who had the most practical influence on Forster's own self-acceptance.

Carpenter (1844-1929), who was born into the upper-middle classes, had taken holy orders at Cambridge before losing his faith in 1874. Unlike

---

[10] See his *A Problem in Greek Ethics* (1883) and *A Problem in Modern Ethics* (1891).

[11] See Phyllis Grosskurth, *Havelock Ellis: A Biography* (London: Quartet, 1981), 184-204. *Sexual Inversion*, which was co-authored by John Addington Symonds, was readied for publication in 1897 as the first volume of Ellis's monumental *Studies in the Psychology of Sex*. A tide of homophobia followed Wilde's release from prison in March of that year, and in the event *Sexual Inversion* was withdrawn just before its general release.

Leslie Stephen, whose similar crisis had made him a passionate advocate of Agnosticism, Carpenter went the direction of a millenarian mysticism, espousing in time most of the progressive ideas that period had to offer, including women's rights, sexual reform, vegetarianism, Whitmanesque spiritual democracy, and a socialism compounded of the ideas of William Morris and Leo Tolstoy. Most importantly, he pleaded for a more compassionate understanding of homosexual (or "Uranian") affection, which he himself believed might be the basis for a future class-free society.

Forster visited Carpenter and his working-class lover, George Merrill, at their farm in Millthorpe in the autumn of 1913. Inspired by what he saw and felt there, Forster almost immediately began to compose *Maurice*. It was the creative breakthrough he so desperately needed, and following closely on *Howards End*, it in a sense fulfilled the physical passion that novel recommended but could not deliver. The prevailing social circumstances that would, as a matter of course, prevent Forster's publishing *Maurice* pervade the novel as an integral part of its theme. Chief of these is the very fact that Clive Durham, who awakens Maurice to love, cannot in the end allow himself to love. The unrelieved sexual tension, the idealization of erotic affection into something else, and at last, Clive's poignant rejection of feeling in favor of propriety, lend a dark and unhappily realistic note to a book often charged with being merely a fantasy or a bit of wish-fulfillment.

In fact, *Maurice* has been treated rather harshly by critics since its publication in 1971, a year after its author's death. Only very recently has it received the serious critical attention it deserves, and efforts to incorporate it fully into Forster's canon are still challenged. But if *Maurice* falls short of

Howards End in nuance and depth, it is nonetheless a fully realized novel, and in some respects far more focused than the preceding ones. One could easily argue, in retrospect, that a homosexual subtext underlies all the other novels; certainly it is barely concealed in the love of Ansell for Rickie, while Philip Herriton, Cecil Vyse, and perhaps Tibby Schlegel with their aestheticism and unspecified sexuality, could well be construed as homosexual characters. In *Maurice*, the subject simply rises to the surface, becoming explicit rather than covert.

Forster would have had no trouble imagining his two principal characters, Maurice Hall and Clive Durham. They are young Cambridge men of the sort Forster knew well enough – intelligent, though not brilliant, financially secure through inheritance, and socially assured of a place among the ruling ranks. Nor would their particular kind of friendship have been unfamiliar to him.[12] But he went out of his way, wisely one presumes, to make his hero Maurice as unlike himself as possible. For Maurice Hall is a fairly pedestrian individual, fine-looking but with little to distinguish him from others of his type. He is in most things orthodox, unquestioning and unoriginal. In fact, he is more than a little obtuse, and his inability to quickly grasp the gist of his situation links him to those other "undeveloped hearts" – Philip Herriton, Lucy Honeychurch, Helen Schlegel – Forster is so fond of saving.

---

[12] "Platonic" male affairs were not at all unusual in the Cambridge of Forster's day and shortly after. The Apostles named these sexless love affairs the Higher Sodomy.

Clive Durham, on the other hand, is much more clever, a lover of books, a Hellenist and a philosopher. In one fell swoop he demolishes Maurice's orthodoxy, pointing him out of the Holy Land toward the blessèd Greeks. Attending a translation class, Clive grows incensed when the dean enjoins a student to skip over "a reference to the unspeakable vice of the Greeks."[13] Fulminating later to Maurice, he remarks that homosexuality was "the mainstay of Athenian society" (*M* 51) as Plato's *Symposium* bears out, and though Maurice has none of Clive's passion for classical scholarship, the mere mention of the forbidden subject is like a breath of fresh air to him.

Reticence on both sides follows the gradual blossoming of their love. Even once accepted, it results in no more than a kiss and a few chaste embraces. Sex, insofar as it rears, is in the nature of the inevitable pressure to propagate, to enter into the world of conventional marriage, and to fulfill those obligations society imposes on such as Maurice and Clive. The latter, especially, as the scion of gentry is expected to take his place at the family estate with a proper wife and child and to enter public life. And Maurice, at heart a bourgeois, hardly questions that he should enter into his deceased father's brokerage. These post-Cambridge developments must at last spell death to the romantic friendship.

The beginning of the end occurs when Clive falls ill while staying with Maurice. His fainting spell produces a rather different conversion from that of Rickie Elliot or Lucy Honeychurch, for he is soon propelled onto the road of heterosexuality and his youthful sexual proclivities along with his Hellenism

---

[13] E. M. Forster, *Maurice* (New York: Norton, 1987) 51. All subsequent quotations from *Maurice* will be cited in the text and refer to this edition.

are eventually jettisoned in favor of a Miss Anne Woods. But for Maurice, slower to wake up to his true nature, the path is very different. Lonely and even suicidally unhappy over losing Clive, he nonetheless cannot deny to himself what he wants.

Among the most convincing scenes in the book are those in which Maurice's erotic desires overwhelm him; he finds himself attracted first to a young house guest of his family's, then to a Frenchman who comes into his office, and later to a working-class boy with whom he boxes in South London. When he goes to hear Tchaikovsky's Symphony Pathétique and is told by a friend that the composer had fallen in love with his nephew and dedicated this masterpiece to him, Maurice rushes to the library for a biography. The book

> thrilled Maurice. . . . He made the acquaintance of "Bob," the wonderful nephew to whom Tchaikovsky turns after the breakdown, and in whom is his spiritual and musical resurrection. The book blew off the gathering dust and he respected it as the one literary work that had ever helped him. (*M* 162)

Not that there is much solace in all of this, for though Maurice occasionally dreams of the possibility of happiness with another man, the likelihood of such a dream's coming true seems remote.

Tormented, Maurice seeks medical help, first from his family's doctor who responds to Maurice's assertion that he is "an unspeakable of the Oscar Wilde sort" with the harsh comment, "Rubbish, rubbish! . . . never let that evil hallucination, that temptation from the devil, occur to you again" (*M* 159). Next, he tries a fashionable hypnotist and succeeds in going into trance, though little comes of it. By the time he returns for a second visit, his fateful encounter with the gamekeeper, Alec Scudder, has occurred, and all attempts to alter his nature will prove futile. The hypnotist, at last, gives him the only sensible advice he has yet received, that is, "to live in some country that had adopted the Code Napoléon, . . . France or Italy, for instance. There homosexuality is no longer criminal." When Maurice, a thorough Englishman, asks "Will the law ever be that in England?" the hypnotist replies, "I doubt it. England has always been disinclined to accept human nature" (*M* 211).

As Maurice leaves the hypnotist's office, confirmed that he will never be other than what he is, an interesting dialogue takes place in his head. Noticing the King and Queen passing through the park, he without thinking doffs his hat, a reaction which he instantly despises. Another part of himself willing to condemn the world of so-called normalcy seems to emerge through the layers of conditioned reflex, as if the earlier trance had worked an effect opposite to the one intended. "It was as if the barrier that kept him from his fellows had taken another aspect. He was not afraid or ashamed anymore. After all, the forests and the night were on his side, not theirs; they, not he, were inside a ring fence" (*M* 214-15). Then, while the old Adam reasserts itself and reminds him he must stick to his class, the new insists on calling up visions of the greenwood and the freedom it might hold.

His reveries are interrupted by a letter from Alec Scudder, Clive's gamekeeper, with whom Maurice has shared a night of sexual passion. Scudder, fearful that he has been snubbed, wants to meet with Maurice in London. Unable to believe that this young man of the working class could have noble intents, Maurice suspects blackmail as the motive. Indeed, Alec Scudder is himself unsure of his own motives, for he has suffered a history of indignities at the hands of such gentlemen as Clive and Maurice. Walking together through the British Museum, Alec and Maurice make an uneasy peace across class lines, a barrier that only the great leveller, sex, can easily bridge. They decide to get a room and spend the night together.

Despite this reconciliation, the forces of society seem too strong for any ultimate happiness to result. Alec has already made plans to emigrate to the Argentine, and Maurice has his stockbrokerage to attend to. Though the two men might fall in love, what of it? Saddened, Maurice decides at least to go see Alec off; he waits at the dock in Southampton with Alec's family, but the gamekeeper never appears. Realizing what has happened, Maurice is delirious with excitement.

> His journey was nearly over. He was bound for his new home. He had brought out the man in Alec, and now it was Alec's turn to bring out the hero in him. He knew what the call was, and what his answer must be. They must live outside class, without relations or money; they must work and stick to each other till death. But England belonged to them. That, besides companionship, was their reward. Her air and sky were theirs, not the timorous millions' who own stuffy little boxes, but never their own souls. (*M* 238-39)

It was a vision Forster would hardly have entertained before he met Edward Carpenter who'd actually made such a life for himself and his lover. Even so, it might be argued that the "happily ever after" ending doesn't quite convince, or rather that it seems too sudden or forced.

In 1960, forty-six years after the novel's completion, Forster appended an interesting note to it that attempts to answer this charge. He said that *Maurice* "belongs to the last moment of the greenwood. . . . Our greenwood ended catastrophically and inevitably. There is no forest or fell to escape to today, no cave in which to curl up, no deserted valley for those who wish neither to reform nor corrupt society but to be left alone" (*M* 254). That his two heroes might live together successfully in the city would have been completely impossible in 1914 and not much less so for many years to come; that they might do so in some remote "greenwood" away from oppressive laws was a fantasy soon to fade. In light of changes in attitudes up to 1960 Forster had this to say: ". . . what the public really loathes in homosexuality is not the thing itself but having to think about it." Since legal reform involves such thinking on the part of officials, radical change seems unlikely in the near future. In the meantime, "police prosecutions will continue and Clive on the bench will continue to sentence Alec in the dock. Maurice may get off" (*M* 255).

IV

NOT LANDS AND SEAS ALONE: *A PASSAGE TO INDIA*

Forster's initial trip to India in 1912 was made in the company of his two old Cambridge Apostle friends, Goldsworthy Lowes Dickinson and R. C. Trevelyan.[1] They had each voyaged out for independent reasons – Dickinson as an observer and social commentator, Trevelyan primarily as an aesthete interested in architecture and Indian poetry, and Forster to visit his friend Syed Ross Masood. And no doubt all three men wished to experience the vast and exotic subcontinent which, for any late-Victorian child brought up on Kipling's tales and visions of the glorious Raj, would have played such a large part in their youthful imaginings.

Forster had met Masood six years earlier in England when he had been employed to tutor the young Muslim in Latin. They had then struck up a passionate friendship, amounting on Forster's side to something more than fondness, and on Masood's to a very loyal and demonstrative devotion. Masood, though heterosexual, had none of the typical English restraint, and he was extravagant in his displays of affection for his new friend. The effect of this intimacy on Forster was that it released him, as he later claimed, from his former emotional timidity, and helped to awaken in him that profound interest in other cultures which he would later weave into his books on India

---

[1] R. C. Trevelyan came of the distinguished family of historians and Anglo-Indian administrators. (See Raleigh Trevelyan's *The Golden Oriole: A 200-Year History of an English Family in India* [New York: Simon, 1987]). His great-uncle was Thomas Babington Macaulay and his brother was G. M. Trevelyan, author of *History of England* (1926), and like R. C. a Cambridge Apostle.

and Egypt. Even before Forster had visited the Orient, Masood declared to him, "my great wish is to get *you* to write a book on India, for I feel convinced from what I know of you that it will be a great book. . . . In you I see an oriental with an oriental view of life . . . ."[2] This compliment is the same as that paid to Mrs. Moore by the witty Dr. Aziz when they first meet in the mosque at Chandrapore.[3]

His friendship with Masood and its resultant introductions allowed Forster to gain a more intricate view of Indian life than the average British traveller would have obtained, and he absorbed it all with his usual combination of wonder and detachment. He also got his first unbiased look at Anglo-Indian politics and the effects certain measures were having on native and Britisher alike. There was a good deal of sight-seeing, too, and it was during this trip that Forster made an excursion by elephant into the Barabar Hills near Bankipore, Bengal, and saw the famous Buddhist caves with their Pali inscriptions and strange echoes.

While in India, Forster chanced to meet another native who would have an influence upon him equally as important as that of Masood, and whose invitation nine years later would bring him back for a sojourn that inspired Forster's last and finest novel, *A Passage to India* (1924). This high-born

---

[2] Quoted in Furbank, *E. M. Forster: A Life* 1: 194.

[3] Syed Ross Masood was both wealthy and socially very confident, coming as he did from a prominent Muslim family. Though Forster's Aziz is of humbler origins, not well-off, and socially insecure, in other respects, he seems modelled on Forster's friend: both exhibit nostalgic feelings for the past glory of Islam; both are highly emotional, both possess great charm, wit, and physical attractiveness; and, finally, both worship, with an almost religious intensity, the idea of friendship.

Indian was the Maharajah of Dewas, at the time of their meeting only twenty-four, who had been groomed by the British, though rather unsuccessfully, to be a model new-style prince. It was not altogether uncommon for Indian rulers of Native States to employ educated Englishmen in one capacity or another, usually as tutors or private companion-secretaries, and it was the latter function that Forster came to fulfill for the Maharajah of Dewas.[4] Formerly acquainted mostly with Moslems, Forster now had an opportunity to gain insights into the Hindu mind. During this second stay he was privileged to witness both court rituals and intrigues as well as the colorful religious festival in honor of Krishna, Gokul Ashtami, a recreation of which forms the final section of *A Passage to India*.

In the years just preceding Forster's 1921 visit, the British government in India had begun to enact a series of very repressive legislations, no doubt in response to the increasing nationalist hostility against their rule. In the event, Forster's sympathies were with the Indians, and his growing distaste for the idea of Empire as well as his disgust with Anglo-Indian officialdom resulted in a far more politically penetrating novel than the unfinished one he had begun to compose after his first trip in 1912.

Forster returned in this book to his abiding theme of the necessity of connection, and here he confronted, as he had in his two previous novels, all the formidable obstacles to that difficult goal. The divisions of social class,

---

[4] Forster tells the full story of this fascinating employment in his *The Hill of Devi* (1953), a book which provides clues to many of the fictional events in *A Passage to India*.

economic status, and philosophical outlook which separate the characters in the earlier books are in *A Passage to India* compounded by racial differences, a rigid caste structure, and antipathetic religious traditions which seem almost unbridgeable. In fact, *A Passage to India* is a leap into an alien world that *Howards End* could only suggest, and one next to which the Edwardian class prejudices and social taboos of *Maurice* pale by comparison. The moral fervor that infuses this novel of India reminds one more of Alan Paton's *Cry, the Beloved Country* or Richard Wright's *Native Son* than of Forster's earlier domestic comedies, and the biting satire that colors the portrayal of the Turtons, Callendars and McBrydes reveals the extraordinary advance in political awareness Forster had made by the 1920s.

For if on its deepest level, *A Passage to India* is about the healing power of spiritual intuition, it is on the surface an angry denunciation of racism and imperialism, and an uncompromising indictment of the assumption of power by light-skinned people over darker in the guise of improving a backward race. The more conservative of his countrymen, including some very prominent people, roundly censured Forster for his anti-British position, and indeed his novel was accused by many of inciting further unrest and sedition in India. But Forster, whose judgment on the matter was far more clear-sighted and carefully considered than his detractors could realize, had seen first-hand the untenability of continued British dominance in such far-flung countries, and he knew that sooner or later the Empire was doomed to fall.[5]

---

[5] That Forster had for some time been thinking of this subject is attested by his general condemnation of "the imperialist" as a type in *Howards*

The political superstructure of *A Passage to India*, firmly grounded as it was in definite historical facts and realities, lent the novel a timeliness that the events of twenty years later – the transfer of power from British to Indian hands and the tragic partition of India into separate Hindu and Moslem nations – would only confirm. Forster, nonetheless, never claimed to be a political analyst of the Orwell sort, and *A Passage to India* is in no sense a polemic for any well-defined program, however much the Bloomsbury insistence on toleration informs it throughout. While the novel seems to acknowledge that certain forced political expedients may be inevitable and necessary, it holds aloof from affirming that they will afford any more than a temporary and limited solution.

What it offers instead, what lies at the very heart of *A Passage to India*, is a profound belief in the redemptive possibilities of personal relationships, of those unmediated human contacts which might, though the power of *caritas*, at last overcome the barriers of race, class and nationality. However simplistic on the face of it, there was in truth nothing naïve or superficial about Forster's oft-stated and cherished creed; he shows himself well aware of the perilous social and psychic consequences involved in the attempt to transgress such forbidden borders. Thus the carefully arranged "bridge party" at the Civil Station, a reluctant effort on the part of Turton to introduce Mrs. Moore and Adela Quested to "acceptable" Indians, is a marked failure; the tea at Fielding's garden-house leaves Professor Godbole and Aziz

---

End. Certainly during the period of that novel, wealthy Edwardians had been enjoying quite a Colonial heyday, in East Africa especially. When Paul Wilcox returns from that country, we are shown the negative effects on his character in the form of racism and arrogance.

physically ill, and engenders a vague apathy in Mrs. Moore and Adela; and, finally, the fateful expedition to the Marabar Caves which Aziz organizes in order to show the English ladies "the real India" ends, to say the least, disastrously.

Yet despite these abortive, and undoubtedly too contrived, attempts at connection, the ideal persists that links can be forged. The scene in chapter II when Aziz, having been rudely snubbed by two British memsahibs, retreats into a mosque "to shake the dust of Anglo-India off his feet"[6] and there encounters Mrs. Moore, is a paradigm for the rest of the book. She herself has absconded from the inanities of an evening at the Civil Station, and slipped for respite into the shadowed courtyard. This fortuitous meeting of two people who on the surface have nothing in common but who find themselves in sudden and inexplicable rapport intimates the more authentic coalescence that neither shared political dogmas nor formal religious affinities can ever replace. Mrs. Moore's instinctive reverence, her certainty that "God is here" (*PI* 20) among the arches of a foreign mosque, inspires Aziz to exclaim, "you are an Oriental" (*PI* 23). Bitterly used to the condescension of the British, Aziz is warmed and elated by the unprecedented kindness this unknown elderly woman accords him. For her part, Mrs. Moore is without prejudice, and only does what is natural to her.

Aziz is undoubtedly the best realized character in the book, but Forster, like Jane Austen, preferred his heroes blemished. So we are shown in Aziz

---

[6] E. M. Forster, *A Passage to India* (New York: Harcourt, 1924), 18. All subsequent quotations from the novel will be cited in the text and will refer to this edition.

a man who, though witty, clever and physically attractive, has his full measure of imperfections. Until he finally becomes rapidly anti-British, Aziz is caught up in ambivalent and contradictory attitudes about the Anglo-Indians, at once admiring them for their modern efficiency and organizational abilities while despising them for lording over his land and people. Outwardly touched by British customs – he plays polo, dresses as a European, considers himself modern and enlightened, practices Western medicine – Aziz is in his heart very much an Oriental. When he later abandons Chandrapore for the Native State of Mau, he is soon regarded as "chief medicine man" and he drops "inoculation and such Western whims" (*PI* 292). As a subordinate in Major Callendar's clinic, he is obliged to perpetually humble himself, "not because his soul was servile but because his feelings – the sensitive edges of him – feared a gross snub" (*PI* 16). And partisan Moslem that he is, Aziz thinks very little better about the Hindus whose caste system and religion seem to him medieval and superstitious.

Instead, Aziz lives in his own nostalgic world of Persian poetry, dreaming of a vanished Mogul greatness. His Mohammedanism, heartfelt though it may be, is confusedly mixed up in his mind with the glory, as well as the pity and pathos of Islamic history. It provides very little in the way of actual religious consolation or enlightenment, and indeed, to some degree, it is a divisive force in his life. Of course, Aziz knew that

> God's unity was indubitable and indubitably announced, but on all other points he wavered like the average Christian; his belief in the life to come would pale to a hope, vanish, reappear, all in a single sentence or a dozen heart-beats, so that the corpuscles of his blood rather than he seemed to

decide which opinion he should hold, and for how long. It
was so with all his opinions. (*PI* 55-56)

Aziz's moody vacillations, indecisions, and his dangerous tendency toward
self-deception, clashing with similar traits in Adela Quested, eventually serve
to bring about his near-tragic undoing at the caves of Marabar.

These caves, like Rickie Elliot's magic dell, the Cadbury Rings, the
Piazza Signoria, and the Sacred Lake are places of psychic transformation.
But unlike the sacred places of the West, the Marabar caves hold a mystery
so profound, so inexpressible, that neither ideas of holiness nor of evil seem
to apply. Their symbolic significance must be left, like that of Virginia
Woolf's lighthouse, open-ended, for no definitive statement could ever
exhaust the multifarious possibilities they embody. As if in defiance of
definition, the caves are almost without attributes and barely distinguishable
one from the next:

> Having seen one such cave, having seen two, having seen
> three, four, fourteen, twenty-four, the visitor returns to
> Chandrapore uncertain whether he has had an interesting
> experience or a dull one or any experience at all. He finds
> it difficult to discuss the caves, or to keep them apart in his
> mind, for the pattern never varies, and no carving, not even
> a bees'-nest or a bat distinguishes one from another.
> Nothing, nothing attaches to them, and their reputation –
> for they have one – does not depend on human speech.
> (*PI* 124)

In a sense, the caves represent all of India, for like that country they are
incredibly old, their history shading into a past before all record and memory.
Like India they at once obscure all divisions and distinctions while at the
same time promoting a separateness and an isolation of the most extreme

variety. The caves seem to evoke a mystery and uncanny power suggestive of spirituality, but the fact is, "they are older than all spirit" (*PI* 124). They are reported by some to be Jain, by others, Buddhist. There is also evidence of a past Hindu presence, and it is said that some saddhus once inhabited a cave or two.[7] But all these religious claimants have finally left the Marabar alone, "and even Buddha, who must have passed this way down to the Bo Tree of Gya, shunned a renunciation more complete than his own" (*PI* 124).

The caves are the central pivot of *A Passage to India*. They form a sort of fulcrum upon which the divisions and oppositions of the first part, and the mystical harmonies and attempts at unity of the third are balanced. This tripartite construction of the novel has been much remarked by critics, though with little uniformity of view. While the superimposition of too symmetrical a pattern would be false to the spirit of the book, it is nonetheless tempting to see it as a Hegelian triad of thesis, antithesis and synthesis.[8] Forster, though not in any rigidly schematic way, had a certain bias in favor of the dialectical perspective. We can, without much difficulty, see how he uses it in the former novels by pitting one character type (or the ideas represented by that character) against its opposite, and, in the end, often through the experience of spiritual conversion, bringing the two into a state of relative harmony or synthesis.

---

[7] Significantly, the caves have no relation to India's other dominant religion, Islam, and the Moslem Aziz is left unmoved by them.

[8] As Gertrude M. White does in "*A Passage to India*: Analysis and Revaluation," *Twentieth Century Interpretations of* A Passage to India, ed. Andrew Rutherford (Englewood Cliffs: Prentice, 1970) 50-67.

The opening passages of the book immediately point us to the sort of ironic "playing-off" of opposing views that helps to give *A Passage to India* its special momentum. The town of Chandrapore, on first sight, seems "so abased, so monotonous . . . that when the Ganges comes down it might be expected to wash the excrescence back into the soil" (*PI* 7). And yet, over a rise, "Chandrapore appears to be a totally different place. It is a city of gardens. It is no city, but a forest sparsely scattered with huts. It is a tropical pleasaunce washed by a noble river" (*PI* 8). The pictures are entirely contradictory but they have something in common, something that binds them into a unity that the human eye does not often perceive. This is "the overarching sky [that] settles everything." An infinity of stars and colors, "orange, melting upwards into tenderest purple," the all-enclosing expanse is truly heaven in both the astronomical and theological respects, for "when the sky chooses, glory can rain into the Chandrapore bazaars or a benediction pass from horizon to horizon. The sky can do this because it is so strong and so enormous. Strength comes from the sun, infused in it daily; size from the prostrate earth" (*PI* 8-9). A similar dichotomizing occurs at the beginning of Part II when the caves are said to be beyond description or discrimination, and are then described in exacting detail of length, height and width.

In contrast and opposed to this rational ordering of the world where widely differing elements can at least be brought into some sort of relation, is the more perplexing tendency of India to a complete cancellation of all distinctions. Wasps and other creatures, for instance, have no "sense of an interior. Bats, rats, birds, insects will as soon nest inside a house as out; it is to them a normal growth of the eternal jungle, which alternately produces houses trees, houses trees" (*PI* 35). This is the great paradox of a country where the intricate gradations of caste, plurality of religions, multiplicity of languages, and rigidities of social structure are of such surpassing complexity as to baffle thought.

Certainly, the exclusive rings which encircle the various social groups are the most astonishing example of India's inclination to classify and compartmentalize. One meets, for example, the wealthy proprietor and philanthropist, the Nawab Bahadur, who is admitted into the British club and treated with respect by the English. Above him, ruling their native kingdoms, are the great maharajahs whose splendor seems mythical and godlike, and below, lesser landowners and professional men, each with his carefully allotted position in society. Beneath all of these are infinite grades of subservient castes shading down to the lowliest pariah.

> And there were circles even beyond these – people who wore nothing but a loincloth, people who wore not even that, and spent their lives in knocking two sticks together before a scarlet doll – humanity grading and drifting beyond the educated vision, until no earthy invitation can embrace it. (*PI* 37)

Yet even these overwhelming delimitations are eventually nullified by the levelling that is equally a part of the Indian muddle or mystery. For whereas India's age-old social hierarchy separates and defines,[9] its chief religion,

---

[9] Yet even this is not absolute and among Aziz's various native friends, a weakening of the caste system is evident; ". . . educated Indians visited one another constantly, and were weaving, however painfully, a new social fabric" (*PI* 54).

Hinduism, acts to dissolve every difference in an all-encompassing philosophy of Oneness.

It is upon Hinduism, perhaps seen more as a symbol of unity than as its actual agent,[10] that Forster hinges the potential metaphysical synthesis of *A Passage to India*. As in the previous books, he pits rationalism/common sense/materialism against mysticism/intuition/idealism, but here he elevates the debate to an even higher plane of discourse. Whereas in *Howards End* he had declared inadequate either position by itself, and asserted the necessity of "continuous excursions into either realm," in *A Passage to India* he makes an effort to break the dualistic hold altogether, and to fuse the warring opposites by an appeal to a transcendental Absolute that at once comprehends both sides.

The novel is, in some respects, a tribute to the McTaggart legacy in Forster's thinking, and it recapitulates a variety of McTaggart's non-dualist arguments in a highly unique and creative manner.[11] McTaggart had taught, in *The Nature of Existence*, that each seemingly individual thing in the

---

[10] As an organized religion, it too is full of cleavages: "Hinduism, so solid from a distance, is riven into sects and clans, which radiate and join, and change their names according to the aspect from which they are approached" (*PI* 292). It is rather in its mystical theology that Hinduism is capable of overcoming all differences.

[11] Most critics have been, perhaps understandably, reluctant to credit McTaggart with any lasting influence on Forster or the rest of Bloomsbury. Yet it is telling that Forster's close friend, G. Lowes Dickinson, whose biography he was shortly to write, remained deeply devoted to the memory of McTaggart. Dickinson's last published book (in 1931) was a memoir and revaluation of this Cambridge Idealist whose philosophy and personality had so influenced him.

universe, no matter how infinitesimal, is related and bears a position of mutual reciprocity or co-operation to everything else. Though substance is plural and of an unlimited divisibility, it is, in the final analysis, subsumed in an all-enclosing relationship of "determining correspondence" to an original, undivided and undifferentiated Substance.[12]

McTaggart expounds this dialectical theory with a scrupulous logic that eventually gives way to his idea of a mystical empyrean or Absolute, a noumenal realm beyond either space or time; it is a sphere as far removed from the here-and-now of Moore's ethical principles as it is from the social interactions and moral dilemmas of Forster's earlier novels. If these latter concern themselves both with the necessity of connection and with the possibility of transformation or conversion, if they occasionally wink at the transcendental, they remain nonetheless within an anthropocentric universe of right and wrong. *A Passage to India*, on the other hand, moves outside the strictly human orb of conduct and its consequences. It includes this, of course, but it throws its net much wider to reach into areas hitherto unfathomed, into a realm of primordial pre-human forces, as well as into an Unseen which can be intimated but not explained.

In order to demonstrate more specifically the manner in which Forster weaves this complex philosophic legacy, an amalgam of Cambridge Idealism,

---

[12] See Rudolf Metz, *A Hundred Years of British Philosophy* (London: Allen, 1938). While rejecting Hegel's theism, it was McTaggart's special claim to reconcile logic and mysticism. He wrote in *Studies in the Hegelian Dialectic*, "All true philosophy must be mystical, not indeed in its methods, but in its final conclusions." There are many points of contact between McTaggart's philosophy and both Buddhism and Hinduism.

Neo-Platonism,[13] and Hinduism, into the fabric of *A Passage to India*, it would be well to consider how he delineates his various characters and the experiences they undergo. Forster's ability to embody ideas and modes of perception in his fictional creations without undermining their credibility as personalities reaches in this novel a perfection not previously attained. One might even say that his masterly adaptation and consolidation of inherited realist methods with the innovative internalizing of character that James Joyce, Virginia Woolf and other Modernists were pioneering, remains among his great contributions to the development of this century's literature.[14]

If Forster's Dr. Aziz can be seen to stand primarily for emotion or sentiment, then intellect or rationalism is in this novel represented by his Cyril Fielding, modelled in part on that arch-rationalist, Leonard Woolf, who had spent several years as an administrator in Ceylon.[15] Like Woolf, Fielding

----

[13] Forster had presented a brief but incisive sketch of Neo-Platonism in his *Alexandria: A History and a Guide* (1922). It was a philosophy which had been and remained close to his heart, and he affixed as motto to his guide book these words of Plotinus: "To any vision must be brought an eye adapted to what is to be seen." An excellent study of Plotinus's *Enneads* in relation to *A Passage to India* is John Drew's essay, "The Spirit behind the Frieze?" *A Passage to India: Essays in Interpretation*, ed. John Beer (Basingstoke: Macmillan, 1985) 81-103.

[14] Forster had been enthusiastically reading Proust during the composition of *A Passage to India* and he wrote much of it, by his own admission, under the influence of this great French Modernist. His fusion of realist with Modernist techniques was a tremendous legacy to such literary descendants as Christopher Isherwood.

[15] See Leonard Woolf, *Growing: An Autobiography of the Years 1904 to 1911* (New York: Harcourt, 1976), for an account of his tenure as a colonial civil servant. He took with him from England only a fox-terrier and "90

is an atheist and thus rather averse to religion, whether occidental or oriental. Nor does he feel any particular piety about either empire or the "white man's burden"; and though he is attracted to India, he has no use for the so-called mystery of the East. "A mystery is just a high-sounding term for a muddle" (*PI* 69), he declares. Nonetheless, Fielding, the Principal of the little college in Chandrapore, is both cultivated and intelligent, traits not calculated to endear him to the philistine Heaslop, Turtons, Callendars and McBrydes. He has set himself even further apart by associating in a non-official manner with Indians and by not observing the expected social codes of the Civil Station. In fact, Fielding seems altogether a representative of Bloomsbury, for "he used ideas by that most potent method – interchange [and] he was happiest in the give-and-take of a private conversation. The world, he believed, is a globe of men who are trying to reach one another and can best do so by the help of good will plus culture and intelligence" (*PI* 62). This is a creditable sentiment, and Fielding is sincere in his application of it. But in India, a country where Fielding will never feel quite at home, such rational ideals are not enough.

A similar, though far less refined, outlook is expressed by Adela Quested, whose personality does not come to the fore until the incident in the cave makes her the focus of attention. Another of Forster's "undeveloped hearts," it is she, aside from Mrs. Moore, who will undergo the most dramatic personal transformation. Adela Quested has come out to

---

large, beautifully printed volumes of Voltaire." Though he fell in love with the East and was devoted to his work, Woolf came to loath the Anglo-Indians, and to have grave misgivings about the morality and future of the British Empire.

India ostensibly to marry Ronny Heaslop, Mrs. Moore's eldest son, but her interest is more in adventure than in romance. Like Lucy Honeychurch before her, Adela conceives of adventure as a purely external experience, and as a result, "she would see India always as a frieze, never as a spirit" (*PI* 47). Indeed, if she is not as attractive, but more mature and certainly more emancipated, Adela shares many traits with that earlier heroine, including the fault of peevishness and a fatal tendency to over-rationalize, hence to misinterpret, her own feelings. These young women are for Forster classic English types – sensible to a degree, sexually repressed, emotionally undemonstrative, yet possessed of a brave curiosity about life – and he delighted in placing them in his over-heated theaters of change. Seekers without a goal, neither Lucy nor Adela in the end altogether gains the sympathy of the reader, yet each has a galvanizing effect on the surrounding atmosphere which highlights the true mettle of all the other characters.

Among these other characters must be mentioned the various Anglo-Indians who play secondary roles in the book. Forster is clearly not in love with them; they are, like Charles Wilcox, imperialists and cultural chauvinists of the worst sort – the women even more so than the men. Unappealing as they are, it is a credit to his genius that Forster paints them so well, giving each one a unique individuality, a definite roundness with contour and depth, while maintaining the sense of mass psychology and collectively held opinion that animates them. They are somewhat like La Bruyère's *caractères* – certainly types, but not merely stereotypes.

He accomplishes a similar feat with the local natives, not forbearing to show both the bright and dark sides of the Indian personality, though in general he is far more sympathetic to the Indians than to the British. In fact, he populates the background with a nameless multitude of obscure native figures. They are the servants, drivers, cooks, messengers, and housekeepers who silently care for and mediate between their superiors. Some, such as Mohammed Latif, are shady and undependable. Others, by simply being what they are, achieve a proportion and beauty "apart from human destinies." When Adela enters the courtroom, she notices immediately the humblest person present, the man pulling the punkah fan.

> Almost naked and splendidly formed, . . . he seemed to control the proceedings. He had the strength and beauty that sometimes come to flower in Indians of low birth. When that strange race nears the dust and is condemned as untouchable, then nature remembers the physical perfection that she accomplished elsewhere, and throws out a god – not many, but one here and there, to prove to society how little its categories impress her. (*PI* 217)

Like the farm laborers in *Howards End* who are "England's hope," these voiceless multitudes will be the true foundation (as Gandhi knew) of any future Indian society.

Finally, one comes to the intuitives, Mrs. Moore on the English side and Professor Godbole on the Indian. They are the unmoved movers of the novel's action; in them we find embodied the two poles of mystical experience. Mrs. Moore is the extrovert, Western mystic, her outer life devoted to duty and to the welfare of her children, and her inner to a sincere practice of her faith. Like her prototype Ruth Wilcox, she is inclined to spontaneous accesses of feeling that bind her to all of life. India, the land of mysteries, has the effect of stimulating these feelings, for while

> In England the moon had seemed dead and alien; here she
> was caught in the shawl of night together with earth and all
> the other stars. A sudden sense of unity, of kinship with
> the heavenly bodies, passed into the old woman and out,
> like water through a tank, leaving a strange freshness
> behind. (*PI* 29-30)

This sense of unity extends not only to nature but to other people, including Indians. When her son Ronny chides her for consorting with natives, she exclaims, "God has put us on earth to love our neighbors and to show it, and He is omnipresent, even in India, to see how we are succeeding" (*PI* 51). Nominally a Christian, Mrs. Moore at first refers her intimations of the beyond to that religion, yet something other than its wordy tenets seems to beckon her.

Professor Godbole, the kindly Indian educator, is, of all the characters, the most self-realized, and the one least troubled by spiritual doubts and apprehensions. A thorough Hindu, Godbole nevertheless fits in as easily with Europeans as with Asians. When we first meet him, he is dressed in "a turban that looked like pale purple macaroni, coat, waistcoat, dhoti, socks with clocks. The clocks matched the turban, and his whole appearance suggested harmony – as if he had reconciled the products of East and West, mental as well as physical, and could never be discomposed" (*PI* 72-73). This harmony is a result of Godbole's complete absorption in the spirit of Brahmanism, a religion that excludes nothing. Unlike Mrs. Moore whose moments of spiritual attunement are sporadic and subject to collapse, Godbole lives perpetually in the realm of mystical experience, and will indeed hold up expeditions and miss trains rather than interrupt his *pujah*.

These figures, in their infinite multiplicity, stand for the entire range of human types. Insolate in themselves, they are bound each to the next in a relationship of "mutually determining correspondence" (to use McTaggart's phrase) which, taken all together, comprises the larger unit of humankind. What lies beyond this human realm must be sought among the caves at Marabar. The caves, too, bear a relationship to the human world, but one not easy to determine. Against the backdrop they provide of geological and elemental forces, the temporal interconnections and interdependencies, whether of the ideal Mrs. Moore/Aziz variety, or the Anglo-Indian "herd instinct" sort, or the caste-bound social orderings of the natives, are entirely vitiated.

The Marabar Caves are, as Wilfred Stone has demonstrated in his persuasive Jungian reading,[16] an expression of the Great Mother archetype. They are the womb of the earth out of which all life emerges and to which it must return. Further, they represent the negative, all-consuming, uroboric aspect of the Feminine, rather than its positive or nurturing side.[17] For this reason the hyperconscious Westerners, Mrs. Moore and Adela, experience

---

[16] Wilfred Stone, *The Cave and the Mountain: A Study of E. M. Forster* (Stanford: Stanford UP, 1966) 298-346.

[17] Cf. ". . . the uroboros, the circular snake biting its tail, is the symbol of the psychic state of the beginning, of the original situation. . . . As symbol of the origin and of the opposites contained in it, the uroboros is the "Great Round," in which positive and negative, male and female, elements of consciousness, elements hostile to consciousness, and unconscious elements are intermingled. In this sense, the uroboros is also a symbol of a state in which chaos, the unconscious, and the psyche as a whole were undifferentiated . . . ," in Eric Neumann, *The Great Mother: An Analysis of the Archetype* (Princeton, N.J.: Princeton UP, 1972) 18.

the caves as annihilating all values and relationships, and as violating that sense of individual selfhood upon which occidental culture is predicated.

Mrs. Moore, better prepared by her innate mystical sense for the underworld journey, is nonetheless plunged into a Dark Night of the Soul. This state, according to Evelyn Underhill, is an "incident of the transition from multiplicity to Unity; of that mergence and union of the soul with the Absolute. . . . It is the last painful break with the life of illusion, the tearing away of the self from that World of Becoming in which all its natural affections and desires are rooted . . . and the thrusting of it into that World of Being where at first, weak and blinded, it can but find a wilderness, a 'dark.'"[18]   The Dark Night, or "mystical death" is characterized, psychologically, by feelings of blankness, aridity and stagnation, by "the disappearance of all the old ardours, now replaced by a callousness, a boredom, which the self detests but cannot overcome."[19]   As this terrifying lassitude takes hold of Mrs. Moore, she finds herself indifferent as to whether or not Adela and Ronny should marry: "Her Christian tenderness had gone, or had developed into a hardness, a just irritation against the human race" (*PI* 199). The annoying echo which had started in the cave "began in some indescribable way to undermine her hold on life. Coming at a moment when she chanced to be fatigued, it had managed to murmur, 'Pathos, piety, courage – they exist, but are identical, and so is filth. Everything exists, nothing has value'" (*PI* 149).

---

[18] Evelyn Underhill, *Mysticism: A Study of the Nature and Development of Man's Spiritual Consciousness* (1911; New York: Dutton, 1961) 401.

[19] Underhill 391.

This, in essence, is the primary metaphysical feature of the Marabar Caves; circular caverns whose only openings are man-made, they contain everything, hence they contain nothing.

> "Boum" is the sound as far as the human alphabet can express it, or "bou-oum," or "ou-boum" – utterly dull. . . . Even the striking of a match starts a little worm coiling, which is too small to complete a circle, but is eternally watchful. And if several people talk at once an overlapping howling noise begins, echoes generate echoes, and the cave is stuffed with a snake composed of small snakes, which writhe independently. (*PI* 147-48)

Within this uroboric void all logical categories, and all dualities become negated, including good and evil. This is a state of affairs clearly incompatible both with Mrs. Moore's Christian religious sense and even more so with Adela's rationality. Whereas the older woman is brought face to face with what Jung calls "the Shadow," Adela is violently confronted with unconscious content of a rather different sort. She misinterprets the cave's overwhelmingly malevolent effect of echoing emptiness as being personally-directed and physically threatening.

In the days preceding the expedition, Adela has been dwelling, naturally enough, on her relationship with Ronny Heaslop. Typically unsure of her feelings, she has talked herself, nonetheless, into marriage. As she climbs over a rock holding Aziz's hand, it occurs to her that she is not in love. "The discovery had come so suddenly that she felt like a mountaineer whose rope had broken. Not to love the man one's going to marry! . . . Not to even have asked oneself the question until now!" In this abstracted mental state, Adela notices Aziz, thinking, "what a handsome little Oriental he was,

. . . and she regretted that neither she nor Ronny had physical charm," and then, to make conversation, she inquires of him "in her honest, decent, inquisitive way: 'Have you one wife or more than one?'" (*PI* 152-53). Aziz who sees himself as modern and up-to-date, is shocked to the core by her implication that he is an exotic with a harem of veiled women. He immediately releases her hand and slips into a cave to hide his embarrassment and confusion. Unconscious of her *faux pas*, Adela enters another cave.

What happens to her in the interval is another of the novel's mysteries. To the relatively omniscient reader it must be clear that Aziz is innocent of any crime, for he is never out of sight.[20] By the time he becomes aware that she is no longer with him, Adela has already been swept away in Miss Derek's car. Mrs. Moore's disturbing and claustrophobic cave experience moments earlier had included a tangible, physical violation as well: ". . . some vile naked thing struck her face and settled on her mouth like a pad." But when she emerges into the daylight, she realizes "that the naked pad was a poor little baby, astride its mother's hip," and further, that "nothing evil had been in the cave" (*PI* 147-48). On the empirical level, something equally as explicable has likely happened to Adela, but with her mind in a muddle about marriage, and with half-unconscious thoughts of sexuality intruding, she imagines that someone has attempted to rape her.

---

[20] Both Santha Rama Rau in her stage play and David Lean in his film of *A Passage to India* make this equivocal "crime" and Aziz's possible culpability the dramatic center of their versions.

The consequences of this hallucination, and Aziz's subsequent arrest, reverberate through the community of Chandrapore, driving an even deeper wedge between the British and the Indians. The trial that follows, with Adela's recantation of her charge and Aziz's acquittal, reveals anew the vast cleavages and incompatibilities that divide the city. But as it draws the Anglo-Indians into an even tighter, more defensive group than before, it also serves to bring about a new Hindu-Moslem entente. Politically, the stage is set for the eventual overthrow of the British government in India. The caves, in themselves empty of meaning, their hollow echoes saying no more than "everything exists, nothing has value" have provoked a profound transformation in the human world.

This transformation is, on the plane of affairs, expressed as dislocation and physical movement from one place to another. Adela Quested has been saved from marriage to Ronny Heaslop, an unenviable fate, and she returns to England. "Although her hard school-mistressy manner remained, she was no longer examining life, but being examined by it; she had become a real person" (*PI* 244-45). As so often in Forster, to abjure marriage is to gain one's appropriate life; Adela's victory is the triumph of integrity, reasonableness, autonomy (she expresses eagerness to return to her own friends and profession) over herd instinct and social pressure.

Indeed, the idea of "return" is crucial in completing the initiatory passage, and Adela has not only become strengthened in her clear-eyed rationality, but she has also paid the proper homage to that which her rationality cannot encompass. As she and Cyril Fielding part, they together wonder:

> Were there worlds beyond which they could never touch, or did all that is possible enter their consciousness? They could not tell. They only realized that their outlook was more or less similar, and found in this a satisfaction. Perhaps life is a mystery, not a muddle; they could not tell. Perhaps the hundred Indias which fuss and squabble so tiresomely are one, and the universe they mirror is one. They had not the apparatus for judging. (*PI* 263)

Though he has made his career in India, Fielding too must make his return to the West to recontact there the Hellenistic and European basis of his own world-view, for "he had forgotten the beauty of form among idol temples and lumpy hills [and] without form, how can there be beauty?" (*PI* 282). An expressed cynic on the subject of love and marriage, he unexpectedly finds love in the person of Mrs. Moore's daughter, Stella, and with her he returns to India.

As for Mrs. Moore, she also embarks for the West, but with an altogether different result. Earlier, she had teetered between her desire for religious resignation, "to be one with the universe," and her Christian sense of duty to others. But in the Marabar Cave she discovered that just as "we can neither act nor refrain from action, we can neither ignore nor respect Infinity." This troubling double-vision propels her down into the very depths of her being where she encounters "something very old and very small. Something snub-nosed, incapable of generosity – the undying worm itself" (*PI* 208).

It is a vision of evil, indeed, but evil not as some cosmic power, but rather as human selfishness, pettiness, and a preoccupation with one's own affairs to the exclusion of all else. Underhill describes this stage of the Dark

Night as one in which the "lowest" part of the self is brought to the surface in order to participate fully in the coming transformation. "In the general psychic turmoil, all the unpurified part of man's inheritance, the lower impulses and unworthy ideas which have long been imprisoned below the threshold, force their way into the field of consciousness."[21] In this state of mind, Mrs. Moore does not seem one bit the sweet elderly lady whom Aziz had met in the mosque. She has become cynical, "a withered priestess" who sees into the harsh truth of material life.

Although she does not physically survive her final transfiguration, that she continues to live is apparent. Her ocean voyage, the archetypal "night-sea journey," would appear to be the last stage of the spiritual crisis initiated in the cave. Somewhere out in the Indian Ocean, as her ship approached the Suez, that bridge between East and West, Mrs. Moore shrugged off her body. But while her corpse is lowered into the ocean depths, she herself is reincarnated, or rather apotheosized, in Chandrapore, into a Hindu goddess without attributes but with her own invocation, "Esmiss Esmoor, Esmiss Esmoor . . . ." She communicates telepathically to Adela, giving her the strength to tell the truth in court; she remains very much alive in Aziz's affections; and she appears to Professor Godbole in one of his moments of mystical exaltation.

Mrs. Moore, by her passage to India, has resolved in a more than social way the fissures between the East and the West. Her task has involved a sacrifice, the sacrifice of her individual life, the life one must lose in order to gain eternal life. The parallel is not far to seek between her

---

[21] Underhill 392.

destiny and that of the Christ, whose religion she positively represents.[22] Like the dying-and-reviving avatar of that faith, she too must undergo trials, lose faith, and descend into a sort of hell before she can be reborn into a transfigured state.

This Christian parallel is carried over into the Hindu world where we re-encounter Aziz and Professor Godbole two years later. A great religious festival is underway in the Native State of Mau and Godbole, as Minister of Education, has a place of honor. Amidst the noisy chaos of several bands playing all at once, of solemnity and hilarity strangely mixed, of a confusing array of lesser gods and saints obscuring Krishna's altar,

> Godbole stands in the presence of God. God is not born yet – that will occur at midnight – but He has also been born centuries ago, nor can he ever be born, because He is the Lord of the Universe who transcends human processes. He is, was not, is not, was. (*PI* 283)

As the Birth ceremony begins, a crèche is brought forward, a representation of Krishna's birthplace, Gokul, "the Bethlehem in that nebulous story"; of King Kansa, "who is Herod, directing the murder of some Innocents"; and then, of "the father and mother of the Lord, warned to depart in a dream"

---

[22] There are in the novel two other exemplars of Christianity as a universal religion. Mr. Graysford and Mr. Sorley are missionaries who do not associate with the Anglo-Indians of the Club and who minister to the very poor out beyond the slaughterhouses. They believe in God's divine hospitality, and that in His house "the incompatible multitudes of mankind [will] be welcomed and soothed." While willing to entertain that perhaps lower forms of life might also be included, they nonetheless feel that "we must exclude someone from our gathering, or we shall be left with nothing" (*PI* 38).

(*PI* 287). Earlier, defending her right to love Indians along with Englishmen, Mrs. Moore had said, "God is love." Now, among the jumble of images heaped on the Hindu altar, the same phrase reappears, accidentally written "God si Love," as if to suggest that not only is God love, but that love itself is God.[23]

Perhaps this is where orthodox Christianity and Hinduism come to a parting of the ways. The former, though saving the elect, excludes all others, be they wasps or heathens. In contrast, Hinduism teaches that, "Infinite Love took upon itself the form of SHRI KRISHNA, and saved the world. All sorrow was annihilated, not only for Indians, but for foreigners, birds, caves, railways, and the stars" (*PI* 287-88). Its embrace, unlike Christianity's, includes both spirit and matter, and all the dualities that fall into those two categories. Everything is enclosed in Brahman, the Absolute, and has its true being there.

Dancing in ecstasy upon his strip of red carpet, Professor Godbole oscillates between dissolution in the All and re-emergence into the manifest world of his individual self, demonstrating the ultimate concord between the two planes of being. Into his mind suddenly comes a vision of "an old woman he had met in Chandrapore days" (*PI* 286).

> He was a Brahman, she Christian, but it made no difference,
> it made no difference whether she was a trick of his memory
> or a telepathic appeal. It was his duty, as it was his desire,
> to place himself in the position of the God and to love her,

---

[23] Indeed, "inverting the names of deities" (*PI* 310) is typical in Hindu prayers and chants.

> and to place himself in her position and to say to the God,
> "Come, come, come, come." (*PI* 290)

Thus the two figures are fused one with the other, East and West, and what unites them is the all-encompassing Absolute that reaffirms what the caves had denied.

Forster, or rather, the narrator, brings us down from this lofty empyrean back into the world of human interactions, that sphere of personal relations without which the world would topple. The two years since the trial in Chandrapore have sadly separated through misunderstandings the two friends, Aziz and Fielding. Aziz is bitter against all English, and Fielding, now married, has resumed his Indian career. On a tour through the native states with his wife, Stella, and his brother-in-law, Ralph Moore, Fielding re-encounters Aziz and the two play out a final attempt to recapture their old intimacy. Neither the atheist Fielding, nor the Moslem Aziz, understands the exotic proceedings of Gokul Ashtami, but the colorful Hindu festival, a backdrop "thick with religion and rain" (*PI* 98), provides an atmosphere conducive to such reconciliations.

The reconciliation, incomplete though it is, is partly effected by the presence of Ralph Moore, a strange young man, who seems to be a spiritual emissary of his mother. Ralph, having been stung by a bee or a wasp (that lowly insect that reappears throughout the book, always to elicit some sympathy), is brought an ointment by Dr. Aziz. Aziz, still smarting from his old grievances against these English, is at first hostile, but then softens, realizing that Ralph, like his mother, is "an Oriental" (*PI* 311). In a sudden rush of his former hospitality, Aziz offers to take Ralph out onto the water to view the remainder of the festival. It is among the finest scenes in the novel with its images of wind and monsoon and the gorgeous confusion of the sacred procession. Out on the water, Aziz suddenly hears "the syllables of salvation that had sounded during his trial at Chadrapore" (*PI* 314), and the cycle that had begun so long ago comes full circle, to begin again.

In the wild tumult of wind and rain, Aziz's boat collides with that of Fielding and Stella, and all are plunged into the water, as if in baptism. These latter two, married though not quite at ease due to differences in outlook, have in Mau also reached a new attunement. "There seemed a link between them at last – that link outside either participant that is necessary to every relationship. In the language of theology, their union had been blessed" (*PI* 318). This would sum up the essential message of *A Passage to India*: that between each individual person or thing or idea in the universe is some relationship, though one not always evident. What is necessary is "that link either outside either participant" that can somehow unite and bind the inevitable differences. Political systems attempt this, but fail. Social structures and organized religions try as well, but fall short. Perhaps it is only in the formless sphere of an authentic spiritual life that the subtle link can be found.

But for Fielding, inevitably bound to his doomed colonial career and his limited rational philosophy, these things

> belonged to the universe that he had missed or rejected. And the mosque missed it too. Like himself, those shallow arcades provided but a limited asylum. "There is no God but God" doesn't carry us far through the complexities of matter and spirit; it is only a game with words, really a religious pun, not a religious truth. (*PI* 276)

As for Aziz, though more content in a Native than in a British administered state, he too remains alienated both from the hated English and the mysterious Hindus. While "the pathos of defeated Islam remained in his blood" (*PI* 293), he can only hope for the future liberation of India, and work towards that end. He does continue to write sad poems with an odd blend of nostalgic emotionality and pleas for an end to the purdah, but only one of these verses finally wins the approval of Professor Godbole. This poem is about neither Islam nor womanhood nor the mother-land, but rather about "internationality" which Godbole translates as "bhakti," the Sanskrit for *caritas* or universal love.

With such divisions of race, religion, and political affiliations against them, there is little chance that Fielding and Aziz can do any more than strike an uneasy truce, but such they do. Riding in the jungle together before Cyril's departure, they heatedly discuss politics, their mutual opposition growing at every shouted phrase. Then, personal affection once more obtruding, they declare their friendship and warmly embrace. As they do so, their horses, like relentless forces of history, suddenly swerve, "sending up rocks through which riders must pass single file . . ." (*PI* 322), and carry their riders in different directions. Love remains, fond memory persists, but the friends themselves must part.

V

DEBUNKING THE VICTORIANS:
LYTTON STRACHEY AND THE NEW BIOGRAPHY

Lytton Strachey was almost twenty-one years old when Queen Victoria died in late January of 1901. He had grown up during the final triumphant years of her reign; he could remember the Golden Jubilee of 1887 when monarchs from all over Europe, a great many of them Victoria's relatives, flocked to London to participate in the days of celebration; and he had, a decade later, just finished his despised public schooling and returned home in time for the Diamond Jubilee which took place on June 22, 1897. The aging Queen of England, Empress of India, had invited no foreign kings to celebrate this occasion. In their stead were the colonial heads of state from Canada, Australia, Cape Colony, Natal, Newfoundland, and New Zealand. The British Crown held dominion over a quarter of the globe, and the colorful processions included brigades of infantrymen from Jamaica and Nigeria, gorgeously attired Bengal Lancers, uniformed soldiers from such exotic places as Sierra Leone, the West Indies, Borneo and British Guiana. Never had Londoners witnessed such a glorious spectacle; never had they seen so many races of people nor so much pomp, and all gathered to honor a diminutive woman in black crepe with a feathered bonnet.

When she died, Victoria had been sovereign of England for sixty-three years; even elderly people could hardly remember a time when her familiar profile had not graced their currency, nor when the strict moral standards associated with her rule were not the norm. How much the imposition of these standards was altogether her own doing it would be hard to say. In her girlhood, before her marriage, she was reported to have liked well enough to dance and to flirt, although opportunities for these diversions were rare. Within the first two decades of her reign, however, any early traces of humor or imagination gave way completely to the solemn dignity and irreproachable poise appropriate to her high station.

Of the last three monarchs who preceded her, George III was, for the last years of his reign, certifiably insane; his son, the Prince Regent, later George IV, "presented a preposterous figure of debauched obesity"[1] and was ill-equipped for his duties, while William IV, who succeeded on his brother's death, had amassed huge debts due to his addiction to gambling and, as a younger son, had not been trained to the task of ruling his country. By the time Victoria ascended to the throne, the monarchy had become very unpopular and in some circles almost completely discredited. The loose court mores of the eighteenth century, which the late kings had done nothing to alter and everything to encourage, were still the fashion among the aristocracy. And yet the rising middle classes, who frowned upon their social superiors' scandalous doings, were gaining more and more power in the government. It was Victoria's fate to be very young (only eighteen), unmarried, and highly susceptible to the political tutoring of the Whig Prime Minister, Lord Melbourne. In addition, she had had a very strict upbringing, had seldom ventured from the precincts of the court, was acquainted only with her extensive royal family and their retinue and, until the day that her accession was announced, slept in the same bedroom as her mother. While

---

[1] Lytton Strachey, *Queen Victoria* (New York: Harcourt, 1921) 7. Subsequent citations will be from this edition.

fully aware of her status, Victoria had been shielded from the autocratic presumptions of her uncles. She came to the throne determined to be good and to do her duty as a proper constitutional monarch.

Perhaps it was her own ingrained decorousness, perhaps it was simply the spirit of the coming age, but in any event, the court that assembled itself around Victoria very little resembled that of her mad grandfather nor of her two dissolute and incompetent uncles. Especially after marrying her attractive cousin, the prim and upright Albert of Saxe-Coberg-Gotha, the young queen became set in a pattern of rigid adherence to formal court etiquette and bourgeois morality. Gone were the mistresses, sexual intrigues and royal self-indulgence of the previous reigns, to be replaced by family values, Christian piety and the lofty duties of state. These qualities allowed her middle- and working-class subjects to identify with their queen in a way impossible before now. She seemed, in many ways, not much different from any matron in a cottage with a large brood of children gathered around her. But

> she was more – the embodiment, the living apex of a new era in the generations of mankind. The last vestige of the eighteenth century had disappeared; cynicism and subtlety were shrivelled into powder; and duty, industry, morality, and domesticity triumphed over them. Even the very chairs and tables had assumed, with a singular responsiveness, the forms of prim solidity. The Victorian Age was in full swing. (*QV* 137-38)

This new age was for England one of unprecedented industrial, economic and imperial expansion. The fearsome spectacle of the French Revolution which had threatened to topple all the crowned heads of Europe in the end left Great Britain intact, its monarchy more secure and stable than ever. The destructive forces of radical change were quickly consolidated and absorbed into the liberal reformism for which the Victorian Age became known, and henceforth whenever social unrest or political agitation became particularly disturbing, means of appeasement were swiftly found. This relative stability, allied with the tremendous material success of the greatly expanded Empire, insured a sense of security and permanence that pervaded all aspects of Victorian life. As a result, in its latter stages the Age grew a crust of hypocrisy, complacency and self-satisfaction that many of the young, especially those growing up in the late 1890s, felt determined to smash. Leonard Woolf has written that

> when in the grim, grey, rainy January days of 1901 Queen Victoria lay dying, we already felt that we ourselves were mortally involved in this revolt against a social system and code of conduct and morality which, for convenience sake, may be referred to as bourgeois Victorianism. We did not initiate this revolt. When we went up to Cambridge, its protagonists were Swinburne, Bernard Shaw, Samuel Butler in *The Way of All Flesh*, and to some extent Hardy and Wells. We were passionately on the side of these champions of freedom of speech and freedom of thought, of common-sense and reason. We felt that, with them as our leaders, we were struggling against a religious and moral code of cant and hypocrisy . . . .[2]

This attitude characterizes all of those people who were to become the Bloomsbury Group. In each of them, whether in the field of painting, aesthetics, economics, political philosophy or literature, was the desire both

---

[2] Leonard Woolf, *Sowing: An Autobiography of the Years 1880 to 1904* (New York: Harcourt, 1960).

to strike a fatal blow at the oppressive Victorian past and to make some solid contribution to the new world its passing would make possible.

In this collective project of deconstructing the past, the work of Lytton Strachey stands out as being more overtly stated than that of the rest. A great admirer of the brevity, wit and rapier-like rhetoric of the eighteenth century, Strachey's tools would be satire and irony turned to his particular iconoclastic purpose. Just as Virginia Woolf would set out a program for the writing of the new novel, so too would Strachey present a fresh guideline for the writing of biography. It was a genre that sadly needed revitalizing. English literature had produced one very great work of biography, Boswell's *Life of Johnson*, and several others of lesser note, but during the nineteenth century the form had become mired in the evasions, concealments and hagiographical pieties of the period. The Victorians, it is true, had churned out countless two-volume "Life and Letters," but these were of such uniform dullness that the eminent personages embalmed in them seemed as stiff and lifeless as the marble angels which guarded their tombs. Strachey's biographies, in contrast, would pursue a different and more subtle strategy entirely, for "it is not by the direct method of scrupulous narration that the explorer of the past can hope to depict that singular epoch [the Victorian Age]."[3] Instead, Strachey will

> shoot a sudden and revealing searchlight into obscure recesses, hitherto undivined. He will row out over that great ocean of material, and lower down into it, here and there, a little bucket, which will bring up to the light of day

---

[3] Lytton Strachey, *Eminent Victorians* (New York: Harcourt, 1918) vii. All following quotations will be from this edition.

> some characteristic specimen, from those far depths, to be
> examined with a careful curiosity. (*EV* vii)

In this case, the characteristic specimen were odd fish indeed, and yet they
were the very models of praise-worthy Victorian public life.

Strachey claimed to have no particular end in mind in choosing the
four subjects of *Eminent Victorians* (1918) and certainly there are others he
might have chosen who would have served his ends as well. But a cleric, a
social reformer, an educator and a military man were the perfect
embodiments of those Victorian institutions he most wished to pillory. And
though he claims in his introduction to be writing "without ulterior
intentions," it quickly becomes apparent that his book is ironic from
beginning to end. Furthermore, his distaste for the age they represent, with
its ambitions disguised as piety, its ruthlessness cloaked in altruism, its
appalling repressions and severities complacently masked as moral
earnestness, and its militant imperialism with all the attendant flag-waving and
slaughter, spills over onto those human figures who so exemplified these
traits.

The first of the essays in *Eminent Victorians* exploits one of the crucial
cultural moments in nineteenth century England, the Oxford Movement,
during which a great many Church of England leaders began to question the
liberal tendencies and secularism which had infected the Anglican religion,
and tried to lead it back to an almost pre-Reformation emphasis on ritual,
sacraments, Apostolic Succession and so on. The episode, lasting over ten
years, led many of its leading figures to convert to Roman Catholicism and

stimulated a renewed interest in the Middle Ages and a vogue for all things Gothic.

The controversy involved many men of note, some of whom are still read, though only one, Cardinal John Henry Newman, remains a well-established figure of English literature. But it was not the kindly, mild-mannered, and ultimately sympathetic Newman whom Strachey chose to illustrate the Oxford Movement, but rather the redoubtable Cardinal Manning. Why? For one, it was because Newman lacked the essential and salient characteristic that so passionately interested Lytton Strachey as a biographer: ambition. For another, in his desire to expose the hypocrisy, the mean-spiritedness, the aggression that lay behind the Victorian façade of piety, Strachey needed a man of Manning's strong-willed temperament, and not one of Newman's evident sincerity.

For Manning was nothing if not ambitious and self-assertive. As Strachey says, "Had he lived in the Middle Ages he would certainly have been neither a Francis nor an Aquinas, but he might have been an Innocent" (*EV* 3). Like that Medieval pope whose political machinations helped to bring the Catholic Church, and himself as its head, immense worldly power, Manning's virtues lay in the direction of administrative acumen, diplomacy and "a superior faculty for gliding adroitly to the front rank" (*EV* 4). As much at home in Mayfair drawing rooms as in a pulpit, Manning, for all his apparent asceticism, had an unerring instinct for coming into contact with the right people. His brother-in-law was Samuel Wilberforce and one of his closest correspondents was William Gladstone, later Prime Minister.[4] By dint of these associations, Manning was to quickly rise in the Church of England and its supreme position, the archbishopric of Canterbury, lay clearly ahead of him.

But this was before the great crisis of faith precipitated by the Oxford Movement. Undoubtedly, Manning's spiritual dilemmas were genuine enough – Strachey shows him spending many agonizing hours poring over the works of the Church Fathers, trying to dispel from his mind the assailing doubts he was beginning to have about his own faith. Such grave questions as Baptismal Regeneration and the exemption from Original Sin of the Blessèd Virgin, upon which Anglicanism pronounced only equivocally, pressed upon Manning's anguished mind and conscience; the certainties of Roman Catholicism began to seem ever more attractive.

But what of his promising career in the Church of England? Were not some of his theological questionings bound up in the ambition that had placed Manning in such a position of power and popularity, and which in the event of his conversion would be dashed to nought?

> The example of Newman, a far more illustrious convert, was
> hardly reassuring: he had been relegated to a complete
> obscurity, in which he was to remain until extreme old age.

---

[4] Son of Clapham Sect reformer and abolitionist, William Wilberforce, Bishop Samuel Wilberforce is now best known for his participation in the controversy spurred by the publication of Darwin's *Origin of Species*. He imprudently asked the pugnacious T. H. Huxley whether it was through his grandfather or grandmother that he claimed descent from an ape. Robert Wilberforce, Samuel's brother, was another of Manning's confidants. Gladstone figures ignominiously in the Gordon essay. His hesitations were blamed for the loss of the Sudan and the death of General Gordon.

> Why should there be anything better in store for Manning? Yet it so happened that within fourteen years of his conversion Manning was Archbishop of Westminster and the supreme ruler of the Roman Catholic community in England. (*EV* 60)

That, of course, is the point, for Newman's conversion, as Strachey sees it, was more purely a question of religious temperament, of a romantic and mystical mind that found in Catholic theology a more compatible basis for its own speculations. Manning, in contrast, is shown immediately bustling off to Rome, arranging audiences with the Pope, securing for himself a place in the select *Accademia Ecclesiastica*, and then rushing back to England where he makes himself invaluable to Cardinal Wiseman, the incumbent Archbishop of Westminster, and insinuates himself into the society of England's Old Catholic aristocracy.

Strachey suggests that since the Oxford Movement had initiated a resurgence of English Catholicism, Manning fully intended to exploit this situation for his own gain. Indeed, he quotes from Manning's diary the confessed "desire to be in such as position (1) as I had in times past, (2) as my present circumstances imply, (3) as my friends think me fit for, (4) as I feel my own faculties tend to" (*EV* 72). Though Manning usually qualified such self-seeking admissions with protestations of his submission to God's will, the documented evidence of his steady and at times unscrupulous bids for power make such yielding and suppliant gestures seem highly suspect if not outright hypocritical. The most damning piece of business that Manning's worldly ambition brought him to was his attempt to thwart Newman's elevation to Cardinal. This was in the end unsuccessful, but it points to a streak of competitiveness and a sense of rivalry altogether opposed to Manning's official and even private image.

It was not without calculation that Strachey put Manning's portrait first in *Eminent Victorians*; not only is it the longest of the four, but it sums up in its pages a particular drive shared by the other figures and one which Strachey felt dominated the whole of the Victorian period. No less than Cardinal Manning are Florence Nightingale, Thomas Arnold and General Gordon pressed to their various missions by a singular belief in the moral and religious righteousness of their purposes. In all the masses of their published correspondence and diaries, there is never a hint of awareness that the prodigious fury with which they pursued their aims might emerge from anything other than a desire to serve God and wretched humanity. The religious instinct, so alive in them and to which they perpetually appealed, would seem to cover a multitude of personal failings, at least in Strachey's view, and the notion that their lives might be governed by more complex and inward drives, by repressed sexuality, by the will-to-power, by latent masochistic and self-destructive urges (as in the case of Gordon), would never have occurred to them.

Certainly, in Florence Nightingale, the legendary Lady with the Lamp, one gets the sense of a woman obsessed almost to the point of madness with asserting her will and getting her own way.

> Beneath her cool and calm demeanour lurked fierce and passionate fires. As she passed through the wards in her plain dress, so quiet, so unassuming, she struck the casual observer simply as the pattern of a perfect lady; but the keener eye perceived something more than that – the serenity of high deliberation in the scope of the capacious

brow, the sign of power in the dominating curve of the thin
nose, and the traces of a harsh and dangerous temper –
something peevish, something mocking, and yet something
precise . . . . (*EV* 156)

The indomitability with which Nightingale was able to subordinate the wishes
of others to her own purpose, to indeed bully men in high command when
she wanted something done appear, in light of Victorian attitudes toward
women, no less than amazing. Such a marshalling of personal forces by one
who for the last forty years of her long life was a semi-invalid suggest a sort
of energy on the surface incompatible with the usual nineteenth century
picture of delicate womanhood.

The fact is, Florence Nightingale never submitted to any man. As the
daughter of socially prominent parents, she had had to fight to remain
unmarried, dreaming instead of "something like a Protestant Sisterhood,
without vows, for women of educated feelings" (*EV* 137). Just as the timely
death of Manning's wife was a fortunate boon which permitted his admission
to the Catholic priesthood and subsequent ascendancy, so too was Florence
Nightingale's chosen celibacy all of a piece with her superhuman
accomplishments in reforming the nursing profession, initiating new standards
of medical hygiene and sanitation, and reorganizing the administration of
military hospitals. Even her later invalidism can be seen, like that of
Elizabeth Barrett, or Alice James or Mary Baker Eddy as a curiously
Victorian "ploy" to maintain independence and self-will.[5]

---

[5] See Sir George Pickering's *Creative Malady* (New York: Delta, 1976)
for a medical view of the Victorian cult of invalidism. Pages 99-182 are
devoted to Florence Nightingale.

> Her illness, whatever it may have been, was certainly not inconvenient. It involved seclusion; and an extraordinary, an unparalleled seclusion was, it might almost have been said, the mainspring of Miss Nightingale's life. Lying on her sofa in the little upper room in South Street, she combined the intense vitality of a dominating woman of the world with the mysterious and romantic quality of a myth. (*EV* 189)

In the end, Strachey takes Florence Nightingale down from the pedestal of sanctity upon which posterity had enshrined her, revealing through his probing and subtle means a character in many ways perverse and less than admirable. Nonetheless, he refrains from diminishing the real value of her life's work. That her reforming zeal and her unsparing efforts resulted in a vast number of permanent improvements in the important area of health care he will not deny. But what lay behind these achievements? Was the Lady with the Lamp a ministering angel fired from above with a holy mission, or was her indomitable energy drawn from more inward and tortuous complexes?

As Florence Nightingale slips into old age and her practical and administrative concerns fall into the hands of others, she again takes up the banner, or one might say cudgel, of evangelical religion. With the same implacability she had applied to the reform of the hospitals in Scutari, she attacks the impiety and freethinking that appear to be overtaking a certain class of people, attempting in three fat volumes to prove incontrovertibly the existence of God. Of course, "her conception of God was certainly not orthodox. She felt towards Him as she might have felt towards a glorified sanitary engineer; and in some of her speculations she seems hardly to distinguish between the Deity and the Drains" (*EV* 193). This is satire, to be sure, and we can have little doubt of the lack of seriousness with which Strachey takes Nightingale's brand of religion; indeed, he sees it as the beginnings of that senility that characterized her final years. Yet while he is poking fun at her theology, he is nonetheless exposing a dangerous fallacy which lay behind such a collusion of evangelical moral fervor and the more earth-bound concerns of the Victorians.

His portrait of Dr. Thomas Arnold, the briefest of the four essays, is a study in this fallacy. Arnold, who in 1827 was made headmaster of Rugby, had suffered in his life one brief period of religious doubt through which he passed to emerge "blessed with perfect piece of mind, and a settled conviction" (*EV* 209). Upon being appointed to the headmastership he took Holy Orders and became a Doctor of Divinity, all this as the natural prelude to his new task. So fortified, Dr. Arnold undertook to reform Rugby as an example to all the great public schools of England. His chiefest desire was to introduce Christian moral principles into the education of boys and to inculcate a gentlemanly respectability and the values of "muscular Christianity" in his young charges. As for academic reform, was Arnold

> to improve the character of his pupils by gradually spreading round them an atmosphere of cultivation and intelligence? By bringing them into close and friendly contact with civilised men, and even, perhaps, with civilised women? By introducing into the life of his school all that he could of the humane, enlightened, and progressive elements in the life of the community? On the whole, he thought not. Such considerations left him cold, and he preferred to be guided by the general laws of Providence. (*EV* 213)

Not only did Arnold's excessive concern for the moral life of his pupils make him disregard to a great extent the real purpose of education, but his Calvinistic views colored in what now seem a vile way his entire attitude toward the boys he was proposing to develop. He saw human nature as so inherently depraved, so sunk in moral evil, that observing the innocent activities of a group of boys, he exclaimed, "It is very startling to see so much of sin combined with so little of sorrow." And further, that "when the spring and activity of youth is altogether unsanctified by anything pure and elevated in its desires, it becomes a spectacle that is as dizzying and almost more morally distressing than the shouts and gambols of a set of lunatics" (*EV* 233).

Of all the portraits in *Eminent Victorians*, "Dr. Arnold" brought down on Strachey's head the most condemnation from those who felt that he was viciously maligning the memory of a great and respected pillar of Victorian society. Michael Holroyd has pointed out that there were softer and more attractive traits in Thomas Arnold that Strachey chose to ignore in favor of accentuating the schoolmaster's lack of humor, "his muddle-headed logic, his transcendent self-confidence, his strenuous obsession with moral righteousness . . . ."[6] Yet it was precisely this set of characteristics, and the last of them in particular, that seemed to sum up all that was worst in Victorianism, and that had most infected certain Victorian institutions. Evidence abounds confirming the detrimental effect the English public school could have upon the minds and characters of young boys, and such eminent Victorians as

---

[6] Michael Holroyd, *Lytton Strachey and the Bloomsbury Group: His Work, Their Influence* (Harmondsworth, Middlesex, England: Penguin, 1971) 216.

Anthony Trollope and John Addington Symonds have left vivid records of the torments they suffered during their early school years. Where the emphasis was all on physical activity and dull rote learning, and where the prefect system,[7] initiated by Arnold, resulted in acts of terrible brutality, there was little chance of instilling an enthusiasm for scholarly or artistic pursuits. While the more robust and aggressive among them may have succeeded in this Spartan environment, for the intellectual, the sensitive or the less athletic boy, the school years tended to be a long period of torment and exile.

This was true for Strachey as it had been for Forster, and they were not able to look back on their public school years with anything but dismay. While doing very little to improve the academic standards, Arnold had been

> the founder of the worship of athletics and the worship of good form. Upon those two poles our public schools have turned for so long that we have almost come to believe that such is their essential nature, and that an English public schoolboy who wears the wrong clothes and takes no interest in football is a contradiction in terms. (*EV* 241)

It is little wonder that Strachey would have vented his bitterness on such a man.

General Gordon, on the other hand, came in for a very different sort of treatment. Despite, or perhaps because of his own physical debility, Strachey was greatly drawn to daring men of action, and as a historian he

---

[7] The prefectorial system put older boys in official charge of younger, even giving boys of the Sixth Form authority to flog and otherwise punish those under the Fifth Form. This, allied with the tradition of fagging, led to the tacitly condoned bullying so frequently mentioned in Victorian school memoirs.

was more deeply interested in military and political affairs than he was, for instance, in the theological complexities of the Oxford Movement. He had written his Cambridge fellowship dissertation on Warren Hastings, the English statesman and Indian administrator, and among his biographical essays are nearly as many on political as on literary figures. Gordon was especially attractive for combining a wildly quixotic and romantic nature with the unyielding and determined character of a great soldier.

But while Strachey has not so obviously set out to denigrate Gordon, he nonetheless shows him to be propelled by almost pathological inner drives and by a religious fanaticism that bordered on madness. Furthermore, the military myth which Gordon personified, with its unquestioned assumption of the divine right of British imperialism, was one which Strachey very much wished to puncture. "The End of General Gordon" begins by showing the solitary figure of the general wandering through the streets of Jerusalem with a Bible under his arm. In this moment of respite shortly before the great events at Khartoum which were to seal Gordon's fate, he was engaged upon locating the exact site of the hill of Golgotha, the Garden of Eden and of Christ's sepulchre. Two years earlier he had claimed to have found the Forbidden Fruit, not an apple but the product of the *coco de mer* tree, while in the Seychelles Islands. Such were the private obsessions of the man who would sacrifice himself for the British Empire in Egypt.

Strachey had more diverse sources for his sketch of Gordon than he had for his other eminent Victorians, but no definitive biography. It was, in fact, the hero-worshipping tone, the unrelieved panegyric, of these earlier books that most provoked Strachey's desire to peek behind the veil of this peculiar individual. What he found, commingled with an undoubted bravery and military acumen, was a man tormented by his puritanical religious beliefs, a man whose Calvinistic hatred of the flesh drove him to shun all pleasure and company, to eat a diet of stale bread and milk, and to view humanity with loathing and contempt.[8] Gordon wrote, "I would be able to condemn a man to death without a qualm . . . and feel that I was as guilty as he. Punish, but with forgiveness and with the knowledge that we are all deserving of the same fate."[9] Such a sentiment, imbued as it was with an apocalyptic vision of human worthlessness before God, went hand in hand with an overwhelming self-destructive urge.

Even later biographers, and there have been many, have not failed to note this unmistakable aspect of Gordon's temperament. Strachey was perhaps the first to hint at its etiology in a deeply repressed homosexuality. It is clear that, very much like T. E. Lawrence, Gordon's propensity was to shun all female influence – he had a horror, especially, of "society" and its finely-dressed women – in favor of the rugged life of camps and tents. On the other hand, "he was particularly fond of boys. Ragged street Arabs and rough sailor lads crowded about him. They made free of his house and garden; they visited him in the evenings for lessons and advice; he helped them, found them employment, corresponded with them when they went out

---

[8] Gordon had also worked out for himself a "mystical and fatalistic" and certainly idiosyncratic personal creed" based upon the narrow foundations of Jewish Scripture, eked out occasionally by some English evangelical manual" (*EV* 258).

[9] Quoted in Herbert Tingsten, *Victoria and the Victorians*, trans. David and Eva Grey (New York: Delacorte, 1972) 469.

into the world" (*EV* 257). Of course, there was (as far as we know) no element of overt sexuality in all of this, and certainly any such thing would have been absolutely contrary to Gordon's religious beliefs. After Gordon's death and rapid rise to cult status, Gordon Boys' Homes and Gordon Boys' Clubs were established in industrial towns all over England to venerate his memory and his saintly devotion to male orphans and waifs.

But there was another aspect to this pacific and benevolent sanctity; though Gordon's solitary musings led him to hold that all was vanity in the world, he was nonetheless "an English gentleman, an officer, a man of energy and action, a lover of danger and the audacities that defeat danger, . . . with the self-assertiveness of independent judgment and the arbitrary temper of command" (*EV* 259). That peculiarly Victorian equation of religious with militant activity, so grotesquely manifest in General Gordon, spurred him on to deeds of rash and suicidal valor. One is easily reminded of Gibbon's descriptions of the early Christians, not as hounded and persecuted victims, but as fanatics so eager for death that they virtually offered themselves for martyrdom.

And so it came about that, surrounded and overwhelmed by the superior forces of his enemy, Gordon, ignoring orders to retreat, waited expectantly for the forces of Divine Fate to bring about an end he himself had long desired. Like Cardinal Manning's submission to the Will of God, General Gordon's fate too would appear more self-orchestrated than otherwise. As Strachey says,

> Fatalism is always apt to be a double-edged philosophy; for while, on the one hand, it reveals the minutest occurrences as the immutable result of a rigid chain of infinitely

> predestined causes, on the other, it invests the wildest
> incoherences of conduct or of circumstance with the sanctity
> of eternal law. And Gordon's fatalism was no exception.
> (*EV* 260)

This seems to be a characteristic of all these prominent Victorians who, in the unreflective conviction of their righteousness, would so often claim divine sanction for behavior that we, in a more psychological age, might find peculiar and questionable.

Though Gordon's heroism was obviously motivated by something other than a crass and jingoistic patriotism, he remains an apt symbol for the twilight years of the British Empire. The swaggering optimism, the confidence in England's right to subjugate and rule, the ultimately self-subverting disregard of the rights and humanity of other races was to prove the undoing, within the next few decades, of all the glory, grandeur and might that had swelled Victoria's kingdom over so much of the globe.

The publication in 1918 of *Eminent Victorians* catapulted Strachey to instant fame. He was reviewed and discussed everywhere. His book rapidly went into its third edition and was translated into all the major European languages. In 1918 many Victorians, eminent and otherwise, were still alive, and it was from this quarter that Strachey received the most dissent. Their outrage at his bumptious beard-pulling, his impious attacks upon the sacred figures of the immediate past, roused such people as Edmund Gosse and Mrs. Humphrey Ward to publicly express their fury. But whatever controversy surrounded it only served to increase the book's popularity and, inevitably, its sales.

The fact is that *Eminent Victorians* had arrived auspiciously. It appeared in the last months of the first World War, an event which had seemed in so many ways the ultimate and hideous outcome of British imperial posturing and fist-shaking. The grandiloquent phrases, the patriotic calls for conscription, the military confidence that had sent so many young men off to be slaughtered in foreign trenches seemed by 1918 empty and meaningless. "When the effort was over," writes Barbara Tuchman, "illusions and enthusiasms possible up to 1914 slowly sank beneath a sea of massive disillusionment. For the price it had paid, humanity's major gain was a painful view of its own limitations."[10] Strachey's book, whatever else it might have been, was the first major literary expression of this "massive disillusionment" with the past and its achievements. The publication of *Eminent Victorians*, coinciding as it did with the Armistice, marked the decisive end of Victorianism. The complacency and security of that era could be no longer; whether the century which lay ahead held more of bright promise or of calamity remained to be seen.

Though Strachey was not yet through with the Victorian Age as a subject, his irreverent propagandizing, so marked in *Eminent Victorians*, no longer seemed necessary. In *Queen Victoria* (1921), his next book, he would more closely follow the impersonal aim he had earlier proposed: ". . . to lay bare the facts . . . as I understand them, dispassionately, impartially, and without ulterior intentions" (*EV* ix). In addition, and perhaps in response to some of the academic criticisms of *Eminent Victorians* – charges that it was

---

[10] Barbara W. Tuchman, *The Proud Tower* (New York: Bantam, 1967) 544.

facile in its judgments and inaccurate in its facts – Strachey decided to take more care in his documentation and research. *Queen Victoria* is, as a result, outfitted with all the reassuring paraphernalia of such scholarship, including copious footnotes on nearly every page, an index, and a large bibliography. Whereas the former book, with its four crisp essays, had relied on readily available published accounts, the more sustained *Queen Victoria* involved sifting through massive volumes of letters, memoirs and historical accounts. As before, Strachey showed his genius for selection, and he managed, out of an almost overwhelming quantity of material, to economically and vividly recreate the subtly changing political atmosphere of Victoria's youth through that of her old age. In *Eminent Victorians* the ironic devices he had employed had the effect of distancing the reader from the subject, but in *Queen Victoria*

> his irony is lowered so that it flows like a sub-current flavouring the whole biography, and giving it its distinctive poise and harmony. In this sense, his prose style is more subtle than in his earlier book, the extreme quietness and depth of both the irony and wit being absorbed as a necessary part of the narrative.[11]

Michael Holroyd's comment can apply not only to *Queen Victoria* but to many of the shorter biographical essays Strachey produced as well. It was his impressive ability to dramatize and harmoniously summarize a life that in the early years of the century seemed such a remarkable innovation, and that has continued to exert a profound influence on subsequent biographical writing. The novelistic, hence highly readable and entertaining quality of

---

[11] Holroyd, *Lytton Strachey and the Bloomsbury Group* 248-49.

Strachey's books was not a feature to be often found in earlier biographies. But with Strachey, a new school was initiated. Harold Nicolson, André Maurois and David Cecil were all early practitioners (some might say, unfairly, imitators) of his novelistic method, and they wrote biographies that are still a delight to read.

Since Strachey's time, the art or craft of biography has developed enormously. It would not be extravagant to say, in fact, that the twentieth century has been a great age of biography. The psychological approach, still nascent when Strachey was writing, came to flower in the 1950s with such books as George Painter's *Marcel Proust*, Leon Edel's *Henry James* and Richard Ellmann's *James Joyce*. These large, exhaustive and even multi-volumed works might seem at first to owe little to those models of brevity penned by Lytton Strachey; in actuality they have a readily discernable common ancestor in such a book as *Queen Victoria* where environment and heredity are shown molding the young future monarch's mind and character, and where deep-seated psychological drives are revealed beneath the outer mask of convention and restraint.

In her essay, "The Art of Biography," Virginia Woolf pointed enthusiastically to the new territory which Lytton Strachey had opened up and which future biographers would be free to explore. Things that had once been impossible to discuss – sex, for instance – might now be made a valuable part of life-writing. Modern psychology would help the biographer to interpret the facts and peculiarities of a subject's life in a way hitherto unfathomed.

Thus the biographer must go ahead of the rest of us, like the miner's canary, testing the atmosphere, detecting falsity, unreality, and the presence of obsolete conventions. His sense of truth must be alive and on tiptoe. Then again, since we live in an age when a thousand cameras are pointed, by newspapers, letters, and diaries, at every character from every angle, he must be prepared to admit contradictory versions of the same face. Biography will enlarge its scope by hanging up looking glasses at odd corners. And yet from all this diversity it will bring out, not a riot of confusion, but a richer unity.[12]

Just as her own innovative methods for the depiction of character in fiction were meant to reflect a new view of personality inspired by the changed outlook of the twentieth century, so should biography follow course by pursuing with honesty, insight, and intelligence a fuller and more enlightened perspective on the figures it chooses to delineate.

This sort of truth-telling was a Bloomsbury code and, allied with the group's passion for personal relationships that pushed aside the restraints of convention, it resulted in the production of a great number of biographical and autobiographical works of the highest quality. Virginia Woolf's life of her friend Roger Fry, while beautifully written, was hampered by her inability to say all that she knew.[13] For her own talents, the strict bondage to facts, mundane events, and a certain chronology were too much of a restraint, but her playful mock-biographies, *Orlando* and *Flush*, demonstrate the sort of fun

---

[12] Virginia Woolf, "The Art of Biography," *The Death of the Moth and Other Essays* (New York: Harcourt, 1942) 195.

[13] Woolf was even obliged, because of Fry's family, to suppress his important affair with her sister Vanessa, and to be less than candid about his sexual life.

she could have with this genre when released to do as she liked. Long after her death the important manuscript, "A Sketch of the Past," was discovered. This and other posthumously published pieces demonstrate how very honest and penetrating Woolf was capable of being in writing of her own life.

Virginia Woolf's sketch was written for the Memoir Club which older Bloomsbury organized during World War I to ensure that the friends should meet periodically.[14] On these occasions they would take turns reading to one another their specially prepared reminiscences. John Maynard Keynes "My Early Beliefs," Molly MacCarthy's *A Nineteenth Century Childhood*, and Lytton Strachey's beautifully evocative "Lancaster Gate,"[15] all written for the Memoir Club, reflect the intelligence, intimacy, and genial good humor of these meetings, as well as the seriousness with which the members took the task of memoir writing.

Forster, though not an avid memoirist, did write two excellent biographies, one of his friend Goldsworthy Lowes Dickinson and the other of his great-aunt, Marianne Thornton. His *The Hill of Devi* and many of the essays in *Two Cheers for Democracy* demonstrate the personal tone, the mood of intimate engagement that was a hallmark of his style and, indeed, of Bloomsbury's in general. Perhaps the most remarkable of all Bloomsbury memoirs is Leonard Woolf's five-volume autobiography which he began at age seventy-nine and completed at age eighty-eight. Not only is his memory astounding, but the obvious and almost sacred regard for the very highest

---

[14] The Memoir Club's final meeting was in 1956.

[15] "Lancaster Gate" has now been published in *The Shorter Strachey*, ed. Michael Holroyd and Paul Levy (Oxford: Oxford UP, 1980) 1-13.

standards of truth, the penetrating self-analysis, the profound (and rigorously agnostic) philosophical reflections, and the candid emotions revealed in this work must stand as exemplary models of the Bloomsbury creed.

If the biographies of Lytton Strachey, whose critical fortune has risen and fallen more dramatically than that of either Forster or Virginia Woolf, survive and continue to be read, it is because of their underlying and essentially noble commitment to these Bloomsbury values. Whatever faults Strachey's books may have exhibited – the heavy-handed irony of *Eminent Victorians*, the excessive romanticizing in *Queen Victoria* – they served to inaugurate a new age in English biography. Strachey's psychological acumen, his artful selectiveness, his novelistic regard for the pleasure of his readers will undoubtedly remain legacies of enduring value to future biographers no matter what direction this important genre might take.

VI

TIME AND *MRS. DALLOWAY*

Two seminal essays, "Modern Fiction," written in 1919 and published in the first *Common Reader* (1925), and "Mr. Bennett and Mrs. Brown," published posthumously in the volume entitled *The Captain's Deathbed and Other Essays* (1950) but originally delivered as a talk in Cambridge in 1924, contain the germ of Virginia Woolf's program for a new fiction. In the latter essay, echoing Shelley's words of a hundred years before, Woolf declares that "we are trembling on the verge of one of the great ages of English literature." Aligning herself with the Georgian writers – E. M. Forster, D. H. Lawrence, Lytton Strachey, James Joyce and T. S. Eliot – in contradistinction to the Edwardians – John Galsworthy, Arnold Bennett and H. G. Wells – Woolf asserts the incompatibility of the past generation's methods with those which the current generation is attempting to explore.

She does this by recounting a personal anecdote, a simple event in which she boarded a railway carriage and became aware at once of having interrupted the conversation of an elderly lady whom she names Mrs. Brown and a man, probably a businessman, whom she calls Mr. Smith. After observing and listening to what passes between these two people, and then feeling acutely the pressure of the woman's character as they sit in the carriage across from one another, Virginia Woolf begins to make up a scenario for Mrs. Brown. This sort of thing is a common enough experience and for the writer, the novelist, it is the seed from which a book might grow. After all, at the core of novel writing is the notion of character and the desire of the novelist to truthfully convey character or, for that matter, many characters to his or her reader.

But of what does character consist?

> You see one thing in character, and I another. You say it means this, and I that. And when it comes to writing each makes a further selection on principles of his own. Thus Mrs. Brown can be treated in an infinite variety of ways, according to the age, country, and temperament of the writer.[1]

The English novelist, says Woolf, would give Mrs. Brown with all her warts, wrinkles, and eccentricities; the French writer would use Mrs. Brown to generalize about human nature and the human condition; the Russian writer, finally, would hardly concern himself with any externality, but would give only the soul of Mrs. Brown, "the soul alone, wandering out into the Waterloo Road, asking of life some tremendous question which would sound on and on in our ears after the book was finished."[2] Each of these particular biases is acceptable, and each of them gives at least some part of Mrs. Brown. But where, finally, is the real Mrs. Brown? And how best to represent her?

From the beginnings of the novel in the early eighteenth century through its great flowering in the nineteenth, there has been one outstanding characteristic distinguishing the genre; Ian Watt calls this "formal

---

[1] Virginia Woolf, "Mr Bennett and Mrs. Brown," *The Captain's Deathbed and Other Essays* (New York: Harcourt, 1950) 102-03.

[2] Woolf, "Mr. Bennett and Mrs. Brown" 102.

realism."[3] Within the framework of formal realism, or the presentation of life in a manner recognizable as somehow true to its model, there have been, from the very outset, at least two general ways of depicting character. One is Fielding's external method which gives the outward traits of a person in such detail that we may deduce a whole being from them. The other is that of Richardson who draws character from within, giving us the thoughts and emotions of a character and bringing us so much into contact with his or her internal life that we imaginatively construe, if the method is successful, a more rounded and visceral picture of the person. These are the poles of an axis around which all novels from Defoe to Joyce have tended to revolve. But within these perimeters, the prerogative of the novel has always remained character itself, the individual in relation to other individuals and to his or her environment.

In the novels of Sterne or Jane Austen, for example, the focus upon character and its activities is so complete as to constitute an entire and self-sufficient world. "But," Virginia Woolf claims, "the Edwardians were never interested in character itself; or in the book itself. They were interested in something outside."[4] To illustrate this, Woolf briefly reimagines her anecdote, this time with the three Edwardian authors riding in the railway carriage with Mrs. Brown. Wells, observing Mrs. Brown's anxious look and shabby

---

[3] ". . . formal, because the term realism does not here refer to any special literary doctrine or purpose, but only to a set of narrative procedures which are so commonly found together in the novel, and so rarely in other literary genres, that they may be regarded as typical of the form itself." Ian Watt, *The Rise of the Novel* (Berkeley: U of California P, 1957) 32.

[4] "Mr. Bennett and Mrs. Brown" 105.

144

appearance, would immediately proceed to a disquisition on the inadequacy of public education, and then to envision a utopian world where, with this condition improved, things would be infinitely "better, breezier, jollier, happier, more adventurous and gallant . . . ."[5] Mr. Galsworthy, on the other hand, might instead notice the factory outside the carriage window which would lead him to picture the plight of the poor women within who make earthenware pots all day at low wages while their rich employers smoke cigars in Surrey. This author "would only see in Mrs. Brown a pot broken on the wheel and thrown in the corner." Only Mr. Bennett of the three Edwardians would remain focused on Mrs. Brown. "He, indeed, would observe every detail with immense care."[6] But Bennett, too, would become sidetracked in his enumeration of copious detail and extraneous information about houses and leases until, in the end, we, his readers, would lose sight of Mrs. Brown and hear only the voice of Mr. Bennett.

So it came to be that the fictional methods of the Edwardians, however well-suited to the highly-padded social novels they were wont to write, seemed merely cumbrous to the Georgian Modernists. Just as the Post-Impressionist painters felt that to get at the reality underlying appearances they must overthrow the naturalism, the carefully outlined and detailed craftsmanship of their predecessors, so too did the Modernists, in their desire to delve more deeply into the inward consciousness and subtle nature of their characters, need to dispense with the formal conventions of the traditional novel. Indeed, the changed sense of human character which

---

[5] "Mr. Bennett and Mrs. Brown" 106.

[6] "Mr. Bennett and Mrs. Brown" 106.

Virginia Woolf dates at around 1910 had everything to do with this shift. The synchronous occurrence of certain shattering forces – Freud's psychoanalysis, Einstein's physics, Bergson's intuitionist philosophy, as well as the undermining of the established social order precipitated by the Great War – all contributed to that profoundly altered perception of the universe and the individual's place within it which the Modernists felt emboldened to body forth in their art.

What Virginia Woolf offers by way of corrective to Edwardian "materialism" is, by her own admission, tentative and still in a nascent state;

> . . . where so much strength is spent on finding a way of telling the truth, the truth itself is bound to reach us in rather an exhausted and chaotic condition. Ulysses, Queen Victoria, Mr. Prufrock – to give Mrs. Brown some of the names she has made famous lately – is a little pale and dishevelled by the time her rescuers reach her.[7]

With so many of the old ways of thinking lying in tatters about them, the Modernist writers needed to recreate, out of the remnants of the past and the insights of the incipient future, a new sort of fiction, poetry and biography. That their unsurpassed achievements, now in themselves a tradition, should yet move us to such wonder and admiration bears out the continuing worth of these efforts at "telling the truth."

From almost the beginning of her writing career Virginia Woolf had wanted to express her strong sense of the individual as not only a movement in space, but as a flow in time. Even her first novel, *The Voyage Out*, shows

---

[7] "Mr. Bennett and Mrs. Brown" 117.

evidence of this concern. When she came to write *Mrs. Dalloway* she had at last hit upon a method that would give to her characters an actual and mobile existence in a definite time and place while opening them, so to speak, into a larger realm, that underlying stream of thought and memory where each person truly lived, despite outer activity and appearance. She felt that it was within this realm that a hope of connectedness, and even the merging of one fundamentally isolated consciousness with another might be possible. Woolf accomplished this partly through her tunneling technique, or as she put it: "How I dig out beautiful caves behind my characters. I think that gives exactly what I want; humanity, humour, depth. The idea is that the caves shall connect and each comes to daylight at the present moment."[8] This notion of the subterranean interconnectedness of human consciousness, and of the simultaneity and continuity of apparently discontinuous events, coincides in remarkable ways with the thinking of an older contemporary of Virginia Woolf, Henri Bergson, the eminent French philosopher who in 1927 was to receive the Nobel Prize for literature.

As early as 1932 in one of the first critical books on Virginia Woolf, the French critic Floris Delattre had pointed out parallels between her work and that of Bergson.[9] In both their outlooks the individual was seen no longer as a discrete and immutable entity, riding as it were upon the course of outer events. Instead, reflecting modern cinematographic as opposed to

---

[8] *The Diary of Virginia Woolf,* ed. Anne Olivier Bell, vol. 2, *1920-1924* (New York: Harcourt, 1978) 263.

[9] Floris Delattre, *Le Roman Psychologique de Virginia Woolf* (Paris: J. Vrin, 1932).

photographic techniques, they construed the person as a process, a "becoming" rather than a static being. This was due, in part, to the influence of new scientific ideas about time and the nature of the universe which the physicists Einstein, Max Planck, Neils Bohr, Rutherford and Heisenberg were then making public. Their revolutionary theories radially revised previous cosmological notions, and the stable Newtonian world-view of the two previous centuries was soon to become a thing of the past. All of this had an impact far outside the field of physics, and intellectuals of all camps were swept into the excitement. Even Cambridge after 1910 moved toward a more relativist and intuitionist outlook with Bertrand Russell's *The Philosophy of Bergson* (1914) which though somewhat critical of the philosopher's views, helped to introduce Bergsonism to an English audience, Karin Stephen's more admiring *The Misuse of Mind* (1922)[10] and Alfred North Whitehead's own exposition of the new philosophy, *Process and Reality* (1929).

The importance of all this to the artists cannot be exaggerated. E. M. Forster, though not greatly interested in the sciences, recounted in his daybook the impact upon him of reading Eddington's *The Nature of the Physical World* which confirmed his intuition "that matter was not solid, that one knew everything through measurements only, that his own 'spasmodic instincts and confusions about Time' had a value."[11] And Stephen Spender,

---

[10] Karin Costelloe Stephen, a graduate of Newham College, Cambridge, was Virginia Woolf's sister-in-law. She was also the niece by marriage of Bertrand Russell, and the step-daughter of Bernard Berenson.

[11] P. N. Furbank, *E. M. Forster: A Life* (New York: Harcourt, 1981) 158.

in his autobiography *World Within World*, tells of a visit to Lady Ottoline Morrell's home, Garsington, where he stood by

> while Yeats sat on the sofa with Virginia Woolf and explained to her that her novel, *The Waves*, expressed in fiction the idea of pulsations of energy throughout the universe which was common to the modern theories of physicists and to recent discoveries in psychic research.[12]

Certainly, all three of James Joyce's novels can be said to be experiments with time and *Finnegans Wake*, especially, is deliberately written on a circular time-scheme, turning back, as it does, upon itself. Of all the Modernists, perhaps the one whose entire *oeuvre* seems most conditioned by the new physics and philosophy is Marcel Proust. A cousin by marriage of Bergson, Proust had studied at the Sorbonne under that scientifically oriented, if decidedly anti-rationalist, philosopher. It has often been remarked that Proust's great work was an application in fiction of Bergson's ideas about time, memory and the flow of consciousness. Proust himself was proud of the oft-noted comparison of his work to that of the new physicists and he, in fact, helped the mathematician Camille Vettard to get published an essay entitled "*Proust et Einstein*." Proust's biographer, George Painter, states,

> *A la Recherche du Temps Perdu* was, indeed, the picture of a relativistic universe expanding and contracting in a space-time continuum; and when Benjamin Crémieux pointed out some apparent anachronisms in *Le Côté de Guermantes*

---

[12] Quoted in Carolyn G. Heilbrun, ed., *Lady Ottoline's Album* (New York: Knopf, 1976) 100.

Proust explained that these were due "to the flattened form my characters take owing to their rotation in time."[13]

Similarly, Virginia Woolf wished to show in her fiction this curious double-life of character which, while making its way from breakfast to dinner, remained unimpeded by that passage – its inner-life a continuous flow of past into present. She had declared as early as 1919 in her essay, "Modern Fiction," that "life is not a series of gig lamps symmetrically arranged; but a luminous halo, a semi-transparent envelope surrounding us from the beginning of consciousness to the end." And further, "is it not the task of the novelist to convey this varying, this unknown and uncircumscribed spirit, whatever aberration or complexity it may display, with as little mixture of the alien and external as possible?"[14]

We might compare this to Bergson's formulation in *Creative Evolution* where he claims that

> The apparent discontinuity of the psychical life is then due to our attention being fixed on it by a series of separate acts. . . . A thousand incidents arise, which seem to be cut off from those that precede them, and to be disconnected from those which follow. Discontinuous though they appear, however, in point of fact they stand out against the continuity of a background on which they are designed, and to which indeed they owe the intervals that separate them. . . . Our attention fixes on them because they interest it

[13] George D. Painter, *Marcel Proust: A Biography*, vol. 2 (New York: Vintage, 1978) 336.

[14] Virginia Woolf, "Modern Fiction," *The Common Reader*, 1st series (New York: Harcourt, 1925) 154.

more, but each of them is borne by the fluid mass of our whole psychical experience.[15]

Bergson goes on to give a corollary to this idea in his notion of time versus duration, the first being mechanical or clock time, an artificial construct useful for ordering life and measuring events but of no ultimate reality, while the second (*la durée*) is fluid and continuous. Duration is identical with what we often call psychological time, our inner experience of time. It is "the continuous progress of the past which gnaws into the future and which swells as it advances."[16]

However abstract such statements may at first appear, they express a deep and visceral perception which came to be an integral part of the Modernist world-view. This view has about it a variable quality, for it tends to see the exterior man (cf. Kafka, Musil) as fragmented and alienated from his culture, as profoundly ill-at-ease in the world, and as perhaps tortured and perplexed by inchoate images emerging from the unconscious. At the same time, it sees his inward being (cf. Jung, Hesse) as a flowing, organic process of self-actualization, intimately bound by psychic ties to all of life, and, in fact (cf. Freud, Joyce), recapitulating in its private history the entire history of the species.

---

[15] Henri Bergson, *Creative Evolution*, trans. Arthur Mitchell (New York: Modern Library, 1944) 5. *L'evolution créatrice* was originally published in 1907 and first translated into English in 1911. It was phenomenally successful.

[16] Bergson, *Creative Evolution* 7.

These seemingly opposed aspects of what is an essentially unified, if pluralistic, viewpoint account for many of the disparities in Modernist (and Post-Modernist) writing. Certainly, the existential "anxiety of meaninglessness" of which Tillich spoke, as well as a rather uneasy intimation of new possibilities and new meanings, both find a place in Virginia Woolf's work. *Mrs. Dalloway*, in particular, fuses a sense of the unassuageable loneliness and isolation of the individual personality with a quasi-mystical feeling for some transpersonal realm where separate selfhood might at last be resolved.

Mrs. Dalloway made her initial appearance aboard the ship sailing to South America in Virginia Woolf's first novel, *The Voyage Out*. She remained in her creator's mind as a special type, one with whom Woolf was familiar and by which she was at once fascinated and repelled. This was the society hostess, a woman skilled at bringing people together, a great giver of parties, adapt at saying the right things in the drawing room, invariably well-married and an ornament to her husband's career. Woolf had models for such women in her old family friend, Kitty Maxse, and in the several famous hostesses of her acquaintance. Having rebelled in her young womanhood against the fashionable society into which her half-brother, George Duckworth, was drawing her, and having suffered acute pangs of shyness at being "exhibited," Woolf had good reasons both to admire and to abhor the sort of character she created in Clarissa Dalloway.

Even before *Jacob's Room* was published, Woolf had been working on two related sketches, "The Prime Minister" and "Mrs. Dalloway in Bond

Street." These short pieces became the nucleus from which the later novel grew. In a diary entry of 19 June 1923, Woolf had some apposite things to say about her composition, tentatively called *The Hours*: "In this book I have almost too many ideas. I want to give life & death, sanity & insanity; I want to criticise the social system, & to show it at work, at its most intense."[17] She intended to accomplish this, not by a detailed exposition in the manner of Galsworthy, but rather through brief flashes of vision and through a focus on the inner lives of two distinct but subjectively related characters.

Jacob's Room, Virginia Woolf's first truly experimental novel, had been the testing ground for many of her new ideas about character and point-of-view. But some time between its publication in 1922 and before she had begun her next book, Woolf gained an insight which profoundly altered her conception of the way she wished to write. It was this insight that brought about the three great masterworks of her mid-career, *Mrs. Dalloway*, *To the Lighthouse*, and *The Waves*. She called this personal discovery at one point,

> my tunnelling process, by which I tell the past by installments as I have need of it. This is my prime discovery so far; & the fact that I've been so long finding it, proves, I think, how false Percy Lubbock's doctrine is – that you can do this sort of thing consciously.[18]

This searching about for a method to disclose character without recourse to the old devices of building up a surface picture had been partially provoked by Arnold Bennett's criticism (he was speaking of *Jacob's Room*) that her

---

[17] *The Diary of Virginia Woolf* 2: 248.

[18] *The Diary of Virginia Woolf* 2: 272.

characters "do not vitally survive in the mind because the author has been obsessed by details of originality and cleverness."[19] She answered with the essay "Mr. Bennett and Mrs. Brown," defending her position with the claim that the old solid ego of the past was no longer, and that the modern, post-Dostoyevskian personality required a new technique in fiction. Nonetheless, she took Bennett's criticism to heart, as well as that of Middleton Murray, who averred that she had written herself into a corner with *Jacob's Room*.

In that novel Jacob Flanders is seen through the eyes of those about him. We never see him directly, but rather reflected in the mirror of others' perceptions. The effect of this, though conveying in an original way the multiplicity of human personality, tends to leave the reader with too diffuse a picture, robbing the main character of some integral and necessary feature. Determined to avoid this pitfall, Woolf embarked upon *The Hours* in a flush of enthusiasm and creative energy. As she put it herself, "I feel my force flow straight from me at its fullest. . . . I think it most important in this book to go for the central things." Yet she admitted to herself, in the same entry, the great difficulty of her plan:

> I foresee, to return to *The Hours*, that this is going to be the devil of a struggle. The design is so queer & so masterful. I'm always having to wrench my substance to fit it. The design is certainly original, & interests me hugely. I should like to write away & away at it, very quick and fierce."[20]

---

[19] Arnold Bennett in the *Criterion*, July 1924, reprinted in Robin Majumdar and Allen MacLauren, *Virginia Woolf: The Critical Heritage* (London and Boston: Routledge, 1975) 113.

[20] *The Diary of Virginia Woolf* 2:248, 249.

As this novel advanced, Woolf grew more confident in her scheme. Put to the test, her intuition seemed to be working, and this is borne out by the greater clarity and fullness of the characters in the novel she began to call *Mrs. Dalloway*.

Here, while retaining some of the experimental features she had developed in the writing of *Jacob's Room*, Woolf shifts the focus much closer to the interior life of her principal characters. Perhaps her earlier reading of Joyce (whom she didn't in every way admire), and of Proust (whose genius stimulated her enormously), coalesced into a personal mode of interior monologue. This can be seen on the first page of *Mrs. Dalloway* when the sensations of a warm June day trigger in Clarissa Dalloway a complex chain of impressions and emotions which carry her back into the past.

We learn that it is some time not long after the Armistice, for the consequences of the late war figure constantly in Clarissa's reflections. She is on her way to Bond Street to purchase flowers for her party later in the evening. As she makes her way through the busy thoroughfares, an upsurge of memory takes hold of her. There is no violent transition from her concentration upon her task to the subtle movement by which her mind shifts into a recollection of events from her youth. We gather there has been a letter from an old beau, Peter Walsh; this, and some feeling in the warm air seem to provoke the memory. The prospect of seeing Peter Walsh causes in Clarissa both pleasure and a slight remorse, for their relationship had gone sour, and she'd chosen to marry Richard Dalloway and become what Peter Walsh had at the time sarcastically called, "the perfect hostess."

These remarks of his never left her; she was always measuring herself against such criticisms, knowing in her heart she'd taken the safer road in marrying the successful Richard Dalloway and rejecting Peter Walsh, "though she had borne about with her for years like an arrow sticking in her heart the grief, the anguish."[21] But Clarissa is buoyed up, exhilarated, by the pleasure of walking through London on a beautiful day. Her memories, however tinged with regret, are a part of her, part of her present life, a life she loves as she goes about "making it up, building it round one, tumbling it, creating it every moment afresh" (*MD* 5). This sense of life's fluid passage and continuity is only briefly interrupted by a concurrent emotion, one of loneliness and personal mortality, for "she had a perpetual sense . . . of being out, far out to sea and alone; she always had the feeling that it was very, very dangerous to live even one day" (*MD* 11).

It is important to note, for the theme runs throughout the novel, how these two sensations, of life's wonder and excitement and of its precariousness and isolation, continually alternate without ever cancelling one another. Clarissa, who is by nature optimistic, asks herself as she walks toward Bond Street, "did it matter that she must inevitably cease completely; all this must go on without her; did she resent it; or did it not become consoling to believe that death ended absolutely?" (*MD* 12). She feels herself so much a part of the ebb and flow of life, of her past, of other people, that,

---

[21] Virginia Woolf, *Mrs. Dalloway* (New York: Harcourt, 1925) 10. All subsequent quotes from this novel will be cited in the text and refer to this edition.

barring an after-life, this communion with things might itself be a kind of survival.

In the midst of such reveries, Clarissa Dalloway stops before crossing Victoria Street. At this juncture, Big Ben strikes: "Out it boomed. First a warning, musical; then the hour irrevocable. The leaden circles dissolved in the air" (*MD* 5). This tolling of a clock (and not any clock, but the imposing, historical Big Ben) punctuates the novel as a reminder of time-as-taskmaster, the time that ages and carries one toward death; not the fluid, inward *durée*, but "leaden circles" which enclose the transcendent self in a finite world.

Here, again, is that recurring juxtaposition of opposing time schemes. Not only is there Clarissa's personal past, her memories and her evanescent sense of self – "she would not say of herself, I am this, I am that" (*MD* 11) – there is also a larger sense of history, especially of the grandeur of British history, and even that is framed by a past before it was and a future when it shall no longer be. As a motor car with drawn blinds makes its way through the throngs of Piccadilly, some collective impersonal voice perceives

> the majesty of England, of the enduring symbol of the state which will be known to curious antiquaries, sifting the ruins of time, when London is a grass-grown path and all those hurrying along the pavement this Wednesday morning are but bones with a few wedding rings mixed up in their dust. . . . (*MD* 23)

But now, as they hurry, they are upheld by the idea that "greatness was seated within . . . removed only by a hand's-breadth from ordinary people" (*MD* 23). In this, there is a real understanding of people's need to buttress the apparent insignificance of their individual selves by an identification with something larger and more permanent.

We are reminded of Virginia Woolf's intention, stated in her diary, "to criticize the social system & to show it at work, at its most intense." In this novel, especially, the social setting is impressionistically painted with an almost Jamesian richness: country houses, befurred women, upholstered gentlemen, Parliament, the Prime Minister. This is the backdrop against which Clarissa Dalloway moves, and even her memories, her values, her inward self are entwined with a strong sense of place, of class, of position. And it is here that one might consider what Clarissa meant to her author, for Woolf is careful not to overbalance the scale. Clarissa is never just a caricature of a socialite, though we are left in no doubt that her life as Mrs. Richard Dalloway, the life of privilege and status, has entered her soul, and brought about a kind of torpor, a narrowness of outlook, a certain deadening of the spirit, that on occasion threaten to overwhelm her. Nonetheless, seeing her as we do from the inside, Clarissa is not really reprehensible. Though her judgments may occasionally be impaired by class bias (evident in her hatred of Miss Kilman), her quality of knowing people by instinct, her surefootedness in social interaction, her refinement, poise and sensitivity are all admirable and endearing traits.

Set in opposition to Clarissa Dalloway's fashionable upper-class existence is the life of Septimus Warren Smith, a young man not long returned from the front who is suffering the delayed effects of shell shock. With him is his twenty-four year old Italian wife, Rezia. He is introduced while that mysterious and impressive grey car pulls up in front of the Bond

Street florist where Clarissa Dalloway is purchasing her flowers. Immediately
we are drawn into Septimus's world by a deft fusing of the outer event with
the inward perception:

> Everything had come to a standstill. The throb of the motor
> engines sounded like a pulse irregularly drumming through
> an entire body. The sun became extraordinarily hot because
> the motor car had stopped outside Mulberry's shop widow.
> (*MD* 20-21)

This strange deduction offers a clue to the frightful derangement of
Septimus's mind, and further, as he stands amidst the crowd observing the
scene, it was

> . . . as if some horror had come almost to the surface and
> was about to burst into flames. . . . It is I who am blocking
> the way, he thought. Was he not being looked at and
> pointed at; was he not weighted there, rooted to the
> pavement, for a purpose? But for what purpose? (*MD* 21)

The synaesthetic nature of the first perception, and the delusional nature of
the second, are a vivid evocation from within of a profoundly disordered
mental process.

Virginia Woolf had herself suffered bouts of insanity, and she knew the
suddenness with which they could overtake the mind. From her own
experience, she knew the horrors of a disease in which the normal and sane
state could exist side by side with acute madness with often, as in her own
case, only a fine line separating the two.[22] Because of this, however bizarre

---

[22] See *The Diary of Virginia Woolf*, ed. Anne Olivier Bell, vol. 3, *1925-
1930* (New York: Harcourt, 1980) 110 for an impressive example of the way

Septimus's perceptions might seem, he is never shown as altogether unlike ordinary people, and his moments of lucidity are revealed to be more penetrating and observant than the duller awarenesses of his wife and his doctors.

Furthermore, our sympathy is enlisted on his side, for Septimus soon begins a confrontation with the medical men Bradshaw and Holmes, two specialists in the field of mental disorders. Their treatment of him, full of condescension and lacking real understanding, forms part of Virginia Woolf's intended criticism of society and its educated professionals. There is considerable bitterness mixed in with the satirical tone in Woolf's portrayal of these men. Enough is known of her biography to believe she had suffered similar humiliations at the hands of incompetent "specialists." Bradshaw, especially, is the very picture of masculine authority as he advises Septimus not to alarm his wife, to think less about himself, to observe "proportion, divine proportion" (*MD* 150). This, as poor Septimus thinks himself "the most exalted of mankind; the criminal who faced his judges; the victim exposed on the heights; the fugitive; the drowned sailor; the poet of the immortal ode; the Lord who had gone from life to death . . ." (*MD* 146-47). That such delusions might be quelled by a glass of warm milk and a few months' rest in the country is ludicrous. Yet it is such counsel that has brought Sir William Bradshaw to the top of his profession, a counsel that, Woolf tells us, masks something more sinister: the imposition of one will over another, and the locking up of those who fail to conform.

Woolf could rationally and analytically observe her fits of madness as they happened.

The visit of Septimus Warren Smith and his wife to Bradshaw's Harley Street office is given in considerable detail of both outward circumstance and inward perception, but we come to realize that the fairly lengthy episode has all happened in the three quarters of an hour Bradshaw allots to each of his patients. This bit of clock time is linked, then, to those proponents of orderliness, of will and of duty. As the couple leave Bradshaw's office, the leaden circles descend upon them:

> Shredding and slicing, dividing and subdividing, the clocks of Harley Street nibbled at the June day, counselled submission, upheld authority, and pointed out in chorus the supreme advantages of a sense of proportion, until the mound of time was so far diminished that a commercial clock, suspended above a shop in Oxford Street, announced . . . that it was half-past one. (*MD*, 152-54)

How different this oppressive and devouring clock time is from the Bergsonian "duration," the inner, fluid continuous time which knows no such diminishment but which stretches out before and behind in a continuous stream. Certainly neither Septimus's insane delusions, nor Clarissa's memories of her youth, nor Peter Walsh's erotic fantasies can be subjected to Bradshaw's tightly scheduled appointments, nor to a commercial clock over a shop in Oxford Street.

What Virginia Woolf does is to show us life suspended in an uncircumscribed space-time continuum where the simultaneity of events rather than their rigid demarcation is the true state of things. True to the actual experience of life, Woolf conveys the emotional density and inward complexity that might pack the two hours between 10:00 a.m. and noon, however inconsequential its surface events – the buying of flowers in Bond Street, or a visit to a doctor in Harley Street – may appear to be. And yet everything is curiously connected, not obviously on the exterior level of appearances, but in a sort of mystical coherence visible within the subtler reaches of consciousness.

We see this in the episode of the sky-writer which soars overhead, leaving a trail of vaporous letters. Everyone's attention is immediately drawn to it, though each person interprets it differently. To Mr. Bentley it seems "an aspiration; a concentration; a symbol . . . of man's soul; of his determination . . . to get outside of his body" (*MD* 41). To Mrs. Dempster it represents the adventure of foreign parts. To Septimus Warren Smith it is a signal to himself, a cosmic message of beauty and inexhaustible charity. To Mr. Bowley it is merely an advertisement for toffee. Then, there is the grey motor car which somehow links all the onlookers by casting a spell of mystery and power over them. Does the car contain the Prime Minister, or the Prince of Wales or perhaps the Queen herself? No one is certain, but "the surface agitation of the passing car as it sunk grazed something very profound" (*MD* 46). Observing the same scene, Clarissa, Sarah Bletchley, Emily Coates and Mr. Bowley each stand outside of their separate identities, feeling themselves part of some greater category: subjects of Her Majesty, citizens of the British Empire, Englishmen. Again, Woolf expresses a deep truth in this universal need of people to subsume their individuality within some larger whole, whether of the state, of a religion, or of a particular political persuasion, as one might say, "I am a Socialist." Paradoxically, this is not a way of losing identity, but of increasing it by identifying with a more all-inclusive category of kinship, class, or nationality, and thereby achieving a more permanent and ideal status.

Thus, within the leaden circles of clock time, on a particular day in June, in a specific year, in the City of London, as well as in the subterranean consciousness where time flows unimpeded, in "the unseen part of us, which spreads wide" (*MD* 232), Virginia Woolf draws her disparate characters together. As the hour of Clarissa's party approaches, a certain tension mounts. Rezia, sadly acquiescing to Septimus's removal to an institution, packs a bag for her husband while Dr. Holmes ascends toward their rooms in a Bloomsbury lodging house to lead the unfortunate man away. But Septimus, refusing to yield, to give himself up, suddenly flings himself from the window onto the railings below just as Holmes bursts into the room. The distraught Rezia is administered a sedative to keep her calm. And Peter Walsh, having dinner at his hotel prior to leaving for Clarissa's party, hears a siren outside and melancholically reflects on loneliness, on suffering and on the brevity of life.

From the tragedy at the Warren Smith's boarding house, we are suddenly plunged into the midst of Clarissa's party – a scene of glittering society, of small talk and gossip, and even, on occasion, of intimacy and genuine emotion. The distinguished, but somehow menacing figure of Sir William Bradshaw appears, though rather late, for as he tells Richard Dalloway, appropos their discussion of the social problem of shell shock (which one must do something about), a young man, recently out of the army, had killed himself. Hearing this instantly freezes Clarissa. At first she is deeply offended at the impropriety of Bradshaw's remark: "in the middle of my party, here's death, she thought" (*MD* 279). But vividly imagining for herself the terrible suicide, she is thrust into an awful awareness of the shallowness and inconsequence of her privileged existence, for truly there was something

> . . . that mattered; a thing wreathed about with chatter, defaced, obscured in her own life, let drop every day in corruption, lies, chatter. This he had preserved. Death was defiance. Death was an attempt to communicate; people feeling the impossibility of reaching the center which, mystically, evaded them; closeness drew apart; rapture faded, one was alone. There was an embrace in death. (*MD* 280)

Recalling how she had once thrown a shilling into the Serpentine, Clarissa in an instant of psychic rapport deeply identifies with the unknown young man, with Septimus Warren Smith who had killed himself.

She realizes that at bottom, underneath her love of and craving for life, there was an awful fear, the fear of death and nothingness, and of being tainted, destroyed morally by the very thing to which she was so attached. Hatred could do this; so could self-love; and, as her unsettling epiphany at her party shows, so could the need for approval and social success. The integrity of spirit which Septimus had preserved by refusing to capitulate, to conform, she herself had lost. And "somehow it was her disaster – her disgrace. It was her punishment to see sink and disappear here a man, there a woman, in this profound darkness, and she forced to stand here in her evening dress" (*MD* 282).

But then, as she moves toward a window and notices in the house opposite an old woman going to bed, turning her lights off while all Clarissa's were blazing, she has an even deeper realization: that life and death, like time and eternity, are not wholly antagonists, but that one permeates the other, includes the other as a complementary opposite. Life was made the brighter by the very darkness of death, and death was given its solemnity, its permanence, in contrast to fleeting life. As Clarissa turns, regaining her composure, to go back to her party,

> she felt somehow very like him – the young man who had killed himself. She felt glad that he had done it; thrown it away. The clock was striking. The leaden circles dissolved in the air. He made her feel the beauty; made her feel the fun. (*MD*, 283-84)

Mysteriously, Septimus's death has broken for her the barrier between the glitter of life and the void beyond it. Clarissa can take up life again and find in its transient dazzle some core of meaning.

In writing *Mrs. Dalloway*, Virginia Woolf had at last achieved what had eluded her in *Jacob's Room*, namely the anchoring of her characters in chronological time while simultaneously linking them, psychically, to the continuous flow of psychological duration. What Einstein and Bergson had articulated for physics and philosophy, Woolf had expressed in the realm of fiction, and she had accomplished this, like James Joyce before her, using the stuff of ordinary life. And just as Joyce had, through his art, elevated the commonplace Leopold Bloom to the status of Everyman, so did Virginia Woolf make the life of a London socialite and that of a mentally disturbed young man her paradigms for all of humanity.

VII

THE PHILOSOPHY OF *TO THE LIGHTHOUSE*

In the fall of 1881 Leslie Stephen, soon to become the editor of the *Dictionary of National Biography*, bought the lease of Talland House in St. Ives, Cornwall. Beginning the following year and until 1895, when his wife Julia died, Leslie Stephen brought his large household here to spend the summer months. It is the recollection of these months that Sir Leslie's daughter, Virginia Woolf, was later to immortalize in what many critics consider her finest novel. Certainly *To the Lighthouse* has about it an atmosphere of human emotion in all its tangled intricacy and a profound sense of what passes between husbands and wives, and between parents and children, which *The Waves*, for all its poetic brilliance, seems to lack. The method, too, is a further consolidation of those discoveries Woolf had put to such good use in *Mrs. Dalloway*, with perhaps a subtler balance between outer description and inner monologue. This greater balance is due to an artistic realization that is here exemplified in the character of Lily Briscoe. Just as Lily is able, at the novel's end, to complete her long-unfinished painting by drawing a line down the center which unifies the previously discordant elements, so too does Virginia Woolf achieve a feat of synthesis in bringing together the opposing and antagonistic terms whose interplay is the motive force of *To the Lighthouse*.

These terms might be variously expressed, but essentially they refer to the disjunction between the masculine as opposed to the feminine consciousness, or between the rational and empirical set of mind as against the intuitive and suprarational. Not that the former, as Woolf points out in

A Room of One's Own, must always be embodied in the male and the latter in the female, but this pattern, due both to biological and social conditioning, is more likely than the reverse. In *To the Lighthouse*, Professor Ramsay becomes the symbol of a divisive, hyper-rational and analytic masculine intelligence, while Mrs. Ramsay represents a more intuitive, fluid and feminine mode of perception.

This was a theme that had a special resonance for Virginia Woolf, and its roots in her own life are not hard to discover. For Virginia Woolf who was, in her own words, "born into a large connection, born not of rich parents, but of well-to-do parents, born into a very communicative, literate, letter writing, visiting, articulate, late nineteenth century world,"[1] felt always that two opposite streams flowed in her veins, and mingled uneasily. The one came from her father and his background of Cambridge rationalism and British Utilitarianism. Behind this paternal inheritance lay a tradition of Clapham Sect evangelicalism, with its reforming earnestness and stern puritan ethic. If Sir Leslie had repudiated, like so many Victorian intellectuals, his Protestant faith, he had retained its severe morality and rigid code of conduct.

Her mother, though of the same upper middle-class social stratum, had been brought up among a less rigorously intellectual, but more artistic people. Young Julia Jackson's milieu was that of Little Holland House, the home of her aunt Sara Prinsep, where the Pre-Raphaelite painters Rossetti, Burne-Jones, and Holman Hunt, the critic Ruskin, the poet Tennyson, and the

---

[1] Virginia Woolf, "A Sketch of the Past," *Moments of Being*, ed. Jeanne Schulkind, 2nd ed. (New York: Harcourt, 1985) 65.

novelist Thackeray were frequent visitors. Here the famous Victorian artist, G. F. Watts, came to stay for three days and remained for thirty years. Sara Prinsep (a matchmaker, as her niece Julia was to be) even managed to bring the beautiful and lively actress, Ellen Terry, into the household as wife to Watts, a match that proved in the end disastrous.[2] Among the most eccentric of Little Holland House's habitués was Sara's sister, Julia Margaret Cameron, who in middle age took up with great fervor the hobby of photography. Revealing a remarkable talent for the new medium, Mrs. Cameron made many studies of Tennyson and other Victorian eminences, and she captured, in her niece Julia Jackson, that austere type of beauty made famous by the Pre-Raphaelites.[3]

So it was that Virginia Woolf's solidly Victorian background incorporated two divergent strains, the puritan-intellectual, and a legacy of the Pre-Raphaelite aesthetic movement with its undertone of mystical religiosity. In themselves, these facts may be of only biographical consequence, but when one comes to consider *To the Lighthouse*, the most patently autobiographical of all Woolf's novels, they take on a much greater significance and, indeed, there is in them much that gives the book its compelling depth and meaning.

While it might be interesting to read *To the Lighthouse* as a sort of *roman à clef*, identifying here and there various figures from Woolf's past, a

---

[2] Virginia Woolf's play, *Freshwater*, is a fanciful account of this affair.

[3] Burne-Jones's painting, "The Annunciation," is among the most well-known of the pictures for which Julia Jackson posed. It reveals that Madonnaesque quality so often remarked of her face and personality.

more rewarding approach has been suggested by Woolf herself in a posthumously published memoir. In it, she tells us that until she wrote *To the Lighthouse*, the memory of her parents, and especially her mother, had obsessed her.

> She was one of the invisible presences who after all play so important a part in every life. This influence, by which I mean the consciousness of other groups impinging upon ourselves; public opinion; what other people say and think; all those magnets which attract us this way to be like that, or repel us the other and make us different from that; has never been analyzed . . . . I suppose that [in writing *To the Lighthouse*] I did for myself what psycho-analysts do for their patients. I expressed some very long felt and deeply felt emotion. And in expressing it I explained it and then laid it to rest.[4]

But what, really, were the influences of her parents, and in what way do these influences bear on Virginia Woolf the writer? These questions cannot be answered simply, but bound up in the complex texture of *To the Lighthouse* are a great many philosophical and psychological issues which shed a most revealing light upon the inner workings of its author. Furthermore, these issues bear directly upon an emerging Modernist aesthetic that is, in so many ways, an outgrowth of *fin-de-siècle* late-Romanticism and a reaction against nineteenth century positivism and materialism.

While one must be cautious of reducing the characters of Mr. and Mrs. Ramsey to ciphers or emblems, merely, of this state of mind or that, it nevertheless seems clear that they represent for Woolf two quite distinct

---

[4] *Moments of Being* 80-81.

modes of apprehension. These separate processes constitute a kind of dialectic between the two poles of which the novel shifts and between which it attempts a balance.

Initially, it is difficult to be fair towards Mr. Ramsay who is made to embody so much of which Woolf was contemptuous: the fact-obsessed intellect, the literal and linear mind, the masculine disregard of human feelings and personal values. Ramsay's pursuit of "truth," though relentless and uncompromising, has too often a devastating effect upon those close to him, and his lofty cerebrations have brought him a sense of frustration and stagnation rather than philosophic understanding. As the novel begins, James, the youngest of the Ramsay children, is being reassured by his mother that, yes, he might go to the lighthouse the next morning if the weather is fine. But Mr. Ramsay, as if deliberately to dash all hope, immediately declares that, no, it won't be fine. Of course, he's likely right, for

> he was incapable of untruth; never tampered with a fact;
> never altered a disagreeable word to suit the pleasure or
> convenience of any mortal being, least of all his own
> children, who, sprung from his loins, should be aware from
> childhood that life is difficult.[5]

But truth of this sort, the bald truth of facts, endears him not one whit to his children.

James, sitting in the warm comfort of his mother's love and encouragement, feels that "had there been an axe handy, or a poker, any

---

[5] Virginia Woolf, *To the Lighthouse* (New York: Harcourt, 1927) 10-11. All subsequent quotes from the novel refer to this edition and are noted within the text.

weapon that would have gashed a hole in his father's breast and killed him, there and then, James would have seized it" (*TL* 10). This scene encapsulates, as do the first chapters of Lawrence's *Sons and Lovers*, that Oedipal rivalry which Freud had recently defined, with its compound of rage and ambivalent desire. James "hates" his father not only for that cruel logic which leaves no room for childhood's fantasy and hopefulness, but also

> for the exaltation and sublimity of his gestures; for the magnificence of his head; . . . but most of all he hated the twang and twitter of his father's emotion which, vibrating round them, disturbed the perfect simplicity and good sense of his relations with his mother. (*TL* 58)

In his devaluation of emotional sensitivity and in his exclusive endorsement of logic and reason, Ramsay has paradoxically made of himself a paragon of intellect and a monster of irrationality.

We have ample evidence that a similar situation obtained with Leslie Stephen. A typical Victorian paterfamilias, Stephen presided, as does Professor Ramsay, over a family of eight children, a wife, and numerous servants with an absolute and autocratic authority. To his friends, colleagues, and protégés (all men, of course), Stephen was a model of reasonableness and sensible opinion. Yet to his family, to his wife and daughters especially, he was capable of displays of uncontrolled and histrionic fury. In his later years, after the death of Julia and many of his close friends, Sir Leslie's domestic behavior grew worse than ever, and the demands upon his two daughters became insupportable. Virginia Woolf wrote of this period that

> at the age of sixty-five he was almost completely isolated, imprisoned. Whole tracts of his sensibility had atrophied.

> He had so ignored, or refused to face, or disguised his own
> feelings, that not only had he no conception of what he
> himself did and said; he had no idea what other people felt.
> Hence the horror and terror of these violent displays of
> rage.[6]

Implicit here, and in her fictionalized version in *To the Lighthouse*, is a criticism of such a dangerous psychological onesidedness and its damaging consequences. The effect is not only emotionally crippling, but intellectually stunting as well. In the same memoir Woolf writes tellingly,

> Give him a thought to analyse, the thought say of Mill or
> Bentham or Hobbes, and he is (so Maynard [Keynes] told
> me) a model of acuteness, clarity and impartiality. Give him
> a character to explain, and he is (to me) so crude, so
> elementary, so conventional that a child with a box of chalks
> could make a more subtle portrait.[7]

This is a harsh indictment of a man who was in his day considered a pre-eminent critic of the English novel as well as a historian of ideas. Other commentators on Leslie Stephen's literary criticism, notably Lytton Strachey and Desmond MacCarthy, have also noted the aesthetic blind spot that prevented his seeing poetry and fiction in any other than rational and moral terms. Noel Annan, Stephen's second biographer, wrote:

> There is something deficient in a critical judgment which
> concludes that Charlotte Brontë could hardly be put in "the
> highest rank amongst those who . . . can help us to clearer
> conceptions"; and there is something bizarre about a critic
> who declares that *Wuthering Heights* was "a baseless

---

[6] *Moments of Being* 146.

[7] *Moments of Being* 146.

nightmare whose author had . . . a feeble grasp of external facts."[8]

How like Professor Ramsay this is, as he stands in the boat exclaiming poetry, yet at the same time sneering at his daughter for not understanding the points of the compass. Stephen, hence Ramsay, does not really believe in art as a necessary and autonomous value. His utilitarian thinking cannot credit art's transcendent function; he feels, rather, "that the arts are merely a decoration imposed on top of human life; they do not express it" (*TL* 67). Certainly the idea of "art for art's sake" is anathema to him, and for such arts as painting and music he has no feeling whatsoever.

It is against this narrow perspective of the Victorians, the notion that art had validity only for its moral qualities, its ability to instruct, that Modernism, and Bloomsbury in particular, set itself. Even Matthew Arnold's desire to put art or culture in the place of discarded religion was repellent to them, for this, too, shackled art to something that was not art. No, rather link art to science, they were inclined to say, than to an outmoded code of morality or ethics.

Considering the tremendous impress of her father upon Virginia Woolf, who was educated entirely out of his library and under his tutelage, it might be profitable to glance momentarily at Leslie Stephen's work. When he took over the editorship of the *Dictionary of National Biography* in 1882, he had already published his *magnum opus*, a *History of English Thought in the Eighteenth Century* (1876). In two massive volumes he had exhaustively

---

[8] Noel Annan, *Leslie Stephen: The Godless Victorian* (New York: Random, 1984) 330.

explored the empiricist tradition in British philosophy, especially as it developed during the eighteenth century Enlightenment. Most importantly for the agnostic Stephen, he had demonstrated how English thought had disentangled itself from the superstitions of religion and theology to emerge, with nineteenth century science, as a usable path to truth about the physical universe.

Among the leading figures of Stephen's *History* are Locke, Berkeley and Hume, the very men upon whom Professor Ramsay is to lecture at Cardiff and over whose philosophies he seems so painfully occupied. Briefly, John Locke, the father of modern empiricism, refuted Plato by claiming that all knowledge derived from sense-impressions and that nothing exists in the mind (at birth a *tabula rasa*) prior to its contact with matter. He thus represents "sensationalism," or a revised form of Lucretian materialism. Bishop Berkeley, on the other hand, argued that if all we can know of matter is our inward perception of it, then there must be only mind and its ideas, and that matter could hence have no independent existence. His is the idealist position in a particularly eighteenth century manifestation. Finally, Hume, pursuing this line of thought to its logical conclusion or to its inevitable impasse, asserted that since all we know of matter is what can be perceived by the mind, and since the mind contains nothing but its sense perceptions derived from matter, then reasonably there can be neither mind nor matter, at least as absolute and independent categories.[9]

---

[9] Respected as Hume was by the intelligentsia, his views were often ridiculed during his lifetime, and this idea in particular became part of the popular folklore of the eighteenth century. It may have given rise to the humorous story over which Professor Ramsay gets a chuckle, that the

This latter thought-arresting skepticism and its attendant and related systems have Ramsay in a state of appalling mental distraction. When Lily Briscoe chances to ask Andrew Ramsay about his father's books, he replies: "subject and object and the nature of reality. . . . And when she said Heavens, she had no notion what that meant, 'Think of a kitchen table then,' he told her, 'when you're not there'" (*TL* 38).[10] No wonder Ramsay is in such despair as he paces up and down the terrace, driving his mind from A to B to C, along an orderly and logical progression, but stopping at Q as though only some leap of faith might get him to R.

Satirical as this picture may be, it serves as a vivid illustration of the aridity of pure logic or rationality when divorced both from the organic world and from some deeper intuition. Sadly, Ramsay himself is aware that there are those, ". . . the gifted, the inspired who, miraculously, lump all the letters together in one flash – the way of genius" (*TL* 55). But this he cannot do, bound as he is to the sequential, that linear series of gig lamps, with each moment or thought separate and circumscribed.

Professor Ramsay inhabits the old Newtonian and perhaps the newer Darwinian universe. It is a world both mechanistic and deterministic from which God has been expelled and where even Nature is relegated to the status of a blind force, "red in tooth and claw," where the survival of the

---

freethinker Hume, who was very corpulent, became stuck in a bog and called to an old peasant woman to pull him free. She refused unless he would repeat The Lord's Prayer.

[10] And of course this is the same problem that exercises the Cambridge undergraduates in Forster's *The Longest Journey*.

fittest is the only motive for evolution. Worst of all, his overly-intellectualized approach to life has made Ramsay nearly oblivious of the real world about him. Mrs. Ramsay comments to herself that while "his understanding often astonished her . . . did he notice the flowers? No. Did he notice the view? No. Did he even notice his own daughter's beauty, or whether there was pudding on his plate or roast beef?" (*TL* 107). This is the crux of Ramsay's problem, this sterile intellectual abstractedness that has brought him to a painful impasse in his thinking and to a decided alienation from his emotions.

In his domestic relations, Mr. Ramsay, like his model, Leslie Stephen, is a troubling as well as a tyrannical figure. The effort of maintaining his academic position and the burden of responsibility for so large a household weigh heavily upon him. He is plagued by unreasonable fears of financial ruin and of failure in his career. His truncated self, split as it is from a sense of its own wholeness, cries out for an emotional sympathy and attention which only a woman can provide. And Mrs. Ramsay is willing to provide it; she sees it as her function in life, "indeed, she had the whole of the other sex under her protection" (*TL* 13). She is a vessel from which they drink, assuaging their aridity with her infusions of tenderness and sympathy; in fact, "she often felt she was nothing but a sponge sopped full of human emotions" (*TL* 51).

This very much accords with what we know of Julia Stephen whose emotions were primarily stirred by the presence of suffering. In an extraordinary document composed to relieve his grief after the death of his wife, Leslie Stephen wrote, "Whenever there was trouble, death or illness in her family, the first thing was to send for Julia, whether to comfort survivors or to nurse the patients."[11] Widowed by her first husband, Herbert Duckworth, at the age of only twenty-four, with two small children and pregnant with a third, Julia had, by the time she married Leslie Stephen, experienced an ample share of sorrow. In marrying Stephen (26 March 1878), she took upon herself not only a husband nearly forty-six years old, but also his seven-year-old mentally deficient daughter.[12] That Julia Stephen was a woman of exceptional character, as well as of outstanding beauty, there can be little doubt. She eventually produced a book out of her nursing experiences which she published under the title *Notes from Sickrooms* (1883), suggesting some desire on her part to make a public statement and a mark outside of her immediate family. Helen Ramsay, likewise, has a secret wish to accomplish some socially redeeming work, but it is a wish that remains largely unfulfilled.

Julia and her fictional counterpart, Helen Ramsay, essentially accept their allotted role of "angel in the house." Although she is a slave to her husband's demands, Mrs. Ramsay at the same time occupies a sort of sacred pedestal in his estimation. Professor Ramsay knows he cannot get by without her, that she is the binding force of his life. And we never get the sense,

---

[11] Alan Bell, ed., *Sir Leslie Stephen's Mausoleum Book* (Oxford: Clarendon, 1977) 40.

[12] Laura Stephen (1870-1945) was the offspring of Leslie Stephen's marriage to William Makepeace Thackeray's younger daughter, Minny, who died in 1875. Laura remained in the Stephen household during most of Virginia Woolf's childhood, but eventually she was committed to an asylum in York.

however ethereal she may appear, that Mrs. Ramsay is simply a passive agent of feeling. One thinks of a line from Sylvia Plath's "Lesbos": "Every day you fill him with soul-stuff, like a pitcher." This is what she does, actively keeping alive the connection between things which the men, on their own, would be unable to do. She feels always that "the whole of the effort of merging and flowing and creating rested on her." And she feels as well, "as a fact without hostility, the sterility of men, for if she did not do it nobody would . . ." (*TL* 126). There is in this an undertone of almost religious resignation, and a hint not so much of a submission to masculine hegemony but to some inner feminine power from which she draws strength and self-renewal.

Whatever the source of her strength, it is a quality perceptible to others, something goddess-like that draws both men and women to pay homage to her. Even "the little atheist," Charles Tansley, sees in her the image of a *Magna Mater*, "with stars in her eyes and veils in her hair, with cyclamen and wild violets" (*TL* 25). And Lily Briscoe, leaning on Mrs. Ramsay's knee, wonders "Was it wisdom? Was it knowledge? . . . or did she lock up within her some secret which . . . people must have for the world to go on at all?" (*TL* 16). This quality exists beneath the exposed surface of her personality, beneath her poise, her charm, her simplicity. It is other than her beauty, too, although her beauty would seem an expression of it, this quality of "knowing," for "she knew without having learnt. Her simplicity fathomed what clever people falsified" (*TL* 46).

As Mrs. Ramsay presides over her table, spooning out the *boeuf en daube* and hearing the others talk of cubes and square roots and "the French system of land tenure" and "Creevey's Memoirs" about which she knows nothing at all, she is upheld and sustained by "this admirable fabric of the masculine intelligence, which ran up and down, crossed this way and that, like iron girders spanning the swaying fabric, upholding the world, so that she could trust herself to it utterly . . ." (*TL* 159). But this is not her mode of knowing, this intellectual knowledge that freezes things into abstract patterns and breaks it into discrete data. Though she defers to it, admires it greatly, Mrs. Ramsay's knowledge comes not through the reasoning mind, but rather through the soul which takes things in their eternal wholeness, allowing life its fullness and continuity.

Her perception is primarily intuitive; one is even inclined to say "mystical," though it is nothing like the systematic mysticism of Yeats. Instead, it is something inarticulate, inexpressible, without reference to mantic devices or higher powers. It is possible, however, to describe her process of introspection, which seems to happen of itself, as she sinks down through the rings of her personality and becomes "a wedge-shaped core of darkness, something invisible to others" (*TL* 95). This mystical state of being is what constitutes her real life, and she exults in the sense of freedom and peace she thus attains: "Losing personality, one lost the fret, the hurry, the stir; there rose to her lips always some exclamation of triumph over life when things came together in this peace, this rest, this eternity" (*TL* 96).

It seems as though by withdrawing herself from the flux of change, by plunging beneath the surface multiplicity of life, Mrs. Ramsay achieves a psychic state quite close to the Bergsonian intuition of duration in which past, present, and future appear as one simultaneous continuum. This is the

time that partakes of eternity; it is the numinous Present that Mrs. Ramsay
perceives when she feels that

> there is a coherence in things, a stability; something she
> meant, is immune from change, and shines out (she glanced
> at the window with its ripple of reflected lights) in the face
> of the flowing, the fleeting, the spectral, like a ruby . . . .
> Of such moments, she thought, the thing is made that
> endures. (*TL* 158)

Her self-transcendence, then, results not in a negation of "things" or of
"materiality," but rather in a seeing of the essential continuity of life, and in
a vision of cosmic unity and wholeness.

By way of linking Mrs. Ramsay's intuitive mode of perception to
Mr. Ramsay's logic, we might evoke the name of William James, a man who
in so many ways bridges the mental world of the nineteenth century with that
of the twentieth. Though not so intimately as his brother Henry James,
William James was well acquainted with Leslie Stephen and the two men
followed one another's work. In fact, James begins his influential essay, "The
Will to Believe," with an anecdote from Stephen's biography of his older
brother, Fitzjames Stephen. The anecdote concerns Fitzjames's being asked,
seriously, as a schoolboy, to "prove the omnipotence of God," the sort of
absurd ontological question against which the eighteenth century empiricists
(especially Hume) fought such a battle.

James goes on to declare that, while he himself is an empiricist, he is
one of a quite different order from the absolutists who usually call
themselves by that name, for "objective evidence and certitude are doubtless

fine ideals to play with, but where on this moonlit and dream-visited planet are they found?"[13] Further, he claims that in our search for truth

> some participation of our sympathetic nature would be logically required. I, therefore, for one, cannot see my way to accepting the agnostic rules for truth-seeking, or wilfully agree to keep my willing nature out of the game. I cannot do so for this plain reason, that a rule of thinking which would absolutely prevent me from acknowledging certain kinds of truth if those kinds of truth were really there, would be an irrational rule.[14]

He argues instead for a more pluralistic faith in possibilities, in the opening of oneself to a variety of experiences that the skeptical empiricist usually blocks by his adherence to what he conceives of as facts.[15]

Moreover, this subdividing of the data of consciousness by the empiricist into discrete chunks is a falsifying of the true nature of things. In his textbook, *The Principles of Psychology*, James wrote,

> Consciousness, then, does not appear to itself chopped up in bits. Such words as "chain" or "train" do not describe it fitly as it presents itself . . . . It is nothing jointed; it flows. A "river" or a "stream" are the metaphors by which it is most naturally described. In talking of it hereafter, let us call it

---

[13] William James, "The Will to Believe," F. O. Matthiessen, *The James Family: A Group Biography* (New York: Random, 1980) 386.

[14] Matthiessen 395.

[15] But Leslie Stephen would have none of this. He wrote, "I have just read a denunciation of the wicked determinists from William James, who is a clever fellow, but, I think, rather flighty. I stick to Spinoza and Jonathan Edwards and Hume and all really clear-headed people." (Quoted in Matthiessen 676.)

the stream of thought, of consciousness, or of subjective life.[16]

Here, for the first time, is the now familiar phrase, "stream of consciousness," that we have come to employ in describing the techniques of Woolf, Joyce, Faulkner, Proust and certain other Modernists. It is not hard to see the parallel between James's view of life and that of Woolf in her similar dictum by which she contrasted her generation's writing with the Edwardians'.

Woolf and William James make similar distinctions between the materialist or Edwardian world view (that of Galsworthy, Bennett and Wells) and the spiritual (that of Woolf and Joyce and Proust), ". . . the former defining the world so as to leave man's soul upon it as a sort of outside passenger or alien, while the latter insists that the intimate and human must surround and underlie . . . ."[17] It is apparent that James, like his disciple Bergson, whose work so influenced the Modernists,

> conceived of reality as a continuing stream of change and movement whose essence, the vital impulse (*élan vital*), is apprehended only by intuition as opposed to the intellect which isolates things from the flow of events, measures and characterizes them by fixed concepts.[18]

So, too, does Virginia Woolf's *To the Lighthouse* represent an intuitive's protest against the domination of intellect and a plea for the claims of an

---

[16] William James, *The Principles of Psychology* (New York: Holt, 1890) 243.

[17] William James, *A Pluralistic Universe* (New York: Longmans, 1912) 23.

[18] Louis Kronenberger, ed. *Brief Lives: A Biographical Companion to the Arts* (Boston: Little, 1965) 55.

inward and unifying perception over the separative sword of the purely rational and empirical mind.

In stressing this, it is important to note that however much *To the Lighthouse* is slanted in favor of the intuitive approach to reality as opposed to the intellectual, it contains, as well, a decided criticism of the mystical mode of perception. We see this in the character of Mrs. Ramsay. For all the richness of her inner life, for all the depth and intensity she brings to the surface of outer existence, Mrs. Ramsay is nonetheless unfulfilled, and she knows it. At one moment she asks herself, "What have I done with my life?" (*TL* 125). She does, after all, have interests and passions of her own. She would like to have campaigned for more hygienic dairies and for a hospital on the Scottish island where they have their summer home. She cares deeply about the plight of the poor and concerns herself with acts of charity. But one feels that despite the domestic successes of her life – a not unhappy marriage, the raising of a large family, her friendships – Mrs. Ramsay has foregone some earlier promise to which she now looks back wistfully. Just as she is buoyed up by "the admirable fabric of the masculine intelligence," so too does she desire that she herself "would cease to be a private woman . . . and become what with her untrained mind she greatly admired, an investigator, elucidating the social problem" (*TL* 18).

In other words, her concern over dairies and health and her sympathy for the poor might have resulted in more tangible action, a kind of action that the mystic or pure idealist can seldom accomplish, and even less so one bound hand and foot to domestic life. While her intuitions and those profound moments of being do inform her personality and endow her with an extraordinary depth of character, they otherwise remain elusive and unexpressed. This may say something about Mrs. Ramsay's belief that everyone should marry. There is an incompleteness or onesidedness about her that demands something more solid on which to lean. The fugitive nature of her awareness needs anchoring to fact and substance without which it remains ineffectual in all but the personal sphere.

Her daughters, Prue, Nancy and Rose, perhaps in reaction to their mother and her role, "sport with infidel ideas which they had brewed for themselves of a life different from hers; in Paris, perhaps; a wilder life; not always taking care of some man or other . . ." (*TL* 14). They will grow up to be the new women of the twentieth century, leaving behind "the angel in the house" for rooms of their own.

This brings us again to the sort of mental process embodied by Mr. Ramsay. Though he fails at finding a rational solution to his philosophical dilemma, he has been able to articulate his ideas, producing a notable book by the age of twenty-five. While his personal limitations are brought forward in a way that Mrs. Ramsay's deficiencies are not, we nonetheless get the sense of a noble and exceptional character behind the severe façade. This becomes more apparent in the final section of the book when Ramsay's honesty and unworldliness, perhaps due to age, mitigate the rather cruel and intimidating personality of ten years earlier.

Even as she satirizes the aridity of a certain type of intellectuality, especially academic intellectuality, Woolf lets us know, through the character of Mr. Ramsay, the true value of a rational approach to life and thought. Both Lily Briscoe and William Bankes sincerely reverence "his power, his gift, suddenly to shed all superfluities" (*TL* 68), and they greatly admire the intensity and profundity of his mind. So, while *To the Lighthouse* is, at least in part, a feminist novel which mocks the deadening side of the masculine mind, it still does not wholly endorse the purely feminine as represented by Mrs. Ramsay.

Instead, what Virginia Woolf seems to suggest is that a fusing of the intuitive and visionary with the rational and intellectual is essential both to individual wholeness and to creativity. The first section of the novel, "The Window," ends with a reconciliation of these opposites. Mrs. Ramsay, very pleased at having sealed the engagement of Paul Rayley and Minta, walks up toward the nursery absorbed in a sense of the continuity of life;

> she felt, with her hand on the nursery door, that community of feeling with other people which emotion gives as if the walls of partition had become so thin that . . . it was all one stream, and chairs, tables, maps, were hers, were theirs, it did not matter whose, and Paul and Minta would carry it on when she was dead. (*TL* 170-71)

She then goes in to her husband who sits reading Sir Walter Scott. It has been a day of considerable contention between them, and she feels Ramsay's need to hear from her that she loves him, "but she could not do it; she could not say it" (*TL* 185). As they sit there in silence something begins to close around them, the painful separate isolations of two people long bound as one. Then, suddenly, "through the crepuscular walls of their intimacy, for they were drawing together, involuntarily, coming side by side, quite close, she could feel his mind like a raised hand shadowing her mind" (*TL* 184).

Love, in this moment of epiphany, breaks the awkward barrier between them: "she had triumphed again. She had not said it: yet he knew" (*TL* 186).

In the central, lyrical section of *To the Lighthouse*, "Time Passes," the dualism of reason versus intuition is transcended by something else, something vaster than any individual consciousness. Here births and deaths are but instances, bracketed within the continuous flux. All life and matter seem precariously poised against nothingness and the absolute effacement of time. The Ramsay's summer home in the Hebrides, now emptied of human inhabitants, gives way to decay. The wallpaper fades; the furniture and teacups collect dust; the floorboards weather and crack. Only old Mrs. McNab, paid to look after the place in the family's absence, witnesses in silence the slow rotting of the deserted house, left "like a shell on a sandhill to fill with dry salt grains now that life had left it" (*TL* 206). Weeds overtake the garden and thorned briars tap at the windows, but "what power could now prevent the fertility, the insensibility of nature?" (*TL* 207).

For nature, with its inexorable cycle of birth and death, is the final term, defying the measurement of reason and too unfathomable for intuition to grasp but a corner. Everything is subsumed in it, including all human loves and griefs: "Mr. Ramsay, stumbling along a passage one dark morning, stretched his arms out, but Mrs. Ramsay having died rather suddenly the night before, his arms though stretched out, remained empty" (*TL* 194). And as nature is ungraspable, all one can hope for are those moments of epiphany, sudden flashes of illumination, like the strokes of the lighthouse beaming across a dark sea.

The final section of the novel, when the remaining family and friends return to the island after ten year's absence, confirms this. With Mrs. Ramsay no longer alive, "the link that usually bound things together had been cut" (*TL* 219). The household is in chaos and Mr. Ramsay, irritable as they prepare for an expedition to the lighthouse, shows a more complex face than he earlier had. Grief over his wife's death and old age have chastened his severity but, at the same time, made him more egotistical, more demanding. At last, Lily Briscoe sees them off, relieved to be shed of Ramsay's "insatiable hunger for sympathy, this demand that she should surrender herself up to him entirely" (*TL* 226), a demand he seemed to make of all women.

Turning, she remembers the painting she had left unfinished ten years ago and the vision of Mrs. Ramsay and James sitting in the window that had been its inspiration. Some frustrating technical problem, some imbalance in the foreground, had prevented her completing it. As she dwells on this, she realizes that it was more than just a technical problem; it was the partiality of her vision. She had, at the time, been in thrall to Mrs. Ramsay who believed that everyone must be married to be complete. And she had been under the spell of Mr. Ramsay, too, who with his penetrating intellect had other answers. "For whatever reason she could not achieve that razor edge of balance between two opposite forces" (*TL* 287).

Standing before her easel and straining to grab hold of the elusive insight, that she might capture it on her canvas, it occurs to her that "the great revelation perhaps never did come. Instead there were little daily miracles, illuminations, matches struck unexpectedly in the dark; here was one" (*TL* 240). The spectral shapes of Mrs. Ramsay and James, vivid and poignant in her memory, then give way to some feeling of undischarged sympathy, and she remembers Mr. Ramsay steering his little expedition to the lighthouse. As she thinks of him, she realizes that things might be viewed just as they are, unadorned, that one might "feel simply that's a chair, that's a table, and yet at the same time, it's a miracle, it's an ecstasy. The problem might be solved after all" (*TL* 300). And then,

> with a sudden intensity, as if she saw it clear for a second, she drew a line there, in the centre. It was done; it was finished. Yes, she thought, laying down her brush in extreme fatigue, I have had my vision. (*TL* 310).

At that very moment, Mr. Ramsay, James and his sister, Cam, arrive at the lighthouse.

James, sitting in the boat, has had his epiphany also. As they reach the stony island, James, "turning back among the many leaves which the past had folded in him" (*TL* 275), recalls the anger and bitterness of ten years before, and the old image of striking his father to the heart returns to him. But he realizes it is not the old man reading a mottled book that he wanted to kill, but something else: "tyranny, despotism, he called it – making people do what they did not want to do, cutting off their right to speak" (*TL* 274). And he, too, like Lily Briscoe, at last reconciles the opposing forces within himself, symbolized by his mother and his father. Looking up at the lighthouse, he sees that "nothing was simply one thing" (*TL* 277). The lighthouse of his childhood's imagination, "a silvery, misty-looking tower with a yellow eye, that opened suddenly, and softly in the evening" (*TL* 275), and this other that they now approached, "a stark tower on a bare rock" (*TL* 301), were both true. And there was no longer any need to choose between them.

VIII

INFIDEL IDEAS: ANDROGYNY AND FEMINISM
IN *ORLANDO* AND *A ROOM OF ONE'S OWN*

Among the most pressing issues which sought attention at the end of the nineteenth century was that one generally called "the woman question." Mary Wollstonecraft, writing one hundred years before this time, had been perhaps the first to forcefully and persuasively articulate the case for women's rights. She wrote,

> It is time to effect a revolution in female manners – time to restore them to their lost dignity – and make them, as part of the human species, labour by reforming themselves, to reform the world.[1]

This self-reformation that Mary Wollstonecraft demanded was no simple matter for it required not only a radical revision of women's place in society, but of her inward perception as well. And while much of eighteenth century enlightenment thinking concerning the nature and rights of man had carried over into a nascent feminist awareness, especially in France and England, very few real political gains were made. In fact, it might be argued that the forces of reaction against feminism were so strong as to diminish rather than increase any actual improvement in women's lot. Certainly the Victorian period is notorious for being the most patriarchal of eras. The entailment of property which prevented women from inheriting land, marital

---

[1] Quoted in Sandra M. Gilbert and Susan Gubar, *The Norton Anthology of Literature by Women* (New York: Norton, 1985) 135.

laws which virtually made women the chattels of their husbands, and the almost complete absence of education or gainful employment for women meant that her claims were made from a position of total disenfranchisement.

Yet this is not to say that protest was not heard, for women, if they had no power, were at any rate beginning to have a voice. The rise of the novel in the eighteenth century and its flowering in the nineteenth were due in large part to an advance in literacy among middle-class women. And having learned to read, women were quick to write. Fanny Burney, Maria Edgeworth, Jane Austen, Mary Shelley, Elizabeth Browning and Christina Rossetti are only the best known of the many women who rushed to the occupation of letters. At times, as in the case of the Brontës, George Sand and George Eliot, women felt compelled to disguise their sex with pseudonyms in order to avoid the cruel epithets used by male critics to dismiss and disparage women's writing. And even when women wrote under their own names or anonymously, an edge of anger and defensiveness often crept into their work, as if the fear of ridicule and censure were ever present.

Beneath the humor and high spirits of all Jane Austen's novels is an undertone of bitterness at the estate of woman who must curry favor with men or risk that worst of social stigmas, spinsterhood. In *Pride and Prejudice* (1813) the Bennet's property has been entailed to a male cousin, underscoring the desperation with which the sisters must seek husbands. Though this is the hinge of a comic plot, its more tragic ramifications are never far from the surface. In Austen's last novel, *Persuasion* (1818), her heroine Anne Elliot debates with Captain Harville the relative strengths of men's and women's affections:

> We certainly do not forget you, so soon as you forget us. It is, perhaps, our fate rather than our merit. We cannot help ourselves. We live at home, quiet, confined, and our feelings prey upon us. You are forced on exertion. You have always a profession, pursuits, business of some sort or other, to take you back into the world immediately, and continual occupation and change soon weaken impressions.[2]

When Harville counters with the fact that "all stories, prose and verse . . . songs and proverbs, all talk of women's fickleness," Anne answers, incontrovertibly, that this is because "men have had every advantage of us in telling their own story. Education has been theirs in so much higher a degree; the pen has been in their hands."[3] All this goes some way in suggesting a feminist subtext to Jane Austen's novels, and if this is true for hers, how much more so for those of a writer like Charlotte Brontë, who had suffered poverty and had chafed under the yoke of the only job open to respectable women, that of governess? Virginia Woolf detected in Brontë's *Jane Eyre* and in *Villette* "an acidity which is the result of oppression, a buried suffering smouldering beneath her passion, a rancour which contacts those books . . . ."[4]

---

[2] Jane Austen, *Persuasion* (Harmondsworth, Middlesex, England: Penguin, 1965) 236.

[3] *Persuasion* 237.

[4] Virginia Woolf, *A Room of One's Own* (New York: Harcourt, 1929) 76. All subsequent quotations will be from this edition.

It was not until the latter decades of the nineteenth century that this protest became more insistently and overtly feminist in tone. Charlotte Perkins Gilman ("The Yellow Wallpaper") and Olive Schreiner (*Story of an African Farm*) expressed in their fiction and in their polemical writings an outrage at the indignities and misfortunes that befell women bereft of legal rights and power and hemmed in by outmoded customs and laws. They also projected a sense of women's extraordinary capabilities and the creativity that might be further unleashed if these social constraints and injustices were removed.

Eventually, a few men began to join in the chorus of agitation for the cause of women's suffrage. John Stuart Mill's *The Subjection of Women* (1869) was an eloquent and impassioned plea for female equality and, later, the work of Havelock Ellis and Edward Carpenter provided psychological and historical arguments for women's emancipation. George Bernard Shaw, always a progressive voice, created brash and headstrong heroines of a far different stripe from the submissive "angel in the house" so beloved of male Victorian writers. He also championed the work of another dramatist, the Norwegian Henrik Ibsen, whose plays so graphically illustrated the boredom, the curtailing of opportunities for emotional and mental development, and the profound psychological, as well as physical, dependency that resulted from women's confinement to the domestic sphere. When Nora, in the final act of Ibsen's *A Doll's House*,[5] slips away from her home, closing the door upon her husband and two children, she in effect closes the door on a whole century of women's oppression. The shock waves caused by this play at the

---

[5] Published in 1879 but not produced in England until the 1890s.

end of the last century may now be difficult to conceive; for that audience, whether approving or outraged, it signalled a departure from which no return would be possible.

Out of all this emerged that freer, more independent and more self-assertive person: the New Woman. Unlike her mother, she was capable of thinking for herself, speaking for herself, managing her own affairs, and perhaps even earning her own money. Little by little, the idea of professions for women began to take hold and more women sought education leading to careers. The 1890s saw further and more violent political struggle for women's suffrage, with pickets and placards and the Pankhursts' being led off to jail. The age of patriarchal culture was at last eroding and a fertile new soil was revealed beneath its accretions.

In the fateful year of 1910, the year of Edward VII's death, the year of the great Liberal victory over the House of Lords, the year of Roger Fry's Post-Impressionist exhibition, that year in which human character forever changed, Virginia Woolf took up her first active political work. It was modest enough, for she had been recruited to address envelopes for the Adult Suffrage Movement, a cause with which she had been in sympathy for some time. Undoubtedly, she found her labor uninspiring and her co-workers an unimaginative lot, and several years later, writing *Night and Day*, she to a degree satirised the feminist movement and the women to whom it was a religion.

Until fairly recently, her seeming equivocation kept contemporary feminists from altogether claiming Virginia Woolf as one of their own. This rejection stemmed naturally enough from the notion that, to the radical feminists of the 1960s, Virginia Woolf did not go far enough in endorsing the autonomy of women's issues. She seemed too bound to class, to an intellectual elite, indeed to codes of social behavior that the separatists were all too ready to read as evidence of her distance from their ranks. Somehow, as the tempers of the time cooled and further advances were made in eliminating bias and sexism, a more moderate if still impassioned feminism replaced the former militant and angry voice. With this change, Woolf's social feminism was reevaluated and found less wanting, was in fact discovered to be far more penetrating than had been previously perceived.[6]

The revelations brought by the publications of all her diaries and letters, as well as by her nephew Quentin Bell's excellent biography, further dispelled the image of "the invalid lady of Bloomsbury," an effete and rarefied individual who took no active part in the great issues of her day. Indeed, what they revealed was an extraordinarily engaged person whose interests ranged well outside literature proper, and a woman for whom friendship and personal discourse were among the most important things in life. It was, in fact, this passion for friendship and a deep commitment to women's spiritual and social emancipation that inspired the two books she wrote after the triumph of *To the Lighthouse*.

---

[6] If anything, Virginia Woolf has now become a patron saint of the new feminist criticism. Many fine essays and books have been published devoted exclusively to this social/political aspect of her writing. One of the most balanced of these is Alex Zwerdling's *Virginia Woolf and the Real World* (Berkeley: U of California P, 1986).

In late 1922, at a party given by her brother-in-law, Clive Bell, Virginia Woolf met the writer Vita Sackville-West. Though a mutual fascination and curiosity marked this first encounter, three years elapsed before their rather casual friendship flowered into something more intimate. This is not the place to retell the permutations of that affair which for both women had a primacy rivalled only by their attachment to their husbands and closest family members. Vita loved Virginia with a passion and intensity she reserved for women, and she admired her as a creative genius of the highest order, one capable of practicing their mutual art not only with consummate skill (a thing Vita herself possessed in great measure), but with a transcendent and brilliant subtlety that Vita could never achieve in her own fiction. For her part, while not greatly admiring Vita's work, Virginia was in awe of her competence, her aristocratic poise, "her capacity I mean to take the floor in any company, to represent her country . . . to control silver, servants, chow dogs; her motherhood . . . her being in short (what I have never been) a real woman."[7]

Vita, it must be allowed, was a passionate and sensuous woman in her early thirties who, though loyal to her husband and sons, was seldom without a female lover. Virginia, on the other hand, was, and had always been, sexually squeamish. Her relationship with Leonard, though entirely devoted, was chaste, and if she was more apt to fall in love with women, these affairs seldom included sexual expression. Thus, for her, the relationship with Vita Sackville-West was the closest she ever came to a romance of both heart

---

[7] *The Diary of Virginia Woolf*, ed. Anne Olivier Bell, vol. 3: *1925-1930* (New York: Harcourt, 1980) 52.

and body. Her memorial to this love was *Orlando* (1928), a book which Vita's son, Nigel Nicolson, called "the longest and most charming love letter in literature."[8] Love letter it was, for in *Orlando* Virginia Woolf imaginatively restored to Vita her beloved ancestral home, Knole, which Vita had lost by its entailment on the death of her father. And love letter, too, in that Woolf played with her hero/heroine, changing her sex as she carried her through three and a half centuries of English history. However playful in spirit, *Orlando* also contained a penetrating analysis both of Vita's complex character and, in some ways, of Virginia Woolf's own deeply androgynous nature.

Doubtless it was her own sexual predilection as well as her wide and varied reading that brought this notion of androgyny to Virginia Woolf's mind long before it entered the common vocabulary of sexual liberation. She may have read the term early on in Coleridge, or perhaps heard of it through Edward Carpenter's essays. Certainly, the idea had been current for some time when, beginning in 1924, Leonard and Virginia Woolf's Hogarth Press undertook to publish the collected works of Sigmund Freud in James Strachey's translation. Though she did not thoroughly read these volumes until years later, Virginia Woolf would have been party to numerous discussions about Freud whose psychoanalytic ideas were at this time absorbing the interest of many of the Bloomsbury group.[9] At any rate, this

---

[8] Nigel Nicolson, *Portrait of a Marriage* (New York: Bantam, 1974) 218.

[9] Not only were Lytton Strachey's brother James and sister-in-law Alix practicing psychoanalysts who had trained in Vienna with Freud, but Virginia Woolf's younger brother, Adrian Stephen, and his wife Karin, also took up analytic practice in 1926.

offers another source for Virginia Woolf's own very modern conception of the essential bisexuality of the psyche.

She had made the creative necessity of integrating the masculine and feminine sides of human nature an overriding theme of *To the Lighthouse*. And it was a theme to which she returned more explicitly in *A Room of One's Own* (1929) where she declared that, "in each of us two powers preside, one male, one female. . . . The normal and comfortable state of being is that when the two live in harmony together, spiritually co-operating" (*Room* 102). That these two aspects are not usually in harmony is implicit in the earlier novel, and overtly stated in *Orlando* and *A Room of One's Own*, for at the core of Virginia Woolf's feminism is the belief that patriarchal, masculinist culture has thwarted and suppressed the feminine, and that this suppression has been responsible for society's general ill-health, its injustices, inequalities and an unchecked tendency to violent aggressiveness that leads eventually to war.

In *Orlando*, though humorously, Woolf gives us a character in whom both sides of human nature, the masculine and the feminine, are more or less equally mixed. She shows us that many of the distinctions between the sexes are merely a matter of conditioning, of learned behavior imposed by shifting social codes. After living the life of a lusty Renaissance nobleman, first as a youth in England, then as ambassador to the Turkish court, Orlando wakes one day to find himself transformed into a woman. Taking sail on a ship returning to England, she realizes to her chagrin

> I shall never be able to crack a man over the head, or tell him he lies in his teeth, or draw my sword and run him through the body, or sit among my peers, or wear a coronet,

> or walk in procession, or sentence a man to death, or lead
> an army. . . . All I can do, once I set my foot on English
> soil, is to pour out tea and ask my lords how they like it.[10]

She realizes, too, that her legs, previously considered her finest feature, must now be kept carefully covered lest a sailor, seeing them, should slip from the masthead to his death. Eternally adaptable, Orlando at last capitulates to the exigencies of this new gender, and she even begins to enjoy it.

> Better is it, she thought, to be clothed with poverty and
> ignorance, which are the dark garments of the female sex;
> better to leave the rule of the world to others; better to be
> quit of martial ambition, the love of power, and all the other
> manly desires if so one can more fully enjoy the most
> exalted raptures known to the human spirit, . . .
> contemplation, solitude, love. (*O* 113)

But the ambiguity remains. That a woman may be ambitious for fame, may indeed crave power, or that a man may wish obscurity and the solitude necessary for poetic inspiration without especial disloyalty to their respective genders is an underlying and pervasive idea of the novel. It, like *To the Lighthouse*, is a protest against a deadening and sterile sexual polarization, as well as a satire on the absurd lengths to which patriarchal culture must go in preserving these artificial distinctions.

A historical perspective is gained on this by showing Orlando primarily during the Renaissance when a sense of androgyny, of the interchangeability of the sexes, curiously obsessed its greatest writer, Shakespeare. The

---

[10] Virginia Woolf, *Orlando* (Harmondsworth, Middlesex, England: Penguin, 1942) 111. All following quotes from *Orlando* will be from the Penguin edition.

cross-dressing of *Antony and Cleopatra*, the gender disguises in *As You Like It* and *The Two Gentlemen of Verona*, the absolute androgyny of Ariel in *The Tempest*, and the sexual ambiguity of the Sonnets all reflect Shakespeare's repeated embodiment of the idea of inherent bisexuality. And Shakespeare is not unique in this; a similar theme can be located in other writers of the period.[11]

Though Woolf believed that during the Renaissance a much more fluid boundary divided the sexes, she nonetheless illustrated in her parable of Shakespeare's hypothetical sister that men, even then, had always the upper hand in education and opportunity and freedom. But it is not until the dawn of the Victorian age that the radical delineation of sex roles, and an insistence on the weakness of women as opposed to the superiority of men, became the social norm.

Accompanying this theme of androgyny is an extended satire on Orlando's creative urge, his or her passionate desire to write which persists throughout the ages, even when thwarted by social position or sex. We see the Renaissance Orlando patronizing ill-bred poets in hopes of learning something of their craft; we see the eighteenth century Orlando (who dresses now as a woman, now as a man, as it suits her convenience) peering with curiosity at the Augustan wits, Mr. Pope, Mr. Addison, Lord Chesterfield, or watching blind Mrs. Williams pouring out tea for Dr. Johnson and Mr. Boswell.

---

[11] Androgyny, the union of the sexes, was an important concept in Medieval and Renaissance alchemy, and it is not unlikely that such esoteric ideas influenced many Elizabethan dramatists, poets and essayists.

When the damp cloud of Victorianism shrouds over the gay and orderly prospects of the eighteenth century, we notice a corresponding change from its clarity and sparkling wit to the dense, swollen prose of the nineteenth century:

> Everywhere the effects were felt. The hardy country gentlemen, who had sat down gladly to a meal of ale and beer in a room designed, perhaps, by the brothers Adam, with classic dignity, now felt chilly. Rugs appeared; beards were grown; trousers were fastened tight under the instep. The chill which he felt in his legs the country gentlemen soon transferred to his house; furniture was muffled; walls and tables were covered; nothing was left bare. . . . But the change did not stop at outward things. The damp struck within. Men felt the chill in their hearts; the damp in their minds. . . . Love, birth, and death were all swaddled in a variety of fine phrases. The sexes drew further and further apart. No open conversation was tolerated. Evasions and concealments were sedulously practised on both sides. . . . The life of the average woman was a succession of childbirths. She married at nineteen and had fifteen or eighteen children by the time she was thirty; for twins abounded. Thus the British Empire came into existence. (*O* 160-61)

"The sexes drew further and further apart." That was part of the damage that Virginia Woolf lay at the feet of Victorianism. It was that era's inability to be honest and direct about human nature, and sexuality especially, that had brought about so many present ills. The consequent bifurcation of the self that set women in one category, men in another, each with utterly distinct and unbridgeable roles, meant that the possibility of achieving wholeness for either sex was immeasurably curtailed.

Bridging Orlando up to the present, to 1928, Virginia Woolf more or less parodies her own style. After the richness of the Renaissance, the clarity and precision of the eighteenth century, and the fertile but gloomy Victorian age, the Modern period seems fragmented and anxious:

> The Old Kent Road was very crowded on Thursday, 11 October 1928. People spilt off the pavement. There were women with shopping bags. Children ran out. There were sales at drapers' shops. Streets narrowed and widened. Long vistas steadily shrunk together. . . . Nothing could be seen whole or read from start to finish. What was seen begun . . . was never seen ended. After twenty minutes the body and mind were like scraps of torn paper tumbling from a sack and, indeed, the process of motoring fast out of London so much resembles the chopping up small of identity which precedes unconsciousness and perhaps death itself that it is an open question in what sense Orlando can be said to have existed at the present moment. Indeed we should have given her over for a person entirely disassembled were it not that here, at last, one green screen were held out on the right, against which the little bits of paper fell more slowly . . . so that her mind regained the illusion of holding things within itself. . . . (*O* 216-17)

What this suggests is a sense of discontinuity and that multifariousness of temper so common to the Modernist world-view.

Both the Dadaist and Surrealist movements made much of this "chopping up small of identity," an attenuation of the modern ego mitigated only by a concurrent influx of unconscious content into what would otherwise be a soul adrift, empty of history and meaning. Certainly, Orlando represents a multiplicity of selves coexisting in one individual, and this multiplicity includes both maleness and femaleness, now one predominating, now the other, irrespective of gender. So while the modern ego may lack the stability and coherence of character let us say before 1910, it is perhaps more various, more pluralistic, and in ways more interesting and full of possibilities than anything dreamed of since the Romantic Age.

Though Orlando and his/her protean sexual identity is a fiction, it is a fiction very much based on fact, for Orlando's model, Vita Sackville-West, had combined in her own life what she wished of both worlds. A passionate and adventurous lover of women, Vita also had a very successful marriage.[12] Perhaps it was her aristocratic disregard for bourgeois social conventions; perhaps it was a deep-seated rebellion against the sort of predatory femininity represented by her mother, the formidable Lady Sackville. In all events, Vita had decidedly gone her own way in arranging for herself a life compatible with her unusual disposition.

A romantic traditionalist, she had agonized since girlhood over the injustice of losing her ancestral property simply because she was born a woman, and she cherished to the end of her life a love for Knole and all it stood for. In her ardent youth, having run off to Paris with Violet Keppel Trefusis (the married daughter of Edward VII's mistress), Vita dressed as a man and called herself Julian. In later life, living happily among her gardens at Sissinghurst Castle with her husband, the writer and diplomatist Harold Nicolson, Vita continued to maintain amorous affairs with various women. She also adopted an unvarying costume of riding breeches and laced boots,

---

[12] See Mitchell A. Leaska's informative and insightful introduction to *The Letters of Vita Sackville-West to Virginia Woolf*, ed. Louise De Salvo (New York: Morrow, 1985).

worn with silk blouses and a long string of pearls, the very picture of androgyny.

Virginia Woolf, too, had long been living in an atmosphere of sexual freedom, a milieu created by her friends in distinct reaction to their strict and repressive Victorian upbringings. In recent decades, with the advent of both the women's and the gay liberation movements, Bloomsbury, even among the non-literary, has come to stand for the possibility of a totally new and experimental code in human sexual relations. Within the group itself, E. M. Forster and Lytton Strachey were both unabashedly homosexual, though Forster rather quietly so. Strachey, who had a varied if unsatisfactory love life, maintained a home with that most Orlando-like individual, the painter Carrington. The Bell ménage, Charleston, was perhaps the most unusual of all, for Vanessa and Clive Bell remained married and continued to share a home long after they were no longer sexual partners. This household included the painter Duncan Grant who, though homosexual, became the father of Vanessa's daughter, Angelica. Angelica, in turn, later married the writer David Garnett who had at one time been in love with each of her parents. That all these permutations were carried out in an atmosphere of openness and minimum jealousy is a great credit to the spirit of these people, and it is doubtful whether many other such experiments in "free love" have been quite as successful.[13]

It was certainly a milieu in which a woman's love for another woman would not have been thought either aberrant or shocking, and Virginia

---

[13] That there were some human troubles in this paradise, however, is borne out by accounts in Angelica Garnett's *Deceived with Kindness: A Bloomsbury Childhood* and in Frances Spalding's biography, *Vanessa Bell*.

Woolf, for her part, did not consider disguising the motive force of the mock-biography, *Orlando* – her love for Vita Sackville-West. Nor did she hesitate, when asked to speak in Cambridge on "Women and Fiction" in October 1928, to bring to bear her considerable passion on this subject. The two lectures Virginia Woolf delivered at Newnham and Girton Colleges became the basis of the published book, *A Room of One's Own*. The book is written in a very formal and personal tone and, as Quentin Bell has pointed out, in it she gets very close to her conversational style.

Though public speaking may have caused her some anxiety, Woolf was, by all accounts, famous for her conversation which combined wit, fantasy, and a certain profundity, all elements which make *A Room of One's Own* one of the most engaging and assimilable polemics ever written. While addressing questions of great importance – the economic deprivation of women, the pervasive prejudice of women's mental inferiority, the social forces and restrictions which have hampered women's accomplishments – Woolf maintains a moderated voice in which stridency and bitterness are carefully submerged. In fact, she weaves the subject of righteous anger into the substance of her essay, for indignation is an emotion not easy to ignore when one approaches the issue of women's thwarted creativity. Pressing forward modern women's demands for education, for equal opportunity, for freedom from an exclusively domestic existence, Woolf holds out always the idea of androgyny, an ideal she claims characterizes the greatest writers, Shakespeare, Keats and Proust.

In order to reach such a state of being, a great deal must be done and a great many obstacles removed. To begin with, no woman can be expected to produce art when she is over-burdened with cares and responsibilities, and has neither a moment nor a quiet place to herself. This latter commodity, Woolf goes on to show, is not easily found, for women have traditionally been barred from those places where such repose might be sought. Woolf describes, by way of example, a visit to "Oxbridge," an all-male college where, having sat down on the banks of a river to ponder her subject, she is immediately asked by some authority to move along, the grass being off-bounds for female visitors. She proceeds across a quadrangle to the famous library, a place where the manuscript of Milton's "Lycidas" is on display, but as she reaches the entrance, she is told that women are not allowed unless accompanied by a man.

Again turned away, she goes on to a college dining room where she is to have lunch. She then describes for us the rather lavish meal of several courses and several wines, a meal at which one might relax and let conversation flow. After this meal, she leaves for the women's college, Fernham, some distance away, where she has been invited to have dinner later that evening. And what a contrast this meal makes to her luncheon at the men's college!

> Here was the soup. It was a plain gravy soup. There was nothing to stir the fancy in that. One could have seen through the transparent liquid any pattern there might have been on the plate itself. But there was no pattern. The plate was plain. (*Room* 17)

After this, there followed not soles in cream and baked partridges, but simple beef and brussels sprouts, as though economy and not pleasure had guided the choice of food. Then prunes and custard served for dessert, a fare not conducive to lighting the lamp of conversation, and indeed, "The meal was over. Everybody scraped their chairs back; . . . soon the hall was emptied of every sign of food and made ready no doubt for breakfast next morning" (*Room* 18).

Why is the difference so marked? Well, for one thing, the men's college is an ancient institution, founded in the Middle Ages, endowed first by kings and, centuries later, by wealthy manufacturers. Here scholarships and fellowships abound. In contrast, the women's college was, with great effort and much opposition, founded in the 1860s on a small budget of money begged from this wealthy woman or that, or raised by sales in some bazaar, yielding hardly enough to erect buildings, much less to provide the barest amenities. Virginia Woolf, or rather the invented narrator of the episode, speculates on all this and decides it is

> useless to ask what might have happened if Mrs. Seton and her mother and her mother before her had amassed great wealth and laid it under the foundations of college and library, because, in the first place, to earn money was impossible for them, and in the second, had it been possible, the law denied them the right to possess what money they earned. (*Room* 23)

So the lack of endowments and bestowals and legacies is due, in large measure, to the fact that women have never had money of their own to leave behind, and they have not had money because they have had no education, and thus no professions or the freedom to seek an independent fortune.

This is the essence of the argument presented by Virginia Woolf: that in order to write fiction "a woman must have money and a room of her own"

(*Room* 4), and that having been so long denied these things, it is a wonder women have written at all. Researching in the British Museum to find answers to such questions as "Why was one sex so prosperous and the other so poor? What effect has poverty on fiction? What conditions are necessary for the creation of works of art?" (*Room* 25), Woolf's narrator finds shelf upon shelf of books by men about women. Each of these elaborates some thesis on "the small size of brain of; the mental, moral and physical inferiority of; weaker muscles of; vanity of;" (*Room* 29) and so on, as if women were some odd biological species recently discovered by men. And she asks, if obliquely, "why this passion on the part of men to assure themselves of women's inferiority, her difference from him?" Surely, it is little different from the insistence on the superiority of one race to another, of one nationality to another, of one class to another. It seems to her related to the martial and Imperial spirit which marches off to conquest confident of the righteousness of its cause, without regard for the humanity and rights of the conquered.

Is this not the same hypertrophy of the masculine intelligence that Woolf illustrates in Professor Ramsay, a onesidedness that, to maintain itself, must deny the feminine, or relegate it to a subservient position? Furthermore, to insist on the weakness and delicacy of women and her need for male protection, not only inflates masculinity out of all proportion, but effectively denies femininity its full measure.

For women's part, the effort to challenge masculine hegemony has, to an extent, drained her creative energy, made her voice strident and angry, and colored her works, her writings especially, with an unhappy bitterness, a dark net out of which something smothered and suppressed is struggling to free itself. Finally, neither the purely masculine nor the purely feminine mind can be fully creative. Instead, to echo Coleridge, "a great mind is androgynous. It is when this fusion takes place that the mind is fully fertilised and uses all its faculties" (*Room* 102). In a more perfect world, the distinctions would be less marked, and the art produced by minds more equally harmonised between the sexes would be infinitely superior to current works.

Unlike the masculine mind, which tends to organize facts and make egoistic assertions, or the feminine, which merely reflects thought and emotion, "the androgynous mind is resonant and porous; . . . it transmits emotion without impediment; . . . it is naturally creative, incandescent and undivided" (*Room* 102). What Virginia Woolf here posits is an aim both personal and cultural. To free oneself, and thus to free society, from a sexism which distorts art and human relationships would be a liberation the effects of which are not yet imaginable. Certainly the benefits for both sexes would be incalculable, and as for society as a whole, only the visionary can project what sort of civilization such a revolution might yield.

Though *A Room of One's Own* is a short book, hardly over one hundred pages, its theme is large. As a contemporary reviewer for the *Spectator* wrote,

> Future historians will place Mrs. Woolf's little book beside Mary Wollstonecraft's *The Rights of Women* and John Stuart Mill's *The Subjection of Women*. It does for the intellectual and spiritual liberation of women what those works did for

the political emancipation. But *A Room of One's Own* outshines them both in genius.[14]

---

[14] *Spectator* 143 (28 Dec. 1929): 985.

IX

MYSTICISM WITHOUT GOD: A VIEW OF *THE WAVES*

Though critical consensus has long placed *The Waves* (1931) at the pinnacle of Virginia Woolf's achievement, the novel remains, of all her work, the least tractable and the most elusive. There is something about it – the curious form (Woolf said it should be called an elegy or a playpoem), the seamless lyricism of its language, the inscrutability of its theme – that while inspiring awe and admiration, tends to defy analysis. To say it is difficult of access, as Joyce's *Finnegans Wake* is, obscures the truth, for *The Waves* almost immediately draws the sensitive reader into its rhythms, which echo waves breaking on a shore and, like the music of Stravinsky or Eric Satie, carry one along to the end perhaps perplexed but invariably beguiled by a sense of something profound and mysterious having occurred.

There is, of course, the central difficulty posed for the reader accustomed to plot and more or less well-delineated characterizations. In *The Waves*, Virginia Woolf has eliminated description and, for the most part, all trace of time-bound plot structure. It was her stated intention to write a book free of superfluities and altogether divested of the merely conventional. Even in the interior monologues or soliloquies which her characters "speak," there is no perceptible change in style from one to the next. There are, however, signposts which clue the reader to the peculiarities of each voice. This technique is not unlike that of William Faulkner in *As I Lay Dying*, a novel exactly contemporary with *The Waves*. Faulkner, in this book, gives to his illiterate and inarticulate characters a sort of interior language which deliberately does not correspond to the ordinary speech of Southern poor whites. The correspondence is rather to a symbolic interior language, the utterance, as it were, of the unconscious. It is reasonable, given the extensive data of psychoanalysis, to presume that the dream life of an uneducated and illiterate person would not markedly differ from that of an educated and highly sophisticated individual. Similar symbols and images should reveal the same psychological complexes and configurations arising from that ground-of-being all people share.

In *The Waves*, this common substratum of psychic life, the collective unconscious, is the true dwelling place of the six lives whose development Virginia Woolf traces. Their language, rather than being composed of the day-to-day palaver of the outer world, consists wholly in symbolic ejaculations from an inner realm, and because there is a certain uniformity to this interior territory, there is a sameness, an undifferentiated quality, to their silent speeches. By retaining the conventional "said Louis; said Rhoda; said Bernard" before each soliloquy, Woolf is able to pursue this method without interjecting extraneous matter and we slowly gather whatever information we are to have about each character purely through the medium of these internal narratives. Their actions and interactions are only obliquely implied.

And yet, these actions hardly matter, for *The Waves* is much less about the passage through life as it is a long meditation on identity and consciousness. In this, the novel is the culmination of that experiment with character that Virginia Woolf had begun ten years before with *Jacob's Room*. There she had seen character as an amalgam of scraps consisting of one's own manifold self-perceptions, as well as those of others. In *Mrs. Dalloway* and in *To The Lighthouse* she had shown character to be a sort of dialectic between a person's inmost being and the social role he or she was obliged to play, or between the conditioned self and something archetypal which strove to act through it. In *Orlando*, individual character is so varied as to, in Whitman's phrase, contain multitudes. Indeed, in that novel it encompasses both the male and female sex, past inheritances, and even future possibilities. In *The Waves*, transcending all these permutations, character or personality has become an almost entirely metaphysical condition, something emerging from the undifferentiated unity of consciousness-at-large and only marking its independence or autonomy with great hesitancy.

Of all her novels, *The Waves* is the one which most fulfills the promise of that early essay, "Modern Fiction" (1919), where Woolf had decried the "materialism" of H. G. Wells, Arnold Bennett, and John Galsworthy, and where she had made a plea for a new fiction, using James Joyce as its most promising exemplar, based not on anything external but rather solely on the imperatives of human psychology. Of Joyce she had said,

> he is concerned at all costs to reveal the flickerings of that innermost flame which flashes its messages through the brain, and in order to preserve it he disregards with complete courage whatever seems to him adventitious, whether it be probability, or coherence or any other of these signposts which for generations have served to support the imagination of a reader when called upon to imagine what he can neither touch nor see.[1]

If the Edwardian materialists labored to create a world in fiction where every

---

[1] Virginia Woolf, "Modern Fiction," *The Common Reader*, 1st series (New York: Harcourt, 1925) 155.

street and every house and the buttons of every coat were to have a solidity so impenetrable that nothing could leak through, the Georgians, who Woolf calls "spiritualists," would do just the reverse. Having learned from the great nineteenth century Russians – from Tolstoy, Dostoyevsky, Chekhov[2] – and from such predecessors as Conrad and Hardy, the Georgians would discard the novelistic conventions of the past and attempt, by pushing their way into territory hitherto unexplored, to convey life as it really appeared to the modern spirit.

As Woolf puts it, "Let us record the atoms as they fall upon the mind in the order in which they fall, let us trace the pattern, however disconnected and incoherent in appearance, which each sight or incident scores upon the consciousness."[3] And so, in *The Waves* there is "no plot, no comedy, no tragedy, no love interest or catastrophe in the accepted style . . . ."[4] Instead, there is only the light of consciousness as impinges upon and is deflected by the conditioning of space and of time. In *The Waves* even these latter categories have diminished in importance, though we gather the location is London or its environs, and the time roughly the 1920s. And since the usual

---

[2] These authors, along with Turgenev, Gogol and Herzen, had only recently been introduced to English readers through the translations of Constance Garnett. Constance Garnett was the wife of Edward Garnett (who, as publisher's reader, had "discovered" and promoted D. H. Lawrence) and mother of the Bloomsbury writer, David Garnett. In 1921 Katherine Mansfield wrote to tell her that "the younger generation owe you more than we ourselves are able to realize. These books have changed our lives, no less."

[3] "Modern Fiction" 155.

[4] "Modern Fiction" 154.

anchors of a definite locale and a specific time have been, to a large degree, lifted, the reality of consciousness is allowed to flood in, infusing the novel with a life drawn not from matter but from the inner world of intuition.

This is not to say that in *The Waves* the outer world has disappeared altogether, but rather that, in the subjective mode of this fiction, the world itself has become more a question of inward perception. In this, *The Waves*, which veers so sharply from past standards of fiction writing, remains nonetheless a quintessentially Modernist production. It must be put on the shelf with *Ulysses*, and with *The Sound and the Fury* or *As I Lay Dying*, for like these exceptional novels, it paves a unique path through the fragmentation and moral chaos of modern existence, all the while applying to some interior category of being or consciousness for its unifying, coherent force. And just as Joyce's Dublin and Faulkner's Yoknapatawpha are at once territories both real and symbolic, so too is Woolf's London real in that one might travel to such a place for oneself, and yet symbolic in that it mirrors, in a way Bennett's Five Towns never do, the very contours of the soul. For Woolf, as for Joyce and Faulkner, setting is important not so much in itself, but for its symbolic associations, for the way it can help lay bare the roots of consciousness which find their soil and atmosphere in a recognizable "real world."

Woolf achieved this effect by a further refinement of her tunneling technique. Digging beneath the personal "stream of consciousness" which she had disclosed for *Mrs. Dalloway* and *To the Lighthouse*, Woolf taps into a deeper stratum of transpersonal awareness. It is her design to show us the outer personality "bubbling up," so to speak, from this transpersonal realm rather than superimposed from without, as in Edwardian fiction, upon a framework of fact and descriptive detail. She had earlier, in "Mr. Bennett and Mrs. Brown," chided the Edwardians for their obsession with such detail – the inexpensive brooch, the mended gloves, the anxious look – as though these things alone could convey to the reader the character of Mrs. Brown. As she puts it, "They have laid an enormous stress upon the fabric of things. They have given us a house in the hope that we may be able to deduce the human beings who live there."[5] But what if the novelist should forego the house, forego the description of frayed gloves and cheap brooches and third-class carriages? What then would serve to indicate Mrs. Brown? Divesting her novel of the sort of scaffolding that had supported the Edwardians in their creation of character, Virginia Woolf turned instead to a poetic language of symbol and metaphor by which she hoped to focus upon the interior reality of human personality.

It is this turning away from materialism, from an excessive focus upon exterior event and physical detail, that however great the differences between them, remains the common denominator of those writers we have come to associate with the modern movement in literature. Even Ernest Hemingway, a novelist on first sight poles apart from Virginia Woolf, said he achieved his effects by elimination, by taking out everything that was not essential and leaving only the tip of the iceberg visible, the rest submerged beneath the surface. And then, as previously noted, the American regional Modernist,

---

[5] Virginia Woolf, "Mr. Bennett and Mrs. Brown," *The Captain's Deathbed and Other Essays* (New York: Harcourt, 1960) 112.

William Faulkner, working independently and with such different material, achieved a remarkable similarity to Virginia Woolf in his experimental prose.[6]

In both these writers, the concern to render interior or psychological time, as well as to convey the workings of mind and memory through the medium of a poeticized prose, resulted in novels that are among the most challenging of this century. What this suggests, for the question of mutual influence remains fairly tenuous, is a simultaneous striving toward like ideals, and a desire on the part of these highly original artists to communicate a new and particularly modern vision of life through fiction.

But the writer, however innovative, must work within the constraints of language if not within the traditional bounds of an established genre. The language of verbal speech must be adapted to serve for the voiceless soundings of the mind communing with itself, and familiar words with all their worn-out associations, must be put in the service of new and unfamiliar concepts. The effort to find appropriate, evocative terms to encompass new visions, new sciences, new technologies became an especial burden of writers and thinkers in the early years of the century. Freud rummaged among the dead languages to find a usable vocabulary for his psychological discoveries. Einstein, Neils Bohr and other physicists likewise coined or invented new words to talk about phenomena never before described. For the Modernist writers, there were several routes to pursue.

---

[6] In 1934 Wyndham Lewis published his vituperative *Men Without Art* in which he linked T. S. Eliot, Faulkner, Hemingway and Virginia Woolf. Three years later, in an untraced review, Faulkner praised Woolf's new novel, *The Years*. Beyond her comments about Lewis's book, there is little evidence that Woolf read or otherwise considered Faulkner's work.

Following the Cubist undermining of traditional spatial relations, Gertrude Stein attempted to subvert the recognizable categories of grammatical association in order to free words from a too strict bondage to established meanings. Joyce, on the other hand, brilliantly saw language as an archaeologist might, with its layer upon layer of accumulated associations; he incorporated this linguistic insight into his technique so that in his prose even the most trivial statement becomes infused with significance. Woolf's inclination was to readapt and mold, like Proust, the traditional usages until they became more pliant to her own purposes. Even in her diaries and letters, we find her again and again using words in ways that seem absolutely original and unexpected, as though they had just been discovered.

After the great popular success of her mock-biography, *Orlando*, Woolf began to meditate a novel that would go further than her previous ones in divesting the form of all extraneous matter, thus allowing her to express certain long-held, if vague feelings that she was wont to call mystical. Her desire to write such a book, one in which her profound intimations of a spiritual reality might predominate, antedated the publication of *To the Lighthouse*. Eric Warner has carefully traced the genesis of *The Waves* (originally called *The Moths*) through several pertinent diary entries in which she tries to define for herself her abstract and visionary notions. "*The Waves*," Warner tells us, "was to be the forum in which she would engage in the restless search for 'it,' undertaking a serious metaphysical quest for the universal and fundamental aspect of 'reality.'"[7] Whatever else, it would be

---

[7] Eric Warner, *Virginia Woolf:* The Waves (Cambridge: Cambridge UP, 1987) 32.

a radical departure from the sort of "holiday book" that had so pleased the readers of *Orlando*:

> Now I could go on writing like that – the tug & suck are at me to do it. People say this was so spontaneous, so natural. And I would like to keep those qualities if I could without losing the others. But those qualities were largely the result of ignoring the others. They came of writing exteriorly; & if I dig, must I not lose them? And what is my own position towards the inner and the outer? I think a kind of ease & dash are good; – yes: I think even externality is good; some combination of them ought to be possible. The idea has come to me that what I want now to do is to saturate every atom. I mean to eliminate all waste, deadness, superfluity: to give the moment whole; whatever it includes. Say that the moment is a combination of thought; sensation; the voice of the sea. Waste, deadness, come from the inclusion of things that dont belong to the moment; this appalling narrative business of the realist: getting on from lunch to dinner: it is false, unreal, merely conventional. Why admit any thing to literature that is not poetry?[8]

This private statement sums up superbly her drive to go beyond mere narrative or story-telling, not because this more traditional aspect of the novel was in any way wrong or mistaken, but because its dominance had tended to hinder or cloud over the possibility of developing character in all its complex inwardness. Even more than this, the external method of writing seemed inimical to that mystical sense of existence Virginia Woolf now wished to convey.

---

[8] *The Diary of Virginia Woolf*, ed. Anne Olivier Bell, vol. 3, *1925-1930* (New York: Harcourt, 1980) 209, 210.

Exactly what this mystical sense is becomes difficult to say, and like the words "materialist" and "spiritualist" that Woolf employs to stand for the older as opposed to the newer world-view, the term "mystical" can at first be somewhat jarring. These words are generally associated with theistic forms of thought, and "spiritualist," especially, calls up images of seances and occult manifestations with which we know Woolf had nothing to do. But the problem is not irrelevant. One has only to turn back to the Cambridge philosophical background upon which the Bloomsbury ethos and frame of mind are based to find the roots of the dilemma.

McTaggart had early on struggled to free his Transcendental Idealism from the "taint" of theology, and to give it a respectable standing within the analytical tradition of Cambridge. He nonetheless retained certain features – reincarnation, immortality, etc. – which can hardly be called other than mystical. And though Bertrand Russell, Alfred Whitehead and G. E. Moore later repudiated McTaggart's metaphysics, they each continued to be deeply concerned with the intersection of logic and science with mysticism.[9]

Undoubtedly the huge appeal that a philosopher like Henri Bergson had for Woolf's generation was that he was able to put intuition on a par with the intellect, and indeed to show that the new Einsteinian physics was a scientific expression of a profoundly intuitive, not to say spiritual,

---

[9] *Mysticism and Logic* (1918) is one of Russell's important early books; Whitehead notably returned late in life to a disenchantment with the mathematically-ordered Newtonian universe he'd previously espoused and thought out a new "philosophy of organism" in such books as *Process and Reality* (1929); G. E. Moore's *Principia Ethica* (1903) was said by Maynard Keynes to be so unworldly that the New Testament was a handbook for politicians by comparison.

world-view in which matter was ultimately equated with pulsating atomic energy. Other contemporary thinkers, however, had more difficulty with the possible confusion of science and mysticism. Freud, for instance, broke with Jung over the latter's alchemical and other arcane interests, writing late in life that his pioneer researches had been clouded by a "threat against our scientific *Weltanschauung*, which, I feared, was bound to give place to spiritualism or mysticism if portions of occultism were proved true."[10]

James Joyce who, like Freud, drew from a vast range of sources, had no qualms about acknowledging his debt to spiritualism and theosophy (as well as to science), and *Ulysses* is peppered throughout with references to esoteric literature.[11] And that other great Irishman, Yeats, whose career spans both the Symbolist and Celtic Twilight period of the 1890s and the Modernist movement, remained his whole life as much a serious occultist as a poet and dramatist. During a visit with Virginia Woolf he told her of his extraordinary psychic experiences, of his occult beliefs (some of which were derived from Plotinus), and that he had been writing in such terms about her recent book:

---

[10] S. Freud, *New Introductory Lectures*, trans. James Strachey (New York: Norton, 1965) 54.

[11] Stuart Gilbert writes that "when we [he and Joyce] chanced to be discussing Eliphas Levi's theories of magic and Mme Blavatsky's entertaining *Isis Unveiled*, he asked me if I had read any of Sinnett's work . . . . Naturally I took the hint and procured his *Esoteric Buddhism* and *Growth of the Soul*, well-written books from which Joyce certainly derived some of his material. He was conversant also with spiritualist literature, I think, but I noticed that while ready enough to talk about theosophy and occultism, he – perhaps because of his Catholic upbringing – shied off this subject." *James Joyce's* Ulysses (New York: Vintage, 1955) vii-viii.

> Certain typical books – *Ulysses*, Virginia Woolf's *The Waves*,
> Mr Ezra Pound's *Draft of XXX Cantos* – suggest a
> philosophy like that of the *Samkara* school of ancient India,
> mental and physical objects alike material, a deluge of
> experience breaking over us and within us, melting limits
> whether of line or tint; man no hard bright mirror dawdling
> by the dry sticks of a hedge, but a swimmer, or rather the
> waves themselves.[12]

If Virginia Woolf was puzzled or surprised by these comments, she gives no hint of it. She said only that she "felt Yeats' extreme directness, simplicity, equality; like his praise; like him: but cant unriddle the universe at tea."[13] Her own mystical beliefs seem quite detached from, or at any rate, not deeply influenced by the formal literature of mysticism, though even of this she could not have been altogether unaware.

After all, Bloomsbury, which had a tradition, inherited from its fathers, of agnosticism, rationalism and indeed open hostility to religion, would have been skeptical of too enthusiastic an interest in even the unorthodox spirituality of Yeats's Golden Dawn. Beyond those leanings, already discussed, in the direction of a Bergsonian intuitionism, Bloomsbury-at-large remained decidedly in favor of the virtues of reason. Nonetheless, in the work of Virginia Woolf, whose sensibility was profoundly intuitive, it is not difficult to discover that contrary tendency which saw rationalism as limited, and which sought means of expressing those reaches of consciousness outside

---

[12] In W. B. Yeats's introduction to his play *Fighting the Waves* (1934), quoted in *The Diary of Virginia Woolf*, ed. Anne Olivier Bell, vol. 4, *1931-1935* (New York: Harcourt, 1982) 255n.

[13] *Diary* 4: 257.

the purview of reason. This tendency was, of course, shared by Forster whose realist techniques often belie an acute interest in the spiritual and mystical side of life. Certain other of the Modernists, T. S. Eliot in particular, could be said to have maintained a curiously dual, even contradictory outlook in this regard.[14]

That there might be a certain danger as well as reward in the pursuit of those inward byways of thought was something Virginia Woolf did not fail to consider. Writing to Forster she once confessed a strange relationship to her mental illnesses: "Not that I haven't picked up something from my insanities and all the rest. Indeed, I suspect they've done instead of religion. But this is a difficult point."[15] Just as there is a subtle relationship between madness and creative genius, perhaps the same might be said for a relationship between so-called insanity and what is claimed to be religious ecstasy. Saints are quite often seen as mad, and madmen often (as Woolf's Septimus Warren Smith does) see themselves prophets and martyrs.

At any rate, while writing *The Waves* Virginia Woolf penned into her diary of 16 February 1930, an even more suggestive comment:

---

[14] Eliot had begun his poetic career under the influence of the French *symbolistes* and the philosophy of Bergson. Though his search for order and stability was to lead him toward orthodox Christianity and conservative political views, it might easily be argued that he remained underneath a kind of romantic. The acknowledged debt to Frazer's *Golden Bough* and Jesse Weston's *From Ritual to Romance* in his footnotes to *The Waste Land* suggest this mythopoeic side of his sensibility.

[15] *The Letters of Virginia Woolf*, ed. Nigel Nicolson and Joanne Trautmann, vol. 2, *1912-1922* (New York: Harcourt, 1976) 499.

> I believe these illnesses are in my case – how shall I express
> it? – partly mystical. Something happens in my mind. It
> refuses to go on registering impressions. It shuts itself up.
> It becomes chrysalis. I lie quite torpid . . . . Then suddenly
> something springs.

Apparently, Woolf saw her bouts of madness, however agonizing, as inroads into regions of consciousness normally inaccessible. It was this visionary domain that Virginia Woolf hoped to capture in her most daring and innovative fictional experiment.

When she came to write *The Waves*, that "eyeless, mystical book" which was to embody her most extreme move away from materialism, Woolf decided to weave more closely into the structure of her novel the sort of lyricism she had exploited in the central "Time Passes" portion of *To the Lighthouse*. The insertion of such lyrical passages ("interludes" she called them) throughout *The Waves* was intended to express "the world seen without a self," an obsessing idea she had longed to put into practice. To accomplish this, she divided *The Waves* into nine sections. The first begins with "The sun had not yet risen. The sea was indistinguishable from the sky . . ."[16] and the final with "Now the sun had sunk. Sky and sea were indistinguishable" (*TW* 341). It is immediately apparent that this large metaphor for life in general – the sun's steady passage across the sky, reflected against the incessantly rolling sea – will be counterpoised against a sense of life in particular as it is seen in the childhood, youth and maturity of the six protagonists.

---

[16] Virginia Woolf, *Jacob's Room & The Waves* [bound in one volume, paginated consecutively from p. 1 of *Jacob's Room* to p. 383 of *The Waves*] (New York: Harcourt, 1923 & 1931) 179. This and all subsequent quotes, noted in the text, are from this edition.

The hour before dawn shows the world in its unmanifest state, one described in all creation myths, before the coming of light. This is the great chaos of the world which precedes the parting of the waters of primal matter; it is the uroboric or alpha state prior to consciousness. As the sun moves above the horizon, a separation is seen: ". . . a dark line lay on the horizon dividing the sea from the sky . . ." and, with this, the ocean's separate waves washing in and drawing out again, ". . . sighing like a sleeper whose breath comes and goes unconsciously" (*TW* 179).

After this first lyrical passage, printed in italics, the six characters are introduced, or rather introduce themselves, with short statements of their perceptions. The first of these are inchoate utterances, describing a sensation either visual or aural, but seemingly disconnected from a knowledge of the thing perceived. The second set of statements, on the other hand, names objects – spider's web, leaves, bird's eyes, caterpillar, snail, stones – as if, between the first and the second, an awareness has taken place allowing the speaker to differentiate between his perception and the objects of that perception.

As the six friends continue their monologues, a deepening complexity is revealed in their statements. Emotion as well as sensation, thought along with intuition begin to figure in their dawning awarenesses. Louis, for instance, declares,

> My roots go down to the depths of the world, through earth
> dry with brick, and damp earth, through veins of lead and
> silver. I am all fibre. All tremors shake me, and the weight
> of the earth is pressed to my ribs. (*TW* 182)

The entire novel is permeated with intuitions such as this, of individual psychic roots deeply entwined beneath the surface of personal consciousness. It represents for Woolf the end result of that great discovery of hers, that tunneling technique through which she had learned to explore, first, the private thought-life of her characters, and now, the unconscious itself from which that thought-life grew. It is for this reason that the word "mystical" is invoked to describe this novel, the inner world assuming here, as it does, a greater reality and coherence than the outer, material world.

In fact, in *The Waves* the life of the imagination takes on a power it has not had since the Romantics. Louis continues,

> . . . my eyes are the lidless eyes of a stone figure in a desert by the Nile. I see women passing with red pitchers to the river; I see camels swaying and men in turbans. I hear tramplings, tremblings, stirrings round me. (*TW* 182)

This hints, it would seem, if not at some idea of reincarnation, at least at a belief that the psychic background of every individual is not bounded by his personal culture, but rather encompasses the entire cultural history of the human race.

The second section of *The Waves*, after describing a seascape in early morning, continues with the individual journeys of the six characters. They are each of them going off to boarding school, leaving their homes and families for the first time. A new stage of life, of self-consciousness, is reached and with it a firmer sense of individual personality. Bernard, for instance, emerges as the most literate of the friends, always making phrases, inventing stories. Neville is the sensitive poet, alienated, making heroes out of the others, sharp in judgment but full of inchoate and unsatisfied yearnings. Louis is the snob, ambitious, eager to shed his Brisbane accent, to become worldly and sophisticated. Of the girls, Susan is the nature-lover; averse to society and the artificial order of school, she dreams always of home, her father, the pleasures of the country. Jinny, on the other hand, is the sensualist, needing the love and approval of others, especially of men. She is the least inhibited sexually, somewhat vain, and very daring. "Jinny dances. Jinny always dances in the hall on the ugly, the encaustic tiles; she turns cartwheels in the playground; she picks some flower forbiddingly, and sticks it behind her ear . . ." (*TW* 202). Rhoda is the most insecure, always watching to see what others do, to follow suit: "Other people have faces; Susan and Jinny have faces; they are here. Their world is the real world. . . . They say Yes, they say No; whereas I shift and change and am seen through in a second" (*TW* 203-04). These passages evince an awareness of others, though it is an awareness of others only in terms of oneself, in the way of adolescence. At this stage, any real involvement with the world of mature relationships is precluded, for the self is, as yet, too enfolded to spread beyond itself.

In addition to these six characters there is another, the silent figure of Percival who broods over the whole of *The Waves*. He has no soliloquies of his own, and halfway through the novel he dies. This is an event which profoundly affects the six friends, coloring their lives with a sense of mortality and transience. Unlike Mr. and Mrs. Ramsay in *To the Lighthouse*, who were based frankly on Virginia Woolf's parents, the characters in *The Waves* are too general to have actual counterparts in real life. Nonetheless, there is something of Lytton Strachey in Neville, something of Virginia Woolf herself in Bernard, perhaps something of Vanessa in Susan. Only Percival, the one character we never actually see or hear directly, seems intentionally to have stood for Virginia Woolf's brother, Thoby. Percival's beauty, courage and monolithic self-possession, are all traits for which Thoby Stephen was fondly remembered, and his early death at the age of twenty-six remained a sad memory for all who knew him. Thoby Stephen had been responsible for bringing his Cambridge friends together in London, and by incorporating his two sisters into that exclusively masculine world he had, in a sense, been the true founder of Bloomsbury. This is Percival's function in *The Waves*; he is a model or ideal around which his friends gather, even after his death.

When Woolf finished *The Waves* she wrote in her diary, "Anyhow it is done; and I have been sitting these 15 minutes in a state of glory, and calm, and some tears, thinking of Thoby and if I could write Julian Thoby Stephen 1881-1906 on the first page. I suppose not."[17] Like *Jacob's Room*, then, *The Waves* is (and Woolf called it such) at least partly an elegy, and a very Keatsian elegy at that, "Where youth grows pale, and spectre-thin, and dies; / Where but to think is to be full of sorrow / And leaden-eyed despairs." Psychologically speaking, one cannot fail to note the significance to Virginia Woolf's work not only of Thoby's untimely death, but of that of Woolf's mother and of her half-sister, Stella, two years later. This surely accounts for the very real presence of death in all her "serious" novels, and the discernible atmosphere of melancholy that surrounds these works. The impact of grief and the consequent sense of mortality upon the sensibility of the young

---

[17] *Diary* 4: 10.

future writer acted to turn her thoughts inward; in Woolf's case, in fact, morbid brooding was a definite symptom of her mental breakdowns and may even help account for her peculiar assertion that these illnesses were "partly mystical," for they put her in touch with a world beyond the physical senses.

In the third chapter, the friends have gone off to college ". . . where the stir and pressure of life are so extreme, where the excitement of mere living becomes daily more urgent" (*TW* 227). At this stage, the need for others becomes markedly more pressing; the sense of community and social commitment draws the friends closer together. This parallels the impersonal opening passage of this chapter where ". . . the birds that had sung erratically and spasmodically in the dawn on that tree, on that bush, now sing together in chorus, shrill and sharp; now together, as if conscious of companionship. . . ." (*TW* 225). So while the allegiances of the friends grow deeper, some in fact into love, the sense of individual identity grows stronger as well. Each of them begins to define his or her place in the world: Neville as poet, Louis as businessman, Susan as country woman, Jinny as a socialite. Their purely internal self-perceptions become crystallized into outer personas.

In the next two chapters, having drifted into separate social spheres, the friends make efforts to maintain their former contact. It is the figure of Percival who draws them together, just as Thoby Stephen, fearing the dispersal of his college friends, had brought them to his home in London. Here, they meet at a French restaurant as a farewell to Percival who is going off to India. The pleasure of this is complicated for each of them by odd feelings about what they are to themselves and to each other.

For Bernard, as his train speeds into London, there is a sense of his face being just one among multitudes. He feels a strong reluctance ". . . to assume the burden of individual life" when it is so much easier to ". . . be carried on by the general impulse." While making his way through "the roar of the traffic, the passage of undifferentiated faces, . . ." Bernard realizes the transience of all individual life, that "we are only lightly covered with buttoned cloth; and beneath these pavements are shells, bones and silence" (*TW* 253-54).

As the friends gather, each of them attempts to assert a familiar identity while existing, somewhat tortuously, in his or her private internal world. Paradoxically, it is within this silent interior that they most truly commingle, somewhere beneath their surface personalities, beneath the halting attempts to communicate, beneath Louis's suave urbanity, Jinny's fashionable glitter, beneath Susan's contempt for clothes and convention, Rhoda's timidity, and Neville's hypersensitivity.

And so the friends proceed through life, balancing between the desire to be individualistic and the pressures and demands of a world which urges conformity. The death of Percival from a riding accident in India draws a curtain of sorrow over them. By dying young, Percival preserves his youth, his beauty and his eternal charm; but he remains also frozen in time, like some figure from classical mythology. For the rest, they must continue to marry, to have children, to administer public offices, to create, to achieve, for "from us every sort of building, policy, venture, picture, poem, child, factory, will spring. Life comes; life goes; we make life" (*TW* 297). While occasionally oppressed by the futility of striving, and bent down by the cares it imposes, the compelling need to do so remains, it seems, both for the sake of individual self-actualization as well as for the more impersonal continuance of the race, and of civilization. As the friends grow older, the carefully forged identities, built up so assiduously in youth, give way again, as in earliest childhood, to a less self-conscious outlook.

Gathering together with his friends one final time to dine in Hampton Court, Bernard summarizes his own life. And yet, as he says,

> what I call "my life," it is not one life that I look back upon;
> I am not one person; I am many people; I do not altogether
> know who I am – Jinny, Susan, Neville, Rhoda, or Louis; or
> how to distinguish my life from theirs. (*TW* 368)

Age, for Bernard, has brought its disillusionments. The bright surface of life, against which he tapped so eagerly, no longer holds his interest. Sitting at the dining table, laid out with its white linen, its carefully ordered silver, its basket of rolls, he achieves, having resigned the world, a sudden transcendence. Looking down, as if from some great height or perhaps from beyond the grave, Bernard perceives the world as an infant must, as pure unconditioned being:

> When I look down from this transcendency, how beautiful
> are even the crumbled relics of bread! What shapely spirals
> the peelings of pears make – how thin, and mottled like
> some sea-bird's egg. . . . I could worship my hand even,
> with its fan of bones laced by blue mysterious veins and its
> astonishing look of aptness, suppleness and ability to curl
> softly or suddenly crush – its infinite sensibility. (*TW* 378)

With this final epiphany, Bernard is ready for death. There may be no personal immortality, no heaven, no God, but there is, he realizes, like the waves that break on the shore, an ". . . eternal renewal, the incessant rise and fall and fall and rise again" (*TW* 383). Like Clarissa Dalloway and Lily Briscoe, he has had his vision, a vision that brings the disparate elements of life and being into some semblance of a unity.

The Waves, written at the end of her most creative period, is Virginia Woolf's ultimate effort to express in fiction a view of life which it is difficult to call other than mystical, though it is a mysticism without the theology of religion or the rituals and systems of Yeats's more formal spiritualism. At the heart of this novel is the belief that life is bounded by forces beyond individual comprehension, and that these forces are what bind the seemingly separate selves of her characters into a unity. In *Mrs. Dalloway*, Clarissa and Septimus are thus mystically linked; in *To the Lighthouse* it is the synthesizing vision of Lily Briscoe which binds together the disparate points-of-view represented by Mr. and Mrs. Ramsay; in *The Waves*, emerging as they do from an undifferentiated common ground-of-being, Woolf's six characters are finally seen as integral units of a greater psychic Whole. This unifying perspective permitted the resolution of a spiritual dilemma which had long troubled Virginia Woolf. By subsuming the apparent solipsistic isolation of individual being into an underlying stream of transpersonal, collective consciousness, by envisioning selfhood as a process and a growth out of one common soil, the tension between what Woolf had called "the I and the not-I" might be relieved. For though death must inevitably overwhelm the one, continuity is assured through the latter.

X

EPILOGUE

THE LEANING TOWER: MODERNISM IN AN AGE OF ANXIETY

No more than Romanticism ended absolutely with the accession of Queen Victoria, nor Victorianism with her death, Modernism's history cannot be said to have come to an end with the great Stock Market crash of 1929 nor even with the advent, ten years later, of World War II. Nonetheless, it is not difficult in retrospect to see some distinct turning point in its fortunes. Certainly, by the early 1930s, the dark and ominous political rumblings from Germany, from Italy and from Spain were becoming daily more audible in England. The severe economic depression that had struck the United States made its way in waves across the Atlantic and by 1931 more than two and a half million of Britain's work force were out of jobs and the government was almost bankrupt. The Labor Party, then in power, collapsed to the despair of the left, and a more conservative National Government took its place. The effect of all this upon intellectuals and artists was twofold: on the one hand, a mood of cynicism and futility overtook the relative optimism and exhilaration of the 1920s; on the other, a new spirit of political urgency, activism and political awareness replaced the creative self-absorption of the previous decade.

The original members of Bloomsbury – Leonard and Virginia Woolf, Clive and Vanessa Bell, Duncan Grant, Desmond and Molly MacCarthy, Lytton Strachey, E. M. Forster and John Maynard Keynes – were by now in their late forties or fifties. Roger Fry was in his mid-sixties. Though they all continued to be productive, on the whole their major achievements lay behind them.[1] They had become successful. Their names were made, and there was a younger generation of novelists, poets and intellectuals eager to take their place in the advance guard.

Among these were Aldous Huxley, George Orwell, Christopher Isherwood, Stephen Spender, Louis MacNeice, Cecil Day Lewis, John Lehmann and W. H. Auden. For them, Bloomsbury's pacifism, rationalism and Francophile culture had come to seem outmoded in light of the threats that faced them. The individualism, heterodoxy and creative experimentalism which had characterized the work of the Modernists yielded to a contrary impulse toward collectivism, social realism and political engagement in the writing of the younger generation. Much of this writing was topical and reportorial, and even the best of it – Auden's poems, Isherwood's *Berlin Stories*, Orwell's essays – shows a worldly engagement profoundly different from the Flaubertian dedication to art for its own sake of James Joyce or Virginia Woolf. But the break between these two generations was of a different quality and kind than the greater rupture which had separated the Modernists from their Victorian forebears. The young writers on the left had no similar need to kill the fathers, and they knew their work had been made possible by the break-throughs of Joyce, T. S. Eliot and E. M. Forster.[2]

---

[1] Strachey died in 1932 and Fry in 1934.

[2] Forster's personal and literary influence upon Isherwood was especially deep. According to P. N. Furbank, Isherwood "saw himself as influenced both by Forster's 'rejection of the humbug that still predominates in English society,' and by the casual easy tone of his novels." Furbank, *E. M. Forster: A Life*, vol. 2 (New York: Harcourt, 1978) 177.

Perhaps the event which most highlighted the change in attitude between Bloomsbury and "the Auden generation" was the Spanish Civil War. A rehearsal for the world-wide holocaust that was soon to follow, the war in Spain encapsulated in compressed form all the political ideologies and camps which since that time have been the rallying points for international dispute. Bloomsbury, as we have seen, can be generally labelled "liberal humanist." There were no Brown Shirts in Bloomsbury, neither were there Bolsheviks. Leonard Woolf, who was always very active politically, had been a Fabian Socialist since 1913, and this brand of left-wing meliorism, with its essentially pacific goals, remained to some extent the loosely-held stance of most of the group. But the jack-booted menace of Franco's Falangists, Mussolini's Italian Fascism and, most frightful of all, the spectre of Hitler's violent and anti-semitic Nazi Party had the effect of mobilizing the young British intelligentsia in a manner previously unknown.

While Maynard Keynes and Leonard Woolf did everything in their power to find peaceful solutions and to reach accords which might stave off the inevitable horror of an international war, Julian Bell, the son of Clive and Vanessa, wrote somewhat belligerently to Forster that, for his part, he would choose the values of militarism

> . . . because they alone will help us in practice, and because they offer us an attitude tolerably proof against disaster and emotion. The soldier's is not perhaps the best of lives for many people: it may not offer a very great number of highly valued states of mind. But it can be a good life . . . .[3]

---

[3] Quoted in P. N. Furbank, *E. M. Forster: A Life*, vol. 1 (New York: Harcourt, 1977) 224.

He enlisted in an ambulance corps and left for Spain where he was killed by a shell in 1937. To one degree or another, this was the attitude of most of his generation, at least for a time. Writing, for them, would not be enough. They wanted to align themselves with some revolutionary Great Cause and to forge a solidarity with the working-class.[4]

Most of these young writers rallied behind the doctrines of Marxism and, until the Nazi-Soviet Pact, were supporters of Soviet Communism. Their efforts in literature reflected these allegiances. In 1931 John Lehmann, Leonard and Virginia Woolf's associate at the Hogarth Press, brought out an anthology of contemporary poets called *New Signatures* which Leonard Woolf claimed "was and still is regarded as that generation's manifesto."[5] The poems in this anthology were characterized by political fervor and an aggressive partisanship, traits distinctly absent from the introspective poetry of Georgian collections published only a few years earlier. Lehmann followed this in 1936 with a semi-annual miscellany called *New Writing* (obviously "new" was a catchword of the period). The contributors, including William Empson, Louis MacNeice, Stephen Spender, W. H. Auden, Isherwood, Julian Bell and Day Lewis, were radically left-wing to a man. That these projects were sponsored by Leonard Woolf must indicate the essential sympathy that existed between older, socialist Bloomsbury and the younger activist writers. But the aesthetic differences were considerable and

---

[4] Julian Bell, of course, had been brought up entirely within the liberal and artistic atmosphere of Bloomsbury, but even the others – MacNeice, Spender, Auden, Isherwood – were solidly middle- or upper-middle-class in background.

[5] Leonard Woolf, *Downhill All the Way* (New York: Harcourt, 1967) 174.

they stamp not only the writing of the 1930s, but the subsequent evolution of Modernism into the latter half of the twentieth century.

Virginia Woolf's late essay "The Leaning Tower" (1940) was a response to what she saw as the historical pressure that had brought about some of these differences. While asserting the danger of theories, she admits the possibility of "some force, influence, outer pressure which is strong enough to stamp itself upon a whole group of different writers so that all their writing has a certain common likeness."[6] The relative economic stability and freedom from local wars of nineteenth century England meant that writers of that period could publish in the full confidence that "life was not going to change; they themselves were not going to change" (134-35). This condition continued until the Great War; prior to that devastating event, the security of the educated middle-classes was such that world affairs hardly troubled the activities of young people at Oxford or Cambridge.

Quoting her Bloomsbury friend, Desmond MacCarthy, Woolf illustrates the unanxious academic atmosphere that formed their minds. Cambridge was a haven, an ivory tower, for the pursuit of learning and friendship:

> We were not very much interested in politics. Abstract speculation was much more absorbing; philosophy was more interesting to us than public causes. . . . What we chiefly discussed were those "goods" which were ends in themselves . . . the search for truth, esthetic emotions, and personal relations. (135)

By the time the war began those people who were to be the representative

---

[6] Virginia Woolf, "The Leaning Tower," *The Moment and Other Essays* (New York: Harcourt, 1948) 129-30. Textual citations are from this edition.

writers of the 1920s had already been molded in the rarefied cloisters of Cambridge. But after the war everything had changed, life had been shattered, the old order dealt a death-blow. The tower, though still intact, had begun to lean.

The generation that followed grew up in a vastly different world.

> When they looked at human life what did they see? Everywhere change; everywhere revolution. In Germany, in Russia, in Italy, in Spain, all the old hedges were being rooted up; all the old towers were being thrown to the ground. (139)

And when they came to write, they could not ignore these changes nor could they indulge themselves in the pleasures of purely aesthetic emotions. "They became communists; they became antifascists" (142). But the influence of political dogma and ideological doctrine upon their writing was not, Woolf suggests, altogether salutary. It often had the effect of adulterating and weakening their art by injecting into it elements foreign and impure, obscuring the light of inspiration much as the Edwardians had done to their novels.

Still, all this must be excused by the fact that "the poet is a dweller in two worlds, one dying, the other struggling to be born" (147). The trail had been broken, it is true, but nothing definite or solid appeared to lie ahead. Unlike the Modernists before them who had turned within and found there a pattern with which to reflect the outer chaos, the poets of the 1930s

> . . . had nothing settled to look at; nothing peaceful to remember . . . . During all the most impressionable years of their lives they were stung into consciousness – into self-consciousness, into class-consciousness, into the consciousness

of things changing, of things falling, of death perhaps about to come. There was no tranquility in which they could recollect. The inner mind was paralysed because the surface mind was always hard at work. (147)

This analysis of the temper of that generation which had grown up entirely in the twentieth century, a witness first to one devastating war and then another, continues to be valid for the current Post-Modern period.

The confidence and enthusiasm with which Bloomsbury could cast off the rusted chains of Victorianism and expect a brave new world to presently emerge sadly gave way, especially after 1939, to a pervasive mood of confusion, doubt and profound despair. There was no going back, but was it really possible to go forward? The revelation, at the end of World War II, of the real horror of Hitler's death camps, and the hideous magnitude of the death and destruction brought about in Hiroshima and Nagasaki by the atom bomb, left very little of optimism or hope.

Shortly before the full enormity of these human crimes became public, E. M. Forster offered his antidote to the political faiths then clamoring for converts. It was a creed he had long preached, and he saw no reason to give it up for another. To others appalled by the unfeeling, inhumane practices everywhere visible, whether perpetuated by Nazis or the Popular Front, he advised the holding out of

> . . . one's own poor little trembling flame, with the knowledge that it is not the only light that is shining in the darkness, and not the only one which the darkness does not comprehend. Personal relations are despised today. They are regarded as bourgeois luxuries, as products of a time of fair weather which is now past, and we are urged to get rid of them, and to dedicate ourselves to some movement or

cause instead. I hate the idea of causes, and if I had to choose between betraying my country and betraying my friend, I hope I should have the guts to betray my country. . . . Probably one will not be asked to make such an agonising choice. . . . and there is even a terror and a hardness in this creed of personal relationships, urbane and mild though it sounds. Love and loyalty to an individual can run counter to the claims of the State. When they do – down with the State . . . .[7]

Forster's young friend, W. H. Auden, disillusioned by what he saw when he went to aid the Republican cause in Spain, came to agree with these sentiments. Exiling himself to New York, the prophet of The Age of Anxiety wrote

There is no such thing as the State
And no one exists alone;
Hunger allows no choice
To the citizen or the police;
We must love one another or die.[8]

The first of these is the voice of a humane rationality chastened by sixty years of observing human folly; the second of a poetic spirit recently liberated from some hampering dogma. The one still echoes the sustaining ethics of Cambridge; the other is hollow with a tortured disbelief.

---

[7] E. M. Forster, "What I Believe," *Two Cheers for Democracy* (New York: Harcourt, 1951) 68-69.

[8] From "September 1, 1939," *Selected Poems*, ed. Edward Mendelson (New York: Vintage, 1979) 88.

BIBLIOGRAPHY

Ackroyd, Peter. *T. S. Eliot: A Life*. New York; Simon, 1984.

Alexander, Jean. *The Venture of Form in the Novels of Virginia Woolf*. Port Washington, New York and London: Kennikat, 1974.

Allen, Walter. *The English Novel*. New York: Dutton, 1957.

---. *The Modern Novel in Britain and the United States*. New York: Dutton, 1965.

Annan, Noel, ed. *Leslie Stephen: Selected Writings in British Intellectual History*. Chicago and London: U of Chicago P, 1979.

---. *Leslie Stephen: The Godless Victorian*. New York: Random, 1984.

Anscombe, Isabelle. *Omega and After: Bloomsbury and the Decorative Arts*. London: Thames and Hudson, 1981.

Apter, T. E. *Virginia Woolf: A Study of Her Novels*. New York: New York UP, 1979.

Auerbach, Erich. *Mimesis, The Representation of Reality in Western Literature*. Garden City, NY: Doubleday, 1957.

Barrett, William. *The Illusion of Technique*. Garden City, NY: Anchor/Doubleday, 1979.

Bazin, Nancy Topping. *Virginia Woolf and the Androgynous Vision*. New Brunswick, NJ: Rutgers UP, 1973.

Beach, Joseph Warren. *The Twentieth Century Novel: Studies in Technique*. New York and London: Appleton, 1973.

Beer, John, ed. A Passage To India*: Essays in Interpretation*. Basingstoke, Hampshire: Macmillan, 1985.

Beja, Morris, ed. *Critical Essays on Virginia Woolf*. Boston: Hall, 1985.

Bell, Alan, ed. *Sir Leslie Stephen's Mausoleum Book*. Oxford: Clarendon, 1977.

Bell, Quentin. *Bloomsbury*. London: Wedenfeld and Nicolson, 1968.

---. *Virginia Woolf: A Biography*. New York: Harcourt, 1972.

Bergson, Henri. *Creative Evolution*. Trans. Arthur Mitchell. New York: Modern Library, 1944.

---. *Duration and Simultaneity with Reference to Einstein's Theory*. Indianapolis: Bobbs, 1965.

Bloom, Harold, ed. *Modern Critical Views: Virginia Woolf*. New York; Chelsea, 1986.

Boyd, Elizabeth French. *Bloomsbury Heritage: Their Mothers and Their Aunts.* New York: Taplinger, 1976.

Bradbury, Malcolm. *Forster: A Collection of Critical Essays.* Englewood Cliffs: Prentice, 1966.

Bradbury, Malcolm, and James McFarlane. *Modernism: 1890-1930.* Harmondsworth, Middlesex, England: Penguin, 1976.

Bullock, Alan, and R. B. Woodings, eds. *Twentieth Century Culture: A Biographical Companion.* New York: Harper, 1983.

Calder, Nigel. *Einstein's Universe.* Harmondsworth, Middlesex, England: Penguin, 1980.

Cavaliero, Glen. *A Reading of E. M. Forster.* Totowa, NJ: Rowman, 1979.

Clements, Patricia, and Isobel Grundy, eds. *Virginia Woolf: New Critical Essays.* London: Vision, 1983.

Collins, Judith. *The Omega Workshops.* Chicago: U of Chicago P, 1984.

Colmer, John. *E. M. Forster: The Personal Voice.* London: Routledge, 1975.

Crabtree, Derek and A. P. Thirlwall, eds. *Keynes and the Bloomsbury Group.* London: Macmillan, 1980.

Daiches, David. *Virginia Woolf.* New York: New Directions, 1963.

Das, G. K., and John Beer, eds. *E. M. Forster: A Human Exploration.* London and Basingstoke: Macmillan, 1979.

De Salvo, Louise, ed. *The Letters of Vita Sackville-West to Virginia Woolf.* New York: Morrow, 1985.

Di Battista, Maria. *Virginia Woolf's Major Novels: The Fables of Anon.* New Haven and London: Yale UP, 1980.

Dowling, David. *Bloomsbury Aesthetics and the Novels of Virginia Woolf.* London and Basingstoke: Macmillan, 1985.

Edel, Leon. *Bloomsbury: A House of Lions.* New York: Avon, 1979.

---. *Literary Biography.* U of Toronto P, 1957.

---. *Stuff of Sleep and Dreams: Experiments in Literary Psychology.* New York: Avon, 1982.

Ellmann, Richard, and Charles Feidelson, Jr., eds. *The Modern Tradition.* New York: Oxford UP, 1965.

Ferns, John. *Lytton Strachey.* Boston: Twayne, 1988.

Ford, Boris, ed. *From James to Eliot.* Vol. 7 of *The New Pelican Guide to English Literature.* Harmondsworth, Middlesex, England: Penguin, 1983.

Forster, E. M. *Abinger Harvest.* New York and London: Harcourt, 1936.

---. *Alexandria: A History and a Guide.* New York: Anchor, 1961.

Forster, E. M. *Aspects of the Novel.* New York: Harcourt, 1927.

---. *Howards End.* Harmondsworth, Middlesex, England: Penguin, 1967.

---. *The Longest Journey.* New York: Vintage, 1922.

---. *Maurice.* New York: Norton, 1987.

---. *A Passage to India.* New York: Harcourt, 1924.

---. *A Room with a View.* Harmondsworth, Middlesex, England: Penguin, 1955.

---. *Two Cheers for Democracy.* New York: Harcourt, 1951.

---. *Where Angels Fear to Tread.* New York: Vintage, 1958.

Foster, Jeannette. *Sex Variant Women in Literature.* 2nd ed. Baltimore: Diana, 1975 (a photo offset reprint of 1st ed., 1956).

Freedman, Ralph, ed. *Virginia Woolf: Revaluation and Continuity.* Berkeley: U of California P, 1980.

Friedman, Melvin. *Stream of Consciousness: A Study in Literary Method.* New Haven: Yale UP, 1955.

Furbank, P. N. *E. M. Forster: A Life.* New York: Harcourt, 1974.

Gadd, David. *The Loving Friends: A Portrait of Bloomsbury.* New York and London: Harcourt, 1974.

Gardner, Philip, ed. *E. M. Forster: The Critical Heritage.* London: Routledge, 1973.

Garnett, Angelica. *Deceived with Kindness: A Bloomsbury Childhood.* San Diego, New York, London: Harcourt, 1985.

Gilbert, Sandra, and Susan Gubar. *The Madwoman in the Attic: The Woman Writer and the Nineteenth Century Literary Imagination.* New Haven and London: Yale UP, 1979.

---, eds. *The Norton Anthology of Literature by Women.* New York: Norton, 1985.

Gillie, Christopher. *A Preface to Forster.* Essex: Longman, 1983.

Glendinning, Victoria. *Vita: The Life of Vita Sackville-West.* New York: Knopf, 1983.

Gordon, Lyndall. *Virginia Woolf: A Writer's Life.* New York: Norton, 1984.

Gransden, K. W. *E. M. Forster.* New York: Grove, 1962.

Grosskurth, Phyllis. *Havelock Ellis: A Biography.* London: Quartet, 1980.

---. *The Memoirs of John Addington Symonds.* Chicago: U of Chicago P, 1984.

---. *The Woeful Victorian: A Biography of John Addington Symonds.* New York: Holt, 1964.

Guiguet, Jean. *Virginia Woolf and Her Works*. New York and London: Harcourt, 1962.

Harper, Howard. *Between Language and Silence: The Novels of Virginia Woolf.* Baton Rouge and London: Louisiana State UP, 1982.

Harrod, R. F. *The Life of John Maynard Keynes*. New York: Avon, 1951.

Heilbrun, Carolyn G., ed. *Lady Ottoline's Album*. New York: Knopf, 1976.

---. *Toward a Recognition of Androgyny*. New York: Knopf, 1973.

Herz, Judith S., and Robert K. Martin, eds. *E. M. Forster: Centenary Revaluations*. Toronto and Buffalo: U of Toronto P, 1982.

Himmelfarb, Gertrude. *Marriage and Morals Among the Victorians*. New York: Vintage, 1987.

---. *Victorian Minds*. New York: Knopf, 1968.

Hoberman, Ruth. *Modernizing Lives: Experiments in English Biography, 1918-1939*. Carbondale: Southern Illinois UP, 1987.

Holroyd, Michael. *Lytton Strachey: A Biography*. New York: Holt, 1967.

---. *Lytton Strachey and the Bloomsbury Group: His Work, Their Influence*. Harmondsworth, Middlesex, England: Penguin, 1971.

Howe, Irving, ed. *The Idea of the Modern in Literature and the Arts*. New York: Horizon, 1967.

Hynes, Samuel. *The Auden Generation: Literature and Politics in England in the 1930s*. New York: Viking, 1977.

Iyengar, Srinivasa. *Lytton Strachey: A Critical Study*. New York: Kennikat, 1967.

James, William. *A Pluralistic Universe*. New York: Longman's, 1912.

---. *Principles of Psychology*. New York: Holt, 1890.

Johnstone, J. K. *The Bloomsbury Group: A Study of E. M. Forster, Lytton Strachey, Virginia Woolf, and their Circle*. New York; Farrar, 1978.

Karl, Frederick R. *Modern and Modernism: The Sovereignty of the Artist 1885-1924*. New York: Atheneum, 1985.

Kronenberger, Louis, ed. *Brief Lives: A Biographical Companion to the Arts*. Boston: Little, 1965.

Kumar, S. K. *Bergson and the Stream of Consciousness Novel*. New York: New York UP, 1963.

Latham, Jacqueline, ed. *Critics on Virginia Woolf*. London: Allen, 1970.

Leaska, Mitchell A. *The Novels of Virginia Woolf: From Beginning to End*. New York: Jay; City U of New York, 1977.

Leaska, Mitchell A. *Virginia Woolf's Lighthouse: A Study in Critical Method.* New York: Columbia UP, 1970.

Lee, Hermione. *The Novels of Virginia Woolf.* New York: Holmes, 1977.

Lehmann, John. *Virginia Woolf and Her World.* New York and London: Harcourt, 1975.

Levenson, Michael H. *A Genealogy of Modernism: A Study of English Literary Doctrine 1908-1922.* Cambridge: Cambridge UP, 1984.

Levine, June Perry. *Creation and Criticism: A Passage to India.* Lincoln: U of Nebraska P, 1971.

Levy, Paul. *Moore: G. E. Moore and the Cambridge Apostles.* New York: Holt, 1979.

Lewis, Thomas S. W., ed. *Virginia Woolf: A Collection of Criticism.* New York: McGraw, 1975.

Love, Jean O. *Virginia Woolf: Sources of Madness and Art.* Berkeley: U of California P, 1977.

Majumdar, Robin, and Allen McLauren, eds. *Virginia Woolf: The Critical Heritage.* London and Boston: Routledge, 1975.

Marcus, Jane, ed. *New Feminist Essays on Virginia Woolf.* Lincoln: U of Nebraska P, 1981.

---. *Virginia Woolf: A Feminist Slant.* Lincoln: U of Nebraska P, 1983.

Marder, Herbert. *Feminism and Art: A Study of Virginia Woolf.* Chicago and London: U of California P, 1968.

Matthiessen, F. O. *The James Family: A Group Biography.* New York: Knopf, 1947.

McDowell, Frederick P. W. *E. M. Forster.* New York: Twayne, 1969.

Meisel, Perry. *The Absent Father: Virginia Woolf and Walter Pater.* New Haven and London: Yale UP, 1980.

---. *The Myth of the Modern: A Study in British Literature and Criticism after 1850.* New Haven and London: Yale UP, 1987.

Mendilow, A. A. *Time and the Novel.* New York: Humanities, 1972.

Meyerhoff, Hans. *Time in Literature.* Berkeley and Los Angeles: U of California P, 1960.

Moers, Ellen. *Literary Women.* New York: Anchor, 1977.

Moore, G. E. *Principia Ethica.* Cambridge: Cambridge UP, 1903.

Moore, Madeline. *The Short Season Between Two Silences: The Mystical and the Political in the Novels of Virginia Woolf.* Boston: Allen, 1984.

Naremore, James. *The World Without a Self: Virginia Woolf and the Novel.* New Haven and London: Yale UP, 1973.

Neumann, Erich. *The Great Mother: An Analysis of the Archetype.* Princeton, NJ: Princeton UP, 1955.

---. *The Origins and History of Consciousness.* Princeton, NJ: Princeton UP, 1970.

Nicolson, Nigel. *Portrait of a Marriage.* New York: Bantam, 1973.

Noble, Joan Russell, ed. *Recollections of Virginia Woolf by Her Contemporaries.* New York: Morrow, 1972.

Painter, George D. *Marcel Proust: A Biography.* 2 vols. New York: Vintage, 1978.

Poresky, Louise A. *The Elusive Self: Psyche and Spirit in Virginia Woolf's Novels.* London and Toronto: Associated UP, 1981.

Regan, Tom. *Bloomsbury's Prophet: G. E. Moore and the Development of His Moral Philosophy.* Philadelphia: Temple UP, 1986.

Richter, Harvena. *Virginia Woolf: The Inward Voyage.* Princeton, NJ: Princeton UP, 1970.

Rose, Phyllis. *Woman of Letters: A Life of Virginia Woolf.* New York: Oxford UP, 1978.

Rosenbaum, S. P. *The Bloomsbury Group.* Toronto: U of Toronto P, 1975.

---. *Victorian Bloomsbury: The Early Literary History of the Bloomsbury Group.* Vol. 1. London: Macmillan, 1987.

Rosenthal, Michael. *Virginia Woolf.* New York: Columbia UP, 1979.

Russell, Bertrand. *A History of Western Philosophy.* New York: Simon, 1945.

Rutherford, Andrew, ed. *Twentieth Century Interpretations of* A Passage to India. Englewood Cliffs: Prentice, 1970.

Singer, June. *Androgyny: Toward a New Theory of Sexuality.* Garden City, NY: Anchor/Doubleday, 1977.

Spalding, Frances. *Roger Fry: Art and Life.* Berkeley and Los Angeles: U of California P, 1980.

---. *Vanessa Bell.* New Haven: Ticknor, 1983.

Spater, George, and Ian Parsons. *A Marriage of True Minds: An Intimate Portrait of Leonard and Virginia Woolf.* New York and London: Harcourt, 1977.

Spender, Stephen. *The Struggle of the Modern.* London: Hamilton, 1963.

Sprague, Claire, ed. *Virginia Woolf: A Collection of Critical Essays.* Englewood Cliffs: Prentice, 1971.

Squier, Susan M. *Virginia Woolf and London: The Sexual Politics of the City.* Chapel Hill and London: U of North Carolina P, 1985.

Stansky, Peter, and William Abrahams. *Journey to the Frontier: Two Roads to the Spanish Civil War.* Boston: Little, 1966.

Stone, Wilfred. *The Cave and the Mountain: A Study of E. M. Forster.* Stanford: Stanford UP, 1966.

Strachey, Lytton. *Eminent Victorians.* New York: Harcourt, 1918.

---. *Queen Victoria.* New York: Harcourt, 1921.

Summers, Claude J. *E. M. Forster.* New York: Ungar, 1983.

Tingsten, Herbert. *Victoria and the Victorians.* Trans. David and Eva Grey. New York: Delacorte, 1972.

Tuchman, Barbara W. *The Proud Tower.* New York: Bantam, 1967.

Underhill, Evelyn. *Mysticism.* 1911. New York: Dutton, 1961.

Vogler, Thomas A., ed. *Twentieth Century Interpretations of* To the Lighthouse. Englewood Cliffs: Prentice, 1970.

Warner, Eric. *The Waves.* Cambridge: Cambridge UP, 1987.

Watt, Ian. *The Rise of the Novel.* Berkeley and Los Angeles: U of California P, 1957.

Wilson, Edmund. *Axel's Castle: A Study in the Imaginative Literature of 1870-1930.* New York: Scribner's, 1931.

Woolf, Leonard. *Beginning Again: An Autobiography of the Years 1911 to 1918.* New York and London: Harcourt, 1964.

---. *Downhill All the Way: An Autobiography of the Years 1919 to 1939.* New York and London: Harcourt, 1967.

---. *Growing: An Autobiography of the Years 1904 to 1911.* New York and London: Harcourt, 1961.

---. *The Journey Not the Arrival Matters: An Autobiography of the Years 1939 to 1969.* New York and London: Harcourt, 1969.

---. *Sowing: An Autobiography of the Years 1880 to 1904.* New York and London: Harcourt, 1960.

Woolf, Virginia. *The Captain's Deathbed and Other Essays.* New York: Harcourt, 1950.

---. *The Common Reader.* 1st and 2nd series. New York: Harcourt, 1925 and 1932.

---. *The Diary of Virginia Woolf.* Ed. Anne Olivier Bell. Vol. 1, *1915-1919.* New York: Harcourt, 1977.

248

Woolf, Virginia. *The Diary of Virginia Woolf.* Ed. Anne Olivier Bell. Vol. 2, *1920-1924.* New York: Harcourt, 1978.

---. *The Diary of Virginia Woolf.* Ed. Anne Olivier Bell. Vol. 3, *1925-1930.* New York: Harcourt, 1980.

---. *The Diary of Virginia Woolf.* Ed. Anne Olivier Bell. Vol. 4, *1931-1935.* New York: Harcourt, 1982.

---. *The Diary of Virginia Woolf.* Ed. Anne Olivier Bell. Vol. 5, *1936-1941.* New York: Harcourt, 1984.

---. *Granite and Rainbow.* New York: Harcourt, 1958.

---. *Jacob's Room* and *The Waves* (published in one volume). New York: Harcourt, 1923 and 1931.

---. *The Letters of Virginia Woolf.* Ed. Nigel Nicolson and Joanne Trautmann. Vol. 1, *1888-1912.* New York and London: Harcourt, 1975.

---. *The Letters of Virginia Woolf.* Ed. Nigel Nicolson and Joanne Trautmann. Vol. 2, *1912-1922.* New York and London: Harcourt, 1976.

---. *The Letters of Virginia Woolf.* Ed. Nigel Nicolson and Joanne Trautmann. Vol. 3, *1923-1928.* New York and London: Harcourt, 1977.

---. *The Letters of Virginia Woolf.* Ed. Nigel Nicolson and Joanne Trautmann. Vol. 4, *1929-1931.* New York and London: Harcourt, 1978.

---. *The Letters of Virginia Woolf.* Ed. Nigel Nicolson and Joanne Trautmann. Vol. 5, *1932-1935.* New York and London: Harcourt, 1979.

---. *The Letters of Virginia Woolf.* Ed. Nigel Nicolson and Joanne Trautmann. Vol. 6, *1936-1941.* New York and London: Harcourt, 1980.

---. *Mrs. Dalloway.* New York: Harcourt, 1925.

---. *The Moment and Other Essays.* New York: Harcourt, 1948.

---. *Moments of Being,* ed. Jeanne Schulkind. 2nd ed. New York: Harcourt, 1985.

---. *Orlando: A Biography.* Harmondsworth, Middlesex, England: Penguin, 1942.

---. *Roger Fry: A Biography.* New York and London: Harcourt, 1940.

---. *A Room of One's Own.* New York and London: Harcourt, 1929.

---. *To the Lighthouse.* New York: Harcourt, 1927.

Zink, David D. *Leslie Stephen.* New York: Twayne, 1972.

Zwerdling, Alex. *Virginia Woolf and the Real World.* Berkeley: U of California P, 1986.

INDEX

Lloyd Davis

SEXUALITY AND TEXTUALITY IN HENRY JAMES
Reading Through the Virginal

Sexuality and Literature. Vol 1
ISBN 0-8204-0599-X   240 pages   hardcover US $ 37.50 *

*Recommended price – alterations reserved

Using Freudian and post-Freudian theories, Henry James's fiction is reinterpreted as an arena of linguistic and sexual interaction. Through readings of novels including *The American* and *The Golden Bowl*, it is argued that James's work, like Freud's itself, can be read as representative and revealing of social and psychological forces, and then reread as a product of these same forces. The emphasis is not biographical but, through employing such theorists as Lacan and Kristeva, textual, wherein textuality becomes the field of disclosure for sexuality. The traditional Jamesian narrative of the passage from innocence is reformulated as both the characterizes virgin's and the texts' entrance into the complexities of the sociosexual order.

« Mr. Davis joins the ranks of brilliant young post-structuralist critics, with a closely-reasoned exposition of sexuality as it controls the weaving of Jamesian narrative . . . Above all, this book comes close to the heart of James' obessional treatment of the links between sex and money, sex and property, sex and social status. A highly literate reading! » (Angus Fletcher, Distinguished Professor of English and Comparative Literature, Graduate School, CUNY)

PETER LANG PUBLISHING, INC.
62 West 45th Street
USA – New York, NY 10036

Virginia R. Hyman

TO THE LIGHTHOUSE AND BEYOND
Transformations in the Narratives of Virginia Woolf

American University Studies: Series IV (English Language and Literature).
Vol. 66
ISBN 0-8204-0620-1   300 pages   hardcover US $ 39.10*

*Recommended price – alterations reserved

Using the psychological and structural dynamics of *To the Lighthouse* as its center, this study explores the variety of ways that Woolf dealt with what she called her «odd family complex». Patterns of conflict that emerge in the earlier narratives, fictional and non-fictional, explain why writing this novel was such a crucial act. Furthermore, the subsequent narratives are revealed as a series of remarkably resourceful strategies for dealing with the unresolved issues raised in *To the Lighthouse*.

«Surely many other readers would be similarly moved – moved by Hyman's analysis, and moved to reread Woolf.» (Dorothy Dinnerstein, Rutgers University)

«Virginia Hyman's original and deeply sensitive study of Virginia Woolf alters markedly the way Woolf will be read and taught from now on ... Hyman's book is a major advance in Woolf scholarship.» (Marvin Magalaner, New York University)

«Its scope is remarkable ... Hyman presents a persuasive and complex analysis of the relation between life and fiction that is lucid, thorough and convincing ... ‹Transformations› is the perfect word for what Hyman wants to do and does do – to show how narrative transforms obsession.» (Claire Sprague, Brooklyn College, CUNY)

PETER LANG PUBLISHING, INC.
62 West 45th Street
USA – New York, NY 10036